POLICING IN JAPAN

SUNY Series in
Critical Issues in Criminal Justice

Gilbert Geis and Donald J. Newman, Editors

POLICING IN JAPAN

A Study on Making Crime

Setsuo Miyazawa

Translated by
Frank G. Bennett, Jr.
with
John O. Haley

STATE UNIVERSITY OF NEW YORK PRESS

Published by
State University of New York Press, Albany

For information, address State University of New York
Press, State University Plaza, Albany, N.Y. 12246

Production by Ruth East
Marketing by Theresa A. Swierzowski

Library of Congress Cataloging-in-Publication Data

Miyazawa, Setsuo, 1947–
    Policing in Japan : a study on making crime / Setsuo Miyazawa ;
translated by Frank G. Bennett, with John O. Haley.
        p.   cm. — (SUNY series in critical issues in criminal
justice)
    Translated from Japanese.
    Includes bibliographical references and index.
    ISBN 0–7914–0891–4 — ISBN 0–7914–0892–2 (pbk.)
    1. Criminal investigation—Japan—Case studies. 2. Detectives—
Japan—Case studies. 3. Criminal justice, Administration of—
Japan—Case studies. 4. Detectives—Japan—Sapporo-shi—Case
studies. I. Title. II. Series.
HV8257.A3M59   1992
363.2'5'0952—dc20
                                                                        91–8617
                                                                        CIP

10 9 8 7 6 5 4 3 2 1

Contents

Foreword

This study of how Japanese police detectives construct crime is a significant contribution to our understanding of law, deviant behavior, and social control. At the same time it adds immeasurably to our understanding of the role of culture and of social organization in explaining differences in the behavior of law and legal agents.

Setsuo Miyazawa's study of the ways that Japanese police detectives construct crime builds on Richard Ericson's seminal study of how detectives in Canada make crime by controlling the construction of information on crime. A principle way to control information on crime, though not the only way of doing so, is to use the procedural rules of criminal law. Law is an *enabling* environment for the social construction of crime. In this work on Japanese detectives, Miyazawa enhances our understanding of the enabling nature of law in the social construction of crime by demonstrating that to a far greater degree than in the United States and Canada, the formal system of criminal law of Japan makes patently illegal tactics unnecessary. They are unnecessary in Japan precisely because the formal rules are designed and implemented to enable detectives to dominate the criminal process and to promote a detective's interest to a far greater extent than is true in the United States or Canada. As he puts it very nicely, "...the more enabling the law is, the less risky the detective's behavior need be."

One might regard this more formally as a general principle in the sociology of law and of deviant behavior and its control. Although social control agents are given responsibility for enforcement of the substantive law, regardless of the content of that law, their capacity to enforce it is limited by the degree to which it enables their enforcement interests. This is true not only for police detectives who enforce the substantive criminal law but for internal revenue agents who enforce the internal revenue code or indeed for all agents responsible for the enforcement of a body of substantive law. From the perspective of the sociology of deviant behavior, the less enabling the law is of agent interests, the more agents will resort to illegal means to enforce the law.

Yet this study also amply demonstrates that the process of law enforcement is not so simple. Although he does not formally address the matter, Miyazawa demonstrates in a variety of ways how important other elements of the culture are in producing this conformity. Not only is the legal culture enabling of agent interests but so are elements of the more general culture. One that seems especially important for confession is the acquiescence of Japanese citizens to authority—their acceptance of *voluntary* compliance. This acquiescence to authority is open to easy manipulation by legal agents. Detectives therefore need not coerce confessions; confessions can be obtained by manipulation of voluntary compliance.

The study of detectives also sheds light on the culture and social organization of work in Japan. Professor Miyazawa raises a puzzling question about detective work in Japan. Why if the law and general culture are so enabling of detective investigation do detectives pursue the solution of cases so aggressively? He discovers that for the Japanese detective failure is impermissible. A detective's own sense of worth is tied imperceptibly but inevitably to the detective's clearance rate.

As we so often see in Japanese society, its citizens are faced with making moral choices where the fate of the individual is closely interwoven with the fate of organizations. Self-blame and shame are the masters of individual fate when the destiny of an organization is at stake. Where, but in Japan, would one expect a high official in a police ministry to commit suicide because he shouldered the blame and shame brought about by a scandal exposing the corruption in a local police department under his general jurisdiction?

Professor Miyazawa' fine work is an excellent example of how the study of an occupation and its organization is an illuminating path into the intricate web of culture and society. Not only does he draw us into an appreciation of the intricate nature of that web in Japan but his rich comparative insights provide a better understanding his readers' own culture. He has given us a framework for such comparisons by guiding us to important dimensions of comparison.

Albert J. Reiss, Jr.
Yale University
Columbus Day, 1990

Preface

It is well known that the crime rate in Japan is far below that of the United States and most other developed nations, while the conviction rate of those brought to trial for criminal activity is near 100 percent. Western analysts have investigated the Japanese police system to find out why it seems to deal with crime so much more successfully. Most such analysts have focused on patrol activities and come away very impressed. The Japanese police are highly motivated and effectively disciplined and are more intimately involved with their neighborhoods and are more visible than Western police. In short, investigators have perceived Japanese police enforcement to be a model worthy of emulation.

Western analysts have failed to investigate other aspects of policing in Japan including criminal investigation. Police detectives work to produce information about the crime and the suspect sufficient to indict, convict, and sentence the suspect to a heavier punishment. They work to construct and justify their version of the event. This process of *making crime* always involves the possibility of violating human rights in any country and, indeed, there has been a series of cases of procedural illegalities committed by Japanese police detectives.

In this book, I show non-Japanese readers this unknown side of Japanese policing. I am the only Japanese investigator ever to have been permitted to observe detective work from the inside. My subjects are police officers in general detective work. I spent months at a Japanese police station, going out on calls with detectives and freely discussing cases with them to draw the most intimate and detailed picture of Japanese detective work available in Japanese or other language.

Here is Japanese police work as it really is: hurried detectives under pressure to clear ever more crimes, torn between following the rules and evading them; a system of detention and questioning that makes it almost impossible for suspects to maintain their innocence; and, at the same time, detectives with a dedication to doing the job right despite all obstacles. It is

ironic that the effective internal control over them, in combination with highly enabling formal legal system, results in many questionable or illegal
actions by the police.

I compare my findings extensively with Anglo-American detective
work researched by Richard V. Ericson, William B. Sanders, Jerome H.
Skolnick, and others, as well as research on Japanese police by David H.
Bayley and Walter L. Ames. I hope that anyone interested in law enforcement or Japanese society will learn something from this book.

Acknowledgments

Innumerable people and several organizations have offered me assistance, encouragement, constructive criticism, and even sheer labor in the process of field research, the publication of the original Japanese study, and the preparation of this English version. In order to name just a few of them, I beg the reader's indulgence in tracing the history of this research endeavor. Publication of an English translation of a non-English book faces many unique problems, and the following acknowledgment demonstrates what any prospective author and publisher of such a book should anticipate.

The field research was carried out in 1974 in the city of Sapporo, the capital of the Hokkaido Prefecture, the northernmost island of Japan. This unprecedented field opportunity was made possible by the permission of the then chief of the Hokkaido Police, Yuichi Tanaka. No police chief in Japan has since allowed a Japanese scholar to conduct an observational study of criminal investigation. I praise his courage and appreciation of the value of scientific studies. If this book has any significant contribution to the study of law enforcement and Japanese society, readers should thank this unusual police chief.

After Chief Tanaka had given me permission, details of the research were handled by Hachio Okamoto, then head of the Bureau of Criminal Investigation, and Masatoshi Hasunuma, then head of the Criminal Planning Department, at the Hokkaido Police Headquarters. They were responsible for the selection of the research site and approval of research methods, particularly of survey questions. There were, of course, some moments of intense exchanges. However, they also understood the value of my research and approved the use of all items I had originally prepared for the questionnaire survey.

My only disappointment with the Hokkaido Police Department came when I asked for comments to my analysis in preparing the Japanese version in 1983 and it did not respond. By that time, Tanaka, Okamoto, and Hasunuma had either retired or been relocated, and no one at the headquarters was directly involved in my research.

My main research site was a police station in Sapporo and I wish to express my greatest appreciation to officers there. Since many of them are still in the force, however, I name only the following two people who are now retired: Kan'ya Sakai, then station chief, and Naoji Ogiya, then assistant station chief in charge of criminal investigation and crime prevention. A remarkably procedure-minded, generally restrained field supervisor, Ogiya was particularly helpful to me. He allowed me to observe some of the most sensitive decisions and explained the purpose of my research to the initially skeptical lower-ranking officers. He even dispatched an undercover police car to transport questionnaires from my office to his station. Without his assurances, officers never would have dispelled their suspicion that I was an undercover agent from the headquarters who had been sent to collect information for the purpose of personal evaluation!

Watching the watchers was really a difficult job. However, I still vividly remember those who worked with me: instructors and students of the Hokkaido Police Academy who invited me to a term-end party; patrol officers at a police box who went out to search for an old man in the middle of a severe snow blizzard; a very aggressive but jovial young detective called "haya-chan" (Mr. Haya) who served as my occasional chauffeur and his old buddy called "tottsan" (dad); an old detective who had been praised as a master detective, yet told me how critical he was about the working condition for lower-ranking officers; and an officer wearing GI haircut who looked more menacing than the gangsters he interrogated. I have kept in touch with some of these men, and there have been some sad news: one of the field supervisors accidentally fell from an office window and died and "haya-chan" was crippled by a car accident. This book does not always praise these men, but rather presents some critical evaluations. I hope, however, they understand that my critique is presented with a sympathy to their situation as workers and citizens, and with the hope that in the near future they will be able to work under improved working conditions and a system that rewards compliance with procedural requirements.

I conducted my field work when I was a research associate in law at Hokkaido University. As a graduate student in criminal law, I was inspired by the Japanese translation of Skolnick's *Justice Without Trial* in 1971 and quickly changed my interest from traditional, German-style doctrinal analysis, to empirical analysis of criminal justice and related matters. In spite of this, Tokuo Kogure, my supervisor at Hokkaido University and a German-trained doctrinal scholar, always defended my approach. He encouraged me to pursue my ambition to carry out an observational study of police, introduced me to the Hokkaido Police Department, and accompanied me to its headquarters. I only hope that I remember to do the same when my own graduate student suggests a research proposal that is totally different from my own interests.

With two stints of graduate study in sociology at Yale immediately after completion of the field research (1975-77 and 1979-81), it took four years (1979–83) to publish the findings in the form of law review article in *Hokkaido Law Review*. It was only after my relocation from Hokkaido to Kobe University in 1983 that I began to contemplate publication of my research in book form. Koichi Miyazawa (unrelated) of Keio University in Tokyo kindly introduced me to a publisher, Seibundo, and the original Japanese version appeared in May 1985. I was most grateful to Seibundo because it published the book against all odds: the book was thick (395 pages of text and 170 pages of appendix), difficult to read, likely to become very expensive, and not expected to sell well as a college textbook.

In the meantime, David H. Bayley and Walter L. Ames had been conducting their respective field work studies approximately the same time I had been completing my own research and analyses. I later learned of their works and examined them, realizing that they had not focused on detective work, and thought that my book might be worth translating into English.

I met Gilbert Geis at an annual meeting of the Law and Society Association at San Diego in June 1985. As he happened to be a series editor for State University of New York (SUNY) Press at the time, Gil kindly promised that he would discuss my project with them. Since then, I have never ceased to be amazed at his extreme generosity.

Michelle Martin, an editor at SUNY Press, wrote me on March 27, 1986, stating that both Gil Geis and David H. Bayley had asked her to write me about submitting a manuscript. No doubt, David knew that my book potentially challenged his pathbreaking work, and I am most grateful to his statesmanship.

I did not have time to translate the book myself and decided to apply for a grant to hire a translator under the Program of Grants-in-Aid for Publication of Scientific Research Result of the Japanese Ministry of Education, Science, and Culture and asked John O. Haley at the University of Washington Law School to supervise translation. John graciously accepted my request, but could not find a suitable translator in his school. He contacted various people, including J. Mark Ramseyer at the UCLA Law School, and asked them to nominate possible candidates. Several people sent me a sample translation, including Frank G. Bennett, Jr., then a third-year student of American and Japanese law at the UCLA Law School. I could not select any specific person that time, however, because the application deadline for a grant from the Education Ministry was November 1986. I received an LL.D. from Hokkaido University for the original Japanese version of the book in March 1987, but heard nothing from the ministry until three months after that.

Rosalie M. Robertson replaced Michelle Martin as my editor at SUNY Press in late 1986. Through correspondence with Rosalie, I began to see a real possibility for the eventual publication of this book. She has been my cheerleader, copy editor, and effective advocate ever since. I believe that no other editor has corresponded with an author as often as she did. This book has been my first exposure to the process of academic publication in the United States, and I have learned a lot from her in that regard.

The Japanese fiscal year starts in April, but the Diet does not usually pass a budget before that. I heard from the Education Ministry in June 1987. My book was one of only eight books receiving a translation grant that year, which included all areas of humanities, social sciences, and sciences. I feel most honored, and relieved, for, without this grant, the whole project may not have been completed.

John O. Haley and I then selected Frank G. Bennett, Jr., for the translation job in September 1987. I have no doubt that this was the beginning of a very difficult task for Frank and his wife, Mieko. While we decided to cut out the entire appendix, the book still was 395 pages long, and the Education Ministry required us to submit a completed translation in March 1988. It is hard to imagine how an American attorney could find time in the middle of his hectic schedule to work on such a project. I was, therefore, both pleased and relieved when I heard later that he had been appointed as a full-time lecturer in Japanese law at the School of Oriental and African Studies (SOAS) in the University of London. I hope that his work on my book was in some way instrumental in the decision by the SOAS.

The initial translation was a densely argued book filled with many tables and technicalities of Japanese law, the pace deliberately slow. Since I expected the frequently heard and powerful response from the Japanese police that my book was just another example of a biased and unrealistic attack against the police by a "leftist" scholar, I presented a massive amount of evidence for every observation and argument. I did not want to preclude any possibility of other scholars doing observational police studies in the future, so even analysis of many policy implications of my findings was presented in a very indirect manner. (Unfortunately, no one has since been granted any such opportunity.) This whole strategy had made the book very difficult to read. Frank sent me the first draft translation in November 1988, and innumerable rounds of drafts, edited drafts, and revised drafts started to make the triangular flight between Los Angeles, Kobe, and Seattle. Frank worked heroically and managed to produce at least the first draft translation for approximately 300 pages of the book. The Education Ministry was benevolent. It accepted the incomplete translation and released the grant to me.

Frank continued to work and I continued to edit his translation. Frank finally produced a full translation in October 1988, and I sent it on to Rosalie at SUNY Press.

I received reviews by three anonymous reviewers in April 1989. Gil, Rosalie, and Frank K. Upham of the Boston College Law School also wrote me their opinions. Obviously the manuscript needed a major revision in many aspects: they particularly recommended condensing data and shortening the book, providing an outline of the legal framework of criminal investigation in Japan, adding comparative and policy analysis, and, most of all, revising the too literal translation. This virtually amounted to writing a new book

My old-time friend and former teacher, Malcolm M. Feeley at the University of California, Berkeley, advised me to find a native English-speaker, not a specialist, but an intellectual person willing to revise the manuscript. I agreed with Malcolm and found an ideal person in Kobe, a few minutes walk from our apartment. He was Michael Les Benedict, a constitutional historian from Ohio State University, who was staying at the Kobe University Law Faculty at that time. Les and his wife, Karen, graciously accepted my request, and, by the time they left Kobe in August 1989, they had reviewed the entire manuscript and made innumerable comments and recommendations for revision.

I closely followed their advice, added comparative materials, and wrote a completely new conclusion. Since Les and Karen were no longer available, I asked Todd Elwyn, an American attorney studying at Kobe, to edit the conclusion.

In the meantime, I realized that the seminal work on Canadian police detectives conducted by Richard V. Ericson provides the analytical framework with which I can most effectively compare my findings with those in North America and in the United Kingdom. It was fortunate that I could discuss his work with him in Hamburg and in Toronto.

I worked on the basis of the computer discs supplied by Frank G. Bennett, Jr. Since I did not have an IBM computer, I purchased two Toshiba, IBM-compatible, portable computers and WordPerfect software. My neighbor, Kazuo Iwasaki of Ritsumeikan University in Kyoto, taught me how to use the machines, and John O. Haley in Seattle helped me to purchase the software. Without additional grant money from the Education Ministry and personal assistance from these friends, I would not have been able to revise the manuscript myself. It has been my practice ever since to carry a computer wherever I go, whether in *shinkansen* (super-express train in Japan) or on a flight to Europe.

I sent the revised manuscript to Rosalie in November 1989 and Rosalie returned a big Christmas present to me in December 1989. The reviewers and editorial board of SUNY Press had approved publication of my book. A contract was signed, and Rosalie and Gil both offered further assistance to copyedit the manuscript. Rosalie sent an edited manuscript to Gil and me in

July 1990 and, to my amazement, Gil returned his own editing just a month after that. Gil Geis kindly edited my manuscript in spite of many of his personal concerns. I never expected that he would personally be involved in the production of my book, for which I am most grateful. Finally, my dissertation supervisor at Yale, Albert J. Reiss, Jr., wrote a perceptive foreword in the middle of his hectic schedule, and my students, Keiichi Ageishi and Hiroto Hata helped me in proofreading.

I thank all of these and other people who helped me at various moments during the process from the beginning of the field research to the final production of this book. I expect, however, that I will not offend them if I dedicate this book to my wife, Nobuko. She is the only person who has been with me for all of these seventeen years.

Setsuo Miyazawa
Kobe University
In the season of cherry blossoms, 1991

Part I

Introduction

1

Making Crime in Japan

This book is a study of the everyday activities of Japanese police detectives as part of their criminal investigations. Police detectives in any country work to "create" criminal cases in which suspects can be indicted, convicted, and sentenced to the maximum possible penalties. The focus of their activity is the construction of information in cases to be presented to prosecutors, judges, the mass media, and, ultimately, the public. Crimes are established as officially recorded social events only after the information put together by police detectives is presented and accepted. This information, thus, makes crimes, and *making crime* (Ericson, 1981) is the job of detectives.

The construction of information on crimes is an interactive process in which actors other than detectives also participate. These actors include victims, witnesses, suspects, defense attorneys, and police supervisors. Detectives and other actors participate in this process with different resources and under varying constraints, and any single piece of information is a result of the complex interactions among these actors. This book describes how Japanese detectives mobilize their resources and deal with constraints in their interactions with other actors, explains their behavior as a response to environmental conditions perceived by them, and compares their behavior with their North American and British counterparts.

Direct observation of criminal investigation is crucial to such a study. As is often the case with large organizations in Japan, whether public or private, the Japanese police provide more opportunities for direct observation to foreigners, particularly American researchers (Bayley, 1976; Ames, 1981; Parker, 1984). Until now, these studies conducted by American researchers have been the only observational studies of the Japanese police published in

1

English, either by foreigners or by Japanese (cf., on the historical background of the modern Japanese police, Westney, 1987: chapter 2).

There was a significant difference among these American researchers in their ability to understand the Japanese language and the length of their observations at a given location. These differences affected their conclusions. Ames spoke Japanese well and unlike others had no need to rely on an interpreter. He also observed a single police station for the longest period of time. It is no wonder, therefore, that his study is more nuanced in both its description and evaluation of the Japanese police. It even includes firsthand information on their relationship with organized crime and social outcasts.

All of these American researchers focused mainly on patrol activities (cf., the first observational study of patrol activities conducted by an independent Japanese researcher, Murayama, 1990). This is understandable given the apparent difference in styles of patrol activities in the United States and Japan. While motorized patrol dominates in the United States, the Japanese style emphasizes foot patrol by officers who are assigned to *koban* or police boxes. Since Japan has had a significantly lower crime rate, the desire to find a more effective style of policing led American researchers to study patrol activities in Japan. However, a series of sophisticated experimental studies in the United States later raised serious doubt about the causal relationship between crime rates and styles and levels of police activities (for a summary of research findings, see Skolnick and Bayley, 1986: 3-5).

In any event, these studies on the Japanese police included no more than a chapter each on criminal investigation (Bayley, 1976: chapter 7; Ames, 1981: chapter 7; Parker, 1984: chapter 5). Among these studies, Bayley offers the most detailed assessment of criminal investigation. Nevertheless, description of investigative activities was not his main concern. This book corrects this dearth of information on criminal investigation in Japan by describing and explaining the routine activities of general police detectives.

Compared to the relative lack of academic interest, the American news media have shown a great deal of interest in criminal investigation in Japan, particularly in its more problematic aspects. On September 20, 1988, for instance, the *New York Times* reported on the lengthy detentions of suspects in police station detention cells, where individuals could be pressured into confessing. The newspaper article stated that "since 1945, 40 people filed suit to overturn verdicts against them on the ground that they were forced to confess crimes they did not commit," and that "since 1963, courts have found 12 cases of false conviction, including 3 people sentenced to death and 3 to life imprisonment." The *Times* also reported on the harsh treatment of persons, including even those accused of minor charges. A female suspect in a loan fraud case was allegedly "stripped naked, subjected twice to a genital search, and forced to urinate while male police officers watched." The police later found that the money had in fact been paid back before her arrest, and she was released without indictment. On May 1, 1989, the *New York Times* again described how Japanese investigative methods relied on interrogations during lengthy pretrial detentions, this time in relation to the investigation of the so-called Recruit bribery scandal by the Special Investigation Team of the Tokyo District Prosecutor's Office, whom *Time* magazine (April 24, 1989) praised as "lonely heroes."

It is tempting to dismiss serious cases of human rights violations as individual actions committed only by the exceptional police officer. I argue in this book, however, that such cases can happen in investigations that follow well-established routines, and that police detectives are working in an environment that constantly tempts them into more aggressive and questionable behavior. I discover basic similarities between detective work in Japan and North America and suggest that similar institutional and utilitarian explanations are applicable to police behavior both in Japan and in North America.

Questionable investigative activities have occurred in a series of cases in Japan and involve forced confessions to false charges, police crimes, and procedural illegalities. Because it is essential for readers to understand the background of this focus, I summarize some examples of such cases.

Forced confessions to false charges repeatedly appear both in the courts and in the news. Four recent examples are summarized below. Two involve convictions several decades ago, but the third and fourth indicate that forced confessions made during pretrial detention at police station detention cells still remain a problem.

On December 31, 1988, the Shizuoka District Court overturned the conviction of Masao Akabori for rape and murder. Police had arrested Akabori for a theft and he eventually admitted to the rape and murder of a six-year-old girl. He was convicted, and the Supreme Court in 1960 upheld the death sentence. Akabori continued to file petitions for retrial from his cell on death row; on his fourth petition the Shizuoka District Court decided in 1986 to retry the case. The court held that Akabori's confession was untrustworthy and found that other evidence was not sufficient to convict him.

On the same day, the Kumamoto District Court overturned the conviction of the late Masao Matsuo, who had been convicted of rape and injury in 1955 and had served a prison term of three years, but continued to seek retrial after his release. The court accepted his thirteenth petition in March 1988. He died soon after, but the retrial continued. As in Akabori's case, the court found the confession untrustworthy.

On March 3, 1989, the Sakai Branch of the Osaka District Court overturned the conviction of a twenty eight-year-old man for the 1979 rape and murder of a woman. In this case, five youths, including this man, had been arrested and sentenced by the trial court in 1982 to prison terms of ten to eighteen years. One of them did not appeal and served the sentence, while the four other defendants appealed and eventually were acquitted in 1986 by the Osaka High Court on the grounds that their confessions were involuntary and untrustworthy and that sufficient evidence was lacking. The remaining defendant who had not initially appealed then requested a retrial that led to his acquittal.

On November 16, 1988, a mother and her seven-year-old son were killed in their apartment in Tokyo. The Tokyo Metropolitan Police found no clue for several months and started a blanket investigation of area youths who had been absent from school early in 1989. They arrested three sixteen-year-old boys in April who admitted to committing the crime. The Tokyo District Prosecutor's Office sent the case to family court in May with recommendations for an adult criminal penalty for one boy and commitment to the juvenile correctional house for the other two. Before the first hearing, however, one of the boys told his mother that he was innocent, and a team of defense attorneys was formed. The attorneys found that one boy had an alibi. He had been working as a painter on the day of the crime in a remote place and his supervisor confirmed this. The Tokyo Family Court held that the confessions were not trustworthy and decided to take no action against the boys. It was revealed that the police had known about the alibi from the beginning, but had pressed the witness to change his statement. The witness's interrogation was terminated only by a writ of habeas corpus.

The police also claimed that a brooch found at one boy's house had been stolen from the victim. However, the attorneys proved that the boy had bought it at a hotel, and the police had not tried to verify this. The boys related to the press that the police had told each of them that the other two boys had confessed at the beginning and therefore they had individually abandoned their resistance. The head of the First Detective Department of the Tokyo Metropolitan Police still maintained to the press that they were guilty.

There have been other cases of police crimes and procedural illegalities, as illustrated in the six cases below.

In the summer of 1982, bars, coffee shops, and gaming machine shops with electric gambling machines were thriving in the Osaka Prefecture, the second largest metropolitan area in Japan. The Osaka Prefectural Police ordered the fifty six police stations under its jurisdiction to search these shops for evidence of illegal gambling. Thirty stations failed to find any, while other stations found evidence in only thirty four shops. It was evident that police information had been leaked. The Special Investigation Team of the Osaka District Prosecutor's Office started its investigation. The main suspect was a veteran officer with fifteen years of experience at the lowest rank of patrolman at the Sonezaki Police Station in downtown Osaka. The Osaka Police planned to relocate him to a southern area of Osaka on November 1. However, realizing this move by the police, the prosecutors asked him to appear in their office on that day. The Osaka Police immediately changed its plan, arrested the officer on the following day, and succeeded in keeping the investigation of its own member internal. The officer was charged with bribery involving thirteen million yen (approximately $52,000 U.S. by the exchange rate in those days).

As is often the case in organizational scandals in Japan, another person, a police sergeant, killed himself on the same day. It was later learned that he also had received money. On November 11, two former officers were arrested for bribery. A few months earlier, one of them had tried to bribe the other upon request from gaming shops. The former eventually received 200,000 yen (approximately $800 U.S.), and the latter divided 7.9 million yen (approximately $31,600 U.S.) with two other officers, including the one who committed suicide. There had been earlier suspicion about their involvement; however, the internal Auditor's Office of the Osaka Police had not arrested them, and, instead, the Osaka Police merely dismissed them for unrelated reasons. The arrest of these former officers was followed by a second suicide. The principal of the National Police Academy in Tokyo killed himself on November 12. He had been chief of the Osaka Police until August of 1982 and it was obvious that corruption had spread during his tenure. By January of 1984, when the Osaka Police closed its investigations, only four active officers of the rank of assistant inspector or lower had been formally charged. More than one hundred officers were dismissed or otherwise disciplined, but only two of them were later indicted. There had been no mention of possible involvement by police executives. The national association of gaming machine manufacturers included many retired police executives. Its president was a former head of the department in charge of regulation of this industry at the Tokyo Metropolitan Police, and its Osaka director was a former police executive in the Osaka area. Moreover, its counselor was a former chief of the National Police Agency and an incumbent cabinet minister.

On November 27, 1986, a wiretap was found on the private phone of Yasuo Ogata, the director of the International Relations Department of the Japanese Communist Party, who lived in Machida City, a suburb of Tokyo. Wiretapping constitutes a crime of obstruction of electric communication punishable by a fine of up to one million yen (approximately $5,880 U.S. by the exchange rate of those days) or a prison term of up to five years. It is also a crime of violation of privacy of electric communication, punishable by a fine of up to 300,000 yen (approximately $1,760 U.S.) or a prison term of up to one year. No law in Japan authorizes the police to wiretap anyone. Since there was a suspicion of police involvement, the Special Investigation Team of the Tokyo District Prosecutor's Office took over the case. By May 1987 the team identified officers at the ranks of patrolman, sergeant, and assistant inspector who had been directly involved in wiretapping. They belonged to the section in charge of national security matters at the Kanagawa Prefectural Police Headquarters. Even local officers work under the direct command of the National Police Agency of the Central Government in the national security area (Ames, 1981). These officers defended their crime as merely following orders from supervisors, but they refused to tell the prosecutors about higher-ranking officers who had ordered or approved the wiretapping.

On May 15, 1987, another police sergeant who had kept records of the wiretapping was found dead in his house, a familiar pattern in organizational crimes in Japan, which involve business corporations, governmental agencies, or political figures. On June 10, 1987, Ogata added to his complaint of wiretapping the abuse of authority by a public official, a crime punishable by a prison term of up to two years. By this time, the Special Investigation Team had expanded its investigation to police executives, and resignations and transfers of several top-level officers followed. The head of the Kanagawa Police Headquarters resigned; the head of its Security Department was transferred to another agency of the Central Government; the head of the Security Division of the National Police Agency resigned; and the head of the subdivision directly involved in this crime was transferred to become the secretary general of the Police Mutual Benefits Association. The police explained that these resignations and transfers had nothing to do with the crime. The media found, however, that the head of the National Police Agency and the head of the Kanagawa Police had sent letters to the Prosecutor's Office, indicating that the resignations of the top officers were the result of their responsibility in the Ogata case and had promised the prosecutors that the police would introduce measures to prevent similar future crimes. Then, on August 4, the Tokyo District Prosecutor's Office announced that there would be no indictment. The office explained that prosecutors could not identify the higher-ranking officers who had ordered or approved the wiretapping and it would be unfair to punish only lower-ranking officers for this type of organizational crime. Ogata filed a civil suit on September 9, 1988, against the state, the Kanagawa Prefecture, and the four identified officers, seeking thirty three million yen (approximately $257,800 U.S.) for damages. The case is still pending.

The background of the prosecutor's decision was exposed by a most unlikely source, the then prosecutor general, Shigeki Itoh, in his memoirs written before his death in March 1988 (Itoh, 1988). In the form of a parable about a "foreign country," Itoh admitted that the investigation had been terminated because of the fear of possible destruction of the prosecutorial system, in its direct confrontation with the much more powerful police system.

He argued that given such a possibility, prosecutors had made the best deal in this case and it was doubtful that they could have indicted anyone where the real suspects were large organizations that have physical force, such as police and the Self-Defense Force (for a partial translation of this "parable," see Miyazawa, 1989).

On February 6, 1988, Michiko Gusoku, the wife of the owner of a small food store in Sakai City of Osaka Prefecture, found a bank envelope containing 150,000 yen (approximately $1,170 U.S.) in her store and reported it to the nearby police box, where a young officer received the money. The owner eventually realized that Gusoku had found the money and went to the main police station to retrieve it. The police told him, however, that the money had not been reported, and opened an investigation with Gusoku as the suspect. Detectives came to question her, bringing a torn bank envelope allegedly found near her store. They asked her doctor if it was safe to take her into custody in spite of her pregnancy, and asked the nearby postal savings office to provide information about her recent financial activities. Gusoku retained an attorney and asked a branch office of the police auditor of the Osaka Prefectural Police Department to investigate the young officer, but the request was refused. Only when newspapers reported this case one month later did the headquarters of the Osaka Police take over the investigation. On March 25 the police admitted that the young officer at the police box had failed to report the money to the station and that Michiko Gusoku was innocent. The officer was dismissed, and, in the subsequent civil suit filed by the Gusokus, the Prefectural Government of Osaka agreed to pay two million yen (approximately $15,000 U.S.) damages. The officer's indictment was suspended by the prosecutor, however, on the grounds that the money was returned and he already had been disciplined.

On December 3, 1988, seven juveniles were arrested for breaking and entering a high school in Hirakata City of Osaka Prefecture. One of the juveniles died less than ninety minutes after the arrest from damage to internal organs. The other juveniles told the newspapers that one of the arresting officers had kicked and thrown the youth down when he had resisted arrest. The Osaka Police Headquarters started an investigation and arrested this officer, a black belt in judo, on the charge of unintentional death caused by physical abuse inflicted by a governmental official in charge of the administration of justice. The officer was dismissed and indicted.

When the gaming shops scandal was exposed in Osaka in 1982, there was suspicion of similar corruption in the neighboring Hyogo Prefecture. A main suspect was an assistant inspector at the Amagasaki Central Police Station. In the process of an investigation in a bribery case, the Kobe District

Prosecutor's Office found that several witness statements prepared by this officer reporting violations of regulations in bars and similar businesses were totally fake, yet the suspects had been indicted and convicted. This was conceivable since such minor cases usually are handled by a summary procedure without trial, and there is no danger that statements will be challenged by the defense attorney. This officer was arrested, indicted, and convicted in 1983 on charges of bribery and forgery of public documents.

In 1986, an officer at the Oi Police Station of the Tokyo Metropolitan Police forged statements by witnesses saying that an American living in Tokyo had possessed marijuana. His supervisor obtained a search warrant based upon these statements, searched the residence of the suspect, and found marijuana there. The police arrested the American at the scene as a flagrant offender. However, the prosecutor discovered the forgery and suspended the prosecution. The officer was dismissed, but his prosecution for forgery was suspended and the police did not disclose this case to the media. The case was reported by a newspaper only in November of 1989.

Among previous studies, Bayley (1976: 4) paints a very different picture of the Japanese police:

> [I]f generality of agreement among people in a country is the mark of truth, then Japanese police behavior is astonishingly good. The incidence of misconduct is slight and the faults trivial by American standards.

Bayley (1976: 152) adds:

> [M]ost informed observers—lawyers, criminal reporters, law professors, and prosecutors—contend that instances of abuse of persons in custody are rare. Celebrated cases have occurred but the incidence is small, especially when compared with the notorious period before 1945. The suspects that seem to be most vulnerable, according to lawyers, are not the poor, as in the United States, but politically active students.

The cases summarized in this chapter suggest that the Japanese police abuse their authority more often than Bayley's Japanese informants led him to believe, and that their victims are not limited to radical students.

In spite of these and other widely reported cases, it is difficult to find English-language literature on police illegalities and questionable police practices in Japan. One exception is a short paper on forced confessions written by a Japanese attorney, Futaba Igarashi (1984; reprinted Igarashi, 1986).

The Japanese Code of Prisons, enacted in 1908, allowed police station detention cells to be used as substitutes for prisons because of the shortage of prisons in those days. This applied as well to detention sections in prisons for suspects and defendants. This system of *daiyo kangoku*, or substitute prisons, still exists today. Because cases of false conviction invariably involved confessions taken during detention in *daiyo kangoku*, the three bar associations in Tokyo formed a committee to investigate practices there and Igarashi served as its chairperson. After surveying thirty people who were known to have been falsely accused between 1949 and 1982, her committee published a book-length report (Tokyo San Bengoshikai, 1984). Igarashi's subsequent paper vividly describes how detained persons were drawn in and eventually themselves contributed to the construction of a version of events the police and prosecutor wanted to present to the court and the public.

However, Igarashi says little about investigative activities outside the police station detention cells. Moreover, highly publicized, serious cases are not the only problems. Less serious, but equally illegal or questionable actions can appear routinely, and such routine cases may provide the background against which more serious cases occur. What is needed, then, is a comprehensive study of general detective work that provides an understanding of the common characteristics of routine investigations that are conducive to questionable police behavior.

There is only one observational study of the Japanese police which focuses on general detective work—the one I conducted in 1974 in Sapporo City of Hokkaido Prefecture in northern Japan. This field research was inspired by Skolnick's (1966) observational study on the American police, and details of research procedure are discussed in chapter 3.

This book is essentially an abridged translation and updated version of the book published in Japanese (Miyazawa, 1985), with a broader comparative perspective. As the cases noted above show, the situation surrounding detective work in Japan has not changed significantly since my field work.

2

The *Enabling* Legal Environment

While there is only one observational study of Japanese police detectives, not many observational studies of general detective work in North America or in England exist, either. More common is research on specialized investigative forces or specific investigative areas. In the United States, for instance, Skolnick's classic study (1966) focused on the vice squad in Oakland, California; Wilson's later work (1978) analyzed investigators for the FBI and the Drug Enforcement Administration; while Manning (1980) studied the policing of narcotics traffic. In England, Hobbs (1988) recently presented a fascinating study on the interaction between community culture and detective culture, but his interest was not in the detective work itself.

We thus find only two works on the everyday activities of general investigation detectives, both conducted in North America. One is a study of an American police force by Sanders (1977) and the other of a Canadian police force by Ericson (1981). Both authors analyze how detectives control the process of information construction to establish the presence of an indictable crime. Ericson's is more comprehensive of the two and provides an additional perspective that is useful to the comparative focus of this book.

Ericson follows McBarnet (1979; cf., 1981), who argued that on the basis of a study on the Scottish system, due process promotes rather than inhibits crime control. The advantage of the police over the accused in reconstructing events, both agree, is inherent in the law itself. Ericson pays much attention to the function of legal and organizational rules, which enable detectives to control the process of event reconstruction according to their own perspective. Ericson sees that low visibility of their work, formal rules of criminal law, internal rules of police organization, and rules developed within their occupational culture are all resources for detectives, who try to

11

control the construction of information on crime and thus the process of "crime making." Despite differences in criminal procedures, he found the forms and results of detective work in Canada and the United States to be similar. According to Ericson, whatever their contents, formal procedural rules are *enabling* for detectives. Detectives everywhere work in such an enabling environment; the difference is only a matter of degree.

Such difference in degree may be significant, however. Despite the apparent similarities of detective work across countries, there might be differences in the effort required on the part of detectives to circumvent or manipulate formal procedural rules to promote their interests, depending on the extent to which formal rules were designed or implemented to enable them to dominate the process. We may hypothesize that the more enabling the law is, the less risky or adventuresome the detective's behavior need be. This is exactly the case in Japan. The detectives I observed, for example, did not use any physical force because they did not need to. Without knowledge of the legal framework of policing in Japan, one may miss the significance of the apparently benign forms of the behavior of Japanese police detectives.

Before outlining the Japanese law of criminal procedure, however, I wish to discuss two other factors which make police work less dangerous and easier in Japan than in many other developed countries. One is well known, namely, the prohibition of firearms. As previous studies on the Japanese police have all noted (Ames, 1981; Bayley, 1976; Parker, 1984), police officers typically do not expect an attack with a firearm in routine cases. In rare incidents someone might want to rob an officer of his gun as happened when an officer was stabbed to death in 1989 in an attempted robbery of his gun. Such an incident is rare, however. The safety of their work definitely contributes to the apparent civility of police behavior.

Another factor that has so far received no attention in previous research, but certainly gives Japanese police detectives an essential advantage is the relatively favorable work load, which allows them time to utilize the formal legal system and other resources to their maximum benefit.

If the police are working with too many cases, it is inevitable that they compromise their investigations in relatively minor cases to reserve time for more serious ones. This in turn may give some leverage to the suspect in a relatively minor crime to negotiate with the police over the disposition of his case. Time constraint due to a heavy work load may rebound to the advantage of the suspect in an even relatively serious crime. For instance, the police may not have time to collect circumstantial evidence sufficient to justify the maximum penalty provided by law or to find other crimes committed by the same suspect so that they can clear numerous crimes by the single investigation.

Readers will learn in the following pages that the police in Japan are probably one of the most fortunate police forces in the world, having a light work load and a highly enabling formal legal system. I will first elaborate on the work load, and then outline the formal legal system of criminal investigation.

1. Work Load of the Japanese Police

The *Keisatsucho,* or the National Police Agency of the Central Government of Japan, issues an annual publication called *Keisatsu Hakusho,* or *White Paper on Police.* Every year this publication claims that the Japanese police have the heaviest work load among police forces of developed capitalist countries, and claims a consistent need to increase the number of officers. The statistics the agency bases its argument on are misleading, however (see Table 2.1). While the agency also reports figures for Great Britain, Italy, and France, here I will compare Japan with the United States and West Germany. Since the Japanese criminal justice system mixes elements of the German and American systems, comparison with these two countries seems most appropriate.

Table 2.1 Police and Crime of Japan, United States, and West Germany in 1985

	JAPAN	U.S.	W. GERMANY
A. Population per police officer (1985) (Note 1)	556	361	317
B. Population (million) (Note 2)	120.8	239.3	54.6
C. Estimated number of police officers (Note 3)	217	663	192
D. Rate of major crimes (per 100,000) (Note 4)	1,328	5,207	6,909
E. Number of major crimes (thousand) (Note 5)	1,608	12,430	4,215
F. Estimated number of major crimes per police officer (Note 6)	7.4	18.7	22.0
G. Clearance rate of major crimes (%) (Note 7)	64.2	20.9	47.2
H. Estimated number of cleared major crimes (thousand) (Note 8)	1,032	2,598	1,990
I. Estimated number of cleared major crimes per police officer (Note 9)	4.8	3.9	10.4
J. Number of homicides (Note 10)	1,847	18,980	2,796
K. Estimated number of homicides per 1,000 police officers (Note 11)	8.5	28.6	14.6
L. Clearance rate of homicides (%) (Note 12)	96.1	72.0	95.0
M. Estimated number of cleared hoimicides (Note 13)	1,775	13,666	2,656

Table 2.1   *(Continued)*

	JAPAN	U.S.	W. GERMANY
N. Estimated number of cleared homicides per 1,000 police officers (Note 14)	8.2	20.6	13.8

Note 1: source, Keisatsucho, 1986: 272.
Note 2: source, Asahi Shinbun, 1989: 748.
Note 3: calculated from line A and line C.
Note 4: Criminal Code offenses except traffic-related unintentional deaths and injuries for Japan, index crimes for the United States, and Straftat except traffic offenses and Staatsschutz-delikte for West Germany; source, Homusho, 1987: 26.
Note 5: definitions and source same to Note 4.
Note 6: calculated from line C and line E.
Note 7: definitions and source same to Note 4.
Note 8: calculated from line E and line G.
Note 9: calculated from line C and line H.
Note 10: source, Homusho, 1987: 27.
Note 11: calculated from line C and line J.
Note 12: source, Homusho, 1987: 26.
Note 13: calculated from line J and line L.
Note 14: calculated from line C and line M.

The National Police Agency in Japan uses statistics for population per police officer (line A) as an indicator of work load and claims that the Japanese police work under the heaviest work load. It maintains that in spite of this, the Japanese police have achieved the highest clearance rate (line G), and this effectiveness has contributed to the lowest crime rate in the world (line D). This path of argument has been so successful in Japan that, as Ames (1981) observed, they have been able to add more police. Ames noted that the authorized national number of police officers increased from 138,000 in 1963 to 197,000 in 1975, with an annual growth rate of more than 3 percent. With the decline of radical movements and the introduction of an increasingly more austere fiscal policy, this growth rate declined thereafter, but it remains positive, the force reaching 220,000 officers in 1987 (Keisatsucho, 1988: 302).

We may question the validity of the argument presented by the Japanese police. A series of sophisticated experimental studies in the United States has cast serious doubt on the assumption that a causal relationship exists between the strength of police activities and crime rate (Skolnick and Bayley, 1986: 1-6). The argument of the Japanese National Police Agency also assumes that most people are potential criminals and therefore targets of daily surveillance or investigation by the police. Otherwise, it does not make sense to measure the police work load by population size per police officer.

Ames (1981: 225) had already pointed out that in claiming the heaviest work load, the Japanese police "failed to note that Japan also has the lowest crime rate and the highest arrest [clearance] rate" of the major capitalist countries. A more realistic indicator of the police work load may be the number of crimes police *must* clear, and a more meaningful measure of police efficiency may be the number of crimes they *actually clear*. Taking this line of analysis, a different picture of the Japanese police emerges.

First, the number of crimes per police officer (Table 2.1, line F) is smallest in Japan, less than a half of that in the United States, and only about one third of that in West Germany. When we compare statistics on homicides (line K), which often require the largest investigative effort, a similar pattern appears, except that the American police have the heaviest work load this time, more than three times that of Japan.

Second, although police productivity is routinely measured by clearance rate, clearance rate also seems to be irrelevant as an indicator of relative productivity, unless one holds constant the number of crimes with which each police force has to deal. A high clearance rate should not be surprising if the number of crimes to be cleared is small to start with. An alternative, more direct measure of productivity could be the absolute number of crimes actually cleared, and, in this regard (line I) the Japanese police cannot claim the highest productivity, for the West German police are more than twice as productive. Turning to homicides (line N), the American police also appear to be more than twice as productive as the Japanese police.

To summarize, the Japanese police have the fewest crimes to clear, and these crimes are, on the average, the least serious. Therefore, the Japanese police can afford to spend more time and use more officers to clear cases. The Japanese police are in a fortunate position in that they can produce the apparently highest clearance rate in the world simply because of the high degree of law-abidingness of the people.

One may argue, of course, that since Japan does not allow plea-bargaining, police have to collect complete evidence in every case. Therefore simple numbers cannot properly measure the higher standard of the quality and quantity of the police work in Japan and the true work load. The West German police, however, also work under a no-plea bargain system, but still clear more crimes than the Japanese. Moreover, most suspects in Japan admit the crime, and rarely challenge the prosecution at their trial (Bayley, 1976). It is safe to maintain that on the average the Japanese police can spend more time and employ more officers in each investigation. The fact that serious crimes such as homicides are more rare in Japan adds to their advantage.

The formal legal system, which appears more enabling in Japan than that in the United States and Canada, works on top of this foundation.

2. The Formal Legal System of Criminal Investigation

As I have already argued, the need for the police to engage in questionable tactics might vary depending on the degree to which the formal legal system is designed or implemented to their advantage. A relatively benign form of police action might still have a forceful impact on a suspect if it were combined with other tactics permitted by a very enabling legal system. We can properly appreciate the significance of police behavior only by understanding the characteristics of the legal system under which the police operate. This section will summarize salient features of the Japanese legal system as it concerns criminal investigation.[1]

a. Voluntary Investigation

Suspects in Japan are subject to two categories of investigative measures, voluntary and compulsory. A previous study on the Japanese police (Bayley, 1976: 146) has shown that police can rely more on the voluntary cooperation of the suspect and other people than on compulsory measures. Ericson observed that in Canada "most suspects unquestioningly submit to police orders" (1981: 138). Not obtaining a warrant could provide the police with "tactical and legal advantages," because "[i]f a suspect consented . . . it gave the enterprise a character of voluntariness" (1981: 154), and helped the police avoid judicial scrutiny of their tactics.

The Japanese police have the great advantage of dealing with generally cooperative suspects. In 1987 (Homusho, 1988: 107), prosecutors received 481,154 suspects for processing, excluding traffic offenses. Only 22.5 percent of these suspects had been arrested. For Criminal Code offenses (349,585 suspects), the lowest arrest rate was 14.9 percent for theft suspects (205,218), while the highest arrest rate was only 70.5 percent for rape suspects (1,907). The rate for homicide suspects was only 41.7 percent (2,952 suspects). These statistics provide a sharp contrast with the United States, where investigation usually starts with an arrest.

The Japanese police may interrogate the unarrested suspect at a police station or a police box on the basis of two statutes.

First, Article 2 of the Police Duties Execution Act provides that an officer may stop and question a person when there is sufficient reason to believe that the person has just committed a crime, is going to commit a crime, or knows about a crime committed or to be committed. The article adds that the officer may ask that person to accompany him to a nearby police station or a police box when questioning on the spot seems disadvantageous to the person or jeopardizes traffic. These tactics are called *shokumu shitsumon,* or duty questioning, and *nin-i doko,* or voluntary accompaniment, and their typical form is field questioning of the previously unknown suspect by a patrol officer, followed by a request to accompany the officer to a nearby police box.

Second, Article 198 of the Code of Criminal Procedure provides that when necessary, an officer may ask the suspect to appear for interrogation. This is called *nin-i shutto,* or voluntary appearance, and its typical form is a phone call or a face-to-face request from a detective for the identified but unarrested suspect to come to a police station for interrogation.

Bayley has suggested (1976: 150-51) the possibility of calculated, utilitarian motives on the part of the Japanese suspect who cooperates, but he places more emphasis on cultural explanations for the voluntary submission of suspects to the police, and stresses the general acceptance of moral authority of the police in Japan, and a sense of moral obligation on the part of the suspect to confess or otherwise cooperate. Bayley (1976: 37) wrote: "The key to success with these tactics [duty questioning and voluntary accompaniment] is to be compelling without being coercive." I shall detail in chapter 6 the actions that detectives take to make the suspect *voluntarily* accompany them to their station, and stay there *voluntarily* until they *voluntarily* confess to the charge, and how compelling or coercive these tactics are.

The Japanese court has interpreted this requirement of voluntariness rather liberally, and police tactics have to be very "compelling" indeed in order to be judged illegally "coercive." The Japanese Supreme Court has held that, depending on actual circumstances, even physical force may be applied legally in the process of voluntary investigation, unless it reaches the level of coercion which requires a specific statutory authorization (March 16, 1976, *Keishu* 30, 187; for abbreviations used by the reporters, see Appendix B). Bayley (1976: 38) observed that "to examine personal possessions . . . is a very delicate matter" when acting without a warrant. The Japanese Supreme Court, however, has ruled that, depending on circumstances, an officer engaged in duty questioning may examine without a warrant things that the questioned person carries, unless the officer is so coercive that he reaches the level at which a warrant is required (June 20, 1978, *Keishu* 32, 670). The Supreme Court has even ruled that it is not illegal to make a suspect spend four nights at a hotel near the police station, subjected to interrogation every day from morning until midnight, as long as the suspect voluntarily agrees to this form of investigation and there is an imminent need to get detailed statements in a short period of time (February 29, 1984, *Keishu* 38, 479).

If voluntary measures are later judged by the court to be virtual arrest, time limitations regarding detention and indictment start from that point. Ericson (1981: 136) explains that in Canada the general test to decide if an arrest has occurred is "whether the suspect perceives he is at liberty to depart from the presence of the police officer if he wishes to do so." Some forms of voluntary accompaniment and appearance in Japan might be judged as virtual arrest by such a test, although the officer does not typically tell the suspect that he is under arrest. Given judicial interpretations of the law, however, Japanese detectives need not be concerned that a voluntary accompaniment will be judged as virtual arrest.

b. Arrest

Compulsory measures of investigation start with arrest. Two forms—warrantless arrest of the flagrant offender and ordinary arrest with a warrant issued by the judge—can be found almost everywhere in the world. Japan has a third type of warrantless arrrest. Article 210 of the Code of Criminal Procedure provides that the police may arrest without warrant a person who, there is a sufficient reason to believe, has committed a crime punishable by imprisonment for three years or more, when there is an urgent need to arrest him and there is no time to apply for a warrant. This is called *kinkyu taiho*, or emergency arrest. The police must apply for warrant immediately after the arrest, and if the judge refuses, the suspect must be released immediately.

Article 33 of the Japanese Constitution, however, provides that no person shall be apprehended except upon a warrant, issued by a competent judicial officer, that specifies the offense with which the person is charged. This raised a question about the constitutionality of such emergency arrests. The Supreme Court has ruled that emergency arrest does not violate the Constitution when performed in accordance with the strict limitations of Article 210 of the Code of Criminal Procedure (December 14, 1955, *Keishu* 9, 2760). The time lapse between the arrest and the application for a warrant has become the main practical issue. For instance, while the Osaka High Court found illegal a lapse of six hours and forty minutes (November 19, 1975, *Hanji* 813, 102), the Hiroshima High Court held six hours acceptable if that time was needed to prepare the minimum evidence necessary to apply for the warrant (February 1, 1983, *Hanji* 1093, 151). It is clear that in practice two or three hours are always acceptable, and gives detectives sufficient time in many cases to obtain a confession, which in turn is used to justify the application for the warrant.

As Bayley (1976: 151) has observed, only a small proportion of suspects are detained in Japan, but once detained, they "have fewer procedural protections in practice than is the case in the United States." To start with, when arrested, the suspect has to be told of his constitutional rights to remain silent and retain counsel. The right to retain counsel is difficult to exercise for most suspects, however, because lawyers are few and expensive, and state-appointed counsel is not provided until indictment. Most suspects are left without counsel during the most crucial time of investigation, when detectives try hard to obtain a confession and collect as much incriminating evidence as possible. Regarding duty solicitors, the British version of state-appointed attorneys, McBarnet (1981: 63) observed that "the value of such schemes can be more symbolic than real," partly because of "the reluctance of solicitors themselves to provide a 24-hour service." They generally "meet prisoners for the first time just before their first court appearance." This British system certainly is enabling for the police (for the recent reform by the Police and Criminal Evidence Act of 1984, see *The Criminal Law Review,* 1985; for an empirical evaluation of its impact on detention and questioning, see Dixon, et al., 1990). But a state-appointed attorney is provided in Japan only after formal indictment which often occurs much later than first court appearance in the British system, so that the Japanese police are able to work under an even more enabling environment.

Arrest must be justified by a specific charge, but detectives sometimes find themselves with no evidence at hand to justify an arrest for the crime they are actually trying to solve. In such a case, the detectives occasionally try to arrest the suspect on a different, usually minor charge, for which they have sufficient evidence. This tactic allows them to interrogate the suspect about the more significant crime they want to solve. Some courts in Japan have found this practice illegal. The Osaka High Court, for instance, did so and ruled that statements secured in this way could not be admitted as evidence at the trial (April 19, 1984, *Kokeishu* 37, 98). The Supreme Court, however, ruled that the practice was not illegal if the minor crime for which the suspect was arrested was related to the major crime (August 9, 1977, *Keishu* 31, 821).

c. Detention at Police Station Detention Cells

Once arrested, the suspect can be confined by the police for forty eight hours before appearing before the prosecutor, and then the prosecutor may confine the suspect for another twenty four hours before applying to the judge for detention. Throughout these seventy two hours, there is no need for the police or the prosector to bring the suspect to the court, and the suspect may be kept in the police station.

Upon application from the prosecutor, the judge may detain the suspect if he does not have a stable residence, if there is a sufficient reason to believe that the suspect will hide or destroy evidence, or if there is a sufficient reason to believe that the suspect will flee. The judge informs the suspect of his constitutional rights and hears his plea. This hearing is the first opportunity for the suspect to appear before the judge. However, it is a closed hearing and the suspect must stand before the judge by himself. The initial period of detention can be up to ten days, and, upon application from the prosecutor, the judge may extend detention for up to another ten days for most crimes.

Statistics indicate that in most cases, once a suspect is arrested, the prosecutor is likely to apply to the judge for detention. In 1987, Japanese prosecutors received 107,895 arrested suspects and subsequently applied for detention for 85.2 percent of them, including 99.2 percent of the arrested homicide suspects and 84.8 percent of the arrested theft suspects (Homusho, 1988: 107). The judge's approval was virtually guaranteed. In 1987, only 143 out of 91,966 applications from the prosecutor were denied. Detectives have ample time for investigation in these cases.

The judge decides where the suspect will be held, and the prosecutor usually asks the judge to detain him at a "substitute prison," namely, *ryuchijo* or detention cells in a police station, except for white collar criminals who are more likely to be held in *kochisho* or regular detention centers as part of the prison system under the control of the Justice Ministry. This is so despite the fact that regular detention centers are not full. In 1982 (Igarashi, 1989: 105), for instance, the daily average of the people detained in substitute prisons was 5,885, a number smaller than the vacancies in detention centers, which were only 59 percent full. In fact in 1988 (Igarashi, 1989: 105), there were only 154 detention centers maintained by the Justice Ministry, compared to 1,254 substitute prisons maintained by the police. Only one detention center was constructed between 1977 and 1988, compared to thirty six substitute prisons established during the same period. As a result of this police effort to add more substitute prisons, the overall capacities of the two detention systems are now the same, with some 16,000 beds each, two or three times as many as needed.

Detention at police station detention cells has a definite advantage for police. While they must make a trip to the detention center if the suspect is detained there, detectives may interrogate him at their convenience if he is detained in their own police station.

Once the detention period expires and if the suspect is indicted, the suspect's legal status changes to that of defendant. The defendant then must be moved to the detention center at an outside prison. In practice, however, the defendant may still remain in the police station. Arrest and detention is justified for each single charge, and if detectives bring in separate charges at proper intervals, the defendant will have a dual status as suspect and defendant for different charges, and can be detained in the police station until detectives finish all the investigations. In 1985 (Igarashi, 1989: 105), for instance, the average daily number of people detained in police station detention cells was 6,553, with 53.4 percent of them already indicted on one or more charges. This system encourages detectives to seek confessions to multiple charges.

The detained suspect, his counsel, family members, and other related persons may ask the judge to disclose the cause of his detention in open court. This procedure is based on Article 34 of the Constitution, which provides that "No person . . . shall be detained without adequate cause; and upon demand of any person such cause must be immediately shown in open court in his presence and the presence of his counsel." This procedure is rarely used, however, because the court has established an interpretation that their job is not to review the legality of detention, but merely to inform the suspect in open court of the cause of his detention. In 1985, for instance, there were only 332 cases following this procedure for the disclosure of the cause of detention at trial courts, including detentions of both suspects and defendants (Nitta and Yasui, 1988).

A prosecutor has admitted, however, that there are cases in which prosecutors try to finish investigation and to release the suspect before the disclosure of the cause of detention is demanded and, to that extent, the procedure has an effect (Masui, 1988). One defense attorney has criticized other attorneys for their reluctance to use this procedure to challenge the judge (Akiyama, 1988). In fact, activist attorneys occasionally demand elaborations of the reasons to detain the suspect and use the open court as a forum to criticize the judge as well as the prosecutor. As a consequence, some judges (Nitta and Yasui, 1988) have proposed to abolish this procedure.

A detained person may file an appeal to the court to which the authorizing judge belongs to challenge the detention decision. This is also rare, however. Attorneys are largely reluctant to advise their client to take this action, because once the court approves the validity of detention, it becomes all the more difficult to get bail after indictment.

d. Interrogations and Confessions

The manner in which the suspect's statements are taken and recorded also is enabling for detectives. The suspect's statements are neither recorded verbatim nor tape recorded. Rather, detectives rewrite statements into coherent stories, and the suspect is simply asked to sign them. Ericson (1981: 114) quoted a case in Canada in which a detective frequently injected his version of events during the victim's verbal description of the crime until the victim signed a statement which reflected the detective's perspective. In Japan, detectives go much further and literally compose all the statements while questioning and listening.

Even when the suspect is wealthy enough to retain counsel, defense counsel has no right to be present at interrogations, and access to counsel itself may be limited for the convenience of the investigation. Article 39 of the Code of Criminal Procedure provides that when necessary for investigation, the prosecutor or the police may designate certain times, places, and durations for meetings between suspects and their counsel. In other words, defense attorneys must acquire the approval of the police or prosecutor in order to see their clients. The code states that such limitations should not unduly restrict the right of the suspect to prepare a defense, but in practice the prosecutors issue orders to the police that unless the counsel brings permission from the prosecutor specifying time, location, and length of the meeting, the police should not let the attorney see his client.

One lower court has held this practice appealable (March 7, 1967, Tottori District Court, *Kakeishu* 9, 375), but another, more influential court ruled that this practice cannot be a subject for appeal, since the prosecutor's order is nothing more than an internal memorandum and does not constitute a governmental action (October 5, 1983, Tokyo District Court, *Hanta* 527, 161). Yet another court has held that this practice is legal, since the prosecutor's order does not necessarily mean complete prohibition, it serves as communication between the prosecutor and the counsel, and the requirement that the counsel secure specific permission from the prosecutor is within the limit of "endurable burden" (February 12, 1985, Gifu District Court, *Hanji* 1165, 184). The Supreme Court's decision was that meetings with counsel may be limited even after indictment, if the reason for the limitation is the need to investigate a separate crime for a later indictment and if the limitation does not "unduly" jeopardize the right of defense for the already indicted crime (April 28, 1980, *Keishu* 34, 178). Some attorneys have since filed civil suits against the state seeking compensation for damages due to their inability to meet their clients, and a few courts have decided in their favor (Wakamatsu, 1987; 1990). But no one has yet succeeded in directly challenging the prosecutor's control while investigation is still in progress. Thus, while the police can freely interrogate the suspect in their own police station, counsel may not see the client freely.

Bayley (1976: 152) states that in general "attorneys are allowed one meeting while the suspect is in police custody and from two to five during the twenty days in prosecutor's custody." Although "they may last as long as half an hour, the average is about fifteen minutes." He added that once "a confession has been made or a charge filed, visits become unlimited." As long as the suspect denies the charge or refuses to talk, meetings will be denied, and confession will become prerequisite to the exercise of his constitutional right. Thus, investigation takes a definite priority over defense.

Control of interrogation of the suspect in custody and regulation of access to defense counsel seem to be common concerns for detectives any-where. Ericson describes (1981: 144-46) comparable practices in Canada. "[T]he police in Canada are under no legal obligation to inform a person that he has a right to counsel before he makes a statement." "Where access was granted to parties other than lawyers, it was typically granted in exchange for co-operation from the suspect."

e. Admissibility of Evidence

After indictment, the defense may attempt to challenge the admissibility of evidence. The attitude of the Japanese court is ambivalent, however. On search and seizure of physical evidence, Article 35 of the Japanese Constitu-tion requires a warrant issued by the judge for adequate cause, particularly describing the place to be searched and things to be seized. But early judicial decisions hesitated to exclude illegally seized evidence. For instance, the Supreme Court held that since the illegality of the procedure does not affect the appearance and nature of such evidence, its value does not change, and therefore it is completely up to the discretion of the court whether or not to admit it (December 13, 1949, *Saibanshu-kei* 15, 349). Twenty-nine years later, however, the Court decided that the evidence would not be admissible if the procedure were gravely illegal, and exclusion of that evidence would be appropriate in the interest of preventing future illegality. At the same time, however, the Court stated that it is unreasonable to exclude all illegally obtained evidence since doing so would jeopardize the search for the truth (September 7, 1978, *Keishu* 32, 1672). This ruling has an element of the exclusionary rule developed in the *Mallorey* case in 1957 in the United States, but the Japanese Supreme Court still hesitates to clearly follow that path.

The situation is similar with regard to the admissibility of confessions. Article 38 of the Constitution provides that no person shall be compelled to testify against oneself; that a confession made under compulsion, torture, or threat, or after prolonged arrest or detention shall not be admitted as evi-dence; and that no one shall be convicted or punished in cases where the only proof against the person is his own confession. Court decisions on confes-sions have fluctuated. In earlier cases, the Supreme Court rarely excluded confessions on the basis of lack of voluntariness or untruthfulness. The Court decided, for instance, that even a confession taken after an unduly long con-finement may be admitted as evidence if there is no causal relationship between the confinement and the confession (June 30, 1948, *Keishu* 2, 715). It held that although the statement was taken during detention following an illegal arrest, this did not by itself deny the voluntariness of the statement (November 25, 1952, *Keishu* 6, 1245). The Court also refused to consider a self-incriminating statement as coerced even when prosecutors interrogated a suspect who had been detained on an eitirely different charge some fifty times in a period of thirty nine days (April 6, 1955, *Keishu* 9, 663). Although meetings with a counsel were not permitted until indictment, the Court ruled that the defendant's right to prepare his defense was not unfairly limited, nor did that fact render a statement involuntary (April 20, 1955, *Hanji* 54, 27).

In the following years a different line of decisions appeared. The Supreme Court decided that when a suspect was prohibited from receiving food from outside, the court should examine the reason for the prohibition and its influence on a confession (May 31, 1957, *Keishu* 11, 1579). If the suspect was interrogated while handcuffed, the court should have a prima facie doubt about the subsequent confession's voluntariness (September 13, 1963, *Keishu* 17, 1703). The Court held that if the prosecutor told the suspect that his indictment would be suspended if he confessed, the voluntariness of the confession was doubtful, and the confession should be excluded (July 1, 1966, *Keishu* 20, 537). When there was a possibility of inducing an untruthful confession by deceit, the Court ruled that the confession should be excluded as involuntary (November 25, 1970, *Keishu* 24, 1670). The Court is still reluctant, however, to exclude a confession on the basis of the illegality of the procedure itself.

As Bayley (1976: 152) observes, "discovery of an involuntary confession is not as damaging to a case [in Japan] as it is in the United States," and "Article 39 [38] of the Constitution . . . is not always observed." This observation applies as well to physical evidence. Given the rarity of retaining counsel before indictment and the limitations on activities of counsel in contested cases, it is extremely difficult for the defense attorney to challenge procedural illegalities and admissibility of evidence. The cases described in chapter 1 illustrated this point. Falsely convicted defendants have had to fight for ten, twenty, or even thirty years to overturn their conviction.

Bayley (1976: 152–54) presents a benign evaluation of the Japanese system. He argues that "the temptation to browbeat unrepentant people would seem to be very great," but that "instances of abuse of persons in custody are rare." "[T]he vulnerable Japanese suspect is handled more considerately in custody by and large than the fortressed American," he concludes, and "[l]ong detentions without charge [indictment] and imperfect access by lawyers to clients has not produced rampant abuse." He asks "Why not?" and his answer is that there is a combination of two factors. One is the ethical norm that encourages suspects to confess, so that the police need not exert much pressure on them. The other is the internalization by the police of their fiduciary role vis-à-vis suspects, which makes the police behave responsibly.

In later chapters I will describe the reality of police behavior in Japan. The fact is that there is no need for the Japanese police to engage in "rampant abuse" of their power, simply because the formal legal system highly favors their interest in crime making. The formal legal system in Japan provides detectives with so many advantages that they rarely need to resort to obviously illegal tactics. In relation to the recent Recruit bribery scandal, *Time* magazine (April 24, 1989: 11) wrote that "[in] a country where laws do not permit the issuing of subpoenas, the granting of immunity or the conducting of undercover operations, a prosecutor must work doubly hard to extract confessions from criminal suspects." It is wrong to infer from such a description that the formal legal environment of criminal investigation in Japan is less enabling than that in the United States. The whole series of enabling features outlined above more than compensate for what *Time* magazine found absent in the Japanese system. The police in Japan do not need to work "doubly hard" to extract confessions. The whole system is designed and implemented in such a way that the suspect will offer apparently voluntary confessions to his captors. It was precisely because of the apparent voluntariness of their confessions that those falsely convicted people discussed in chapter 1 had to fight for so many years to secure their freedom.

In concluding his study of Canadian detectives, Ericson (1981: 213-14) wrote that "criminal process structures are explicitly designed to give detectives the upper hand. Detectives, as rational and pragmatic actors, simply make innovative use of the resources that have been given to them to control the process." Japanese police detectives have even greater formal legal resources. Later chapters will describe how they utilize these and other resources and will explain why they nonetheless engage in questionable tactics when they could easily control the process in most cases well within the bounds of legality.

3

The Process of the Research

1. Exposition of the Research Procedure

To gain an understanding of the meaning of behavior from the actor's own viewpoint, direct observational methods are required. In this chapter I will provide readers with as much information as possible about the context and execution of the research. This should answer questions about the subject organization and whether I was truly able to observe daily activities and grasp the subjective meanings attached to such activities.

Unfortunately, few studies provide this information. In his article, aptly entitled "On Watching the Watchers," Van Maanen (1978: 310), himself a police researcher employing observational research methods, complained that "the actual process by which such information [in many studies] has been generated remains something of a mystery." He particularly criticized "a shroud of silence surrounding the circumstances under which social scientists have been granted permission to conduct research in police settings" and noted that "[v]ery few published studies have discussed the negotiation process by which a specific research site was chosen and secured" (Van Maanen, 1978: 323). Therefore, in the hope that his article would "stimulate others to provide a more comprehensive account for the research that stands behind their results," Van Maanen (1978: 346) described his own research process.

A deeper analysis of this issue may be found in Cicourel's (1976: chapter 1) classic, ethnomethodological study of juvenile justice. He utilized the concept of *objectification,* which denotes "the observer's *and* actor's attempts to convince the reader (or listener) of the credibility of the proper-

27

ties or elements being attended and labelled 'data' for purposes of making inferences and taking further action." In other words, *objectification* of the data about meanings of behavior requires both that the observer-author has information to judge the credibility of the materials provided by the subject-actor and that the reader has information to judge the credibility of the materials provided by the observer.

The fundamental problem is that there is no guarantee that different people will arrive at the same inferences from the same materials. The actor accounts for his own behavior in a truncated form of daily conversation, because he assumes that others share and utilize unspoken tacit knowledge to make sense of his account. The observer will then understand the actor's account on the basis of his own tacit knowledge and present, in his own way of truncated expression, his understanding to the reader, who will in turn bring in his own tacit knowledge to make sense of the materials presented by the observer. Therefore, in presenting research findings, an essential task for the observer is to include the materials received from the actor, and let the reader evaluate the credibility of his conclusions.

Cicourel's practical solution to this problem was to cite many verbatim records of observed incidents along with what he interpreted as the unstated assumptions lying behind them. One chapter of his book (Cicourel, 1976: chapter 4) was devoted to conversational depictions of the social organization of juvenile justice, with direct quotations of observational data. Studies of everyday detective activities do not go that far, but some at least devote a chapter to their research procedure. Sanders, for instance, described his research procedure in his final chapter (1977: chapter 9), while Ericson detailed his research strategy immediately after his introduction (1981: chapter 2), preceding the analytical sections.

The original Japanese version of this book closely followed Cicourel's approach. It first presented all the major cases that had been observed, and always referred to the whole context of the case whenever a fragment of observational data was quoted in the analytical sections of the book. The question of *objectification* is an important one for this research, not simply because the observer-author is an "outsider" to the organization, but also because non-Japanese readers are "outsiders" to the societal context in which the observed and the observer interacted. Therefore, I shall provide a selection of verbatim case records to illustrate the way I observe and deduce implications from my observations. Since the main body of the book will deal with each stage of criminal investigation separately and quote only fragments of observational data, the illustrations also will serve to acquaint non-Japanese readers with the natural sequences of everyday criminal investigation in Japan.

2. The Process of the Research

The duality and centralization of the Japanese police has been well documented in previous studies by American scholars (Bayley, 1976: chapter 9; Ames, 1981: introduction, chapter 10). There exists, first of all, the National Police Agency of the Central Government which in 1987 had 7,588 authorized personnel, including 1,194 sworn police executives and 916 Imperial Palace officers (Keisatsucho, 1988: 302). In addition, each of the forty seven Prefectures into which Japan is divided has its own police force. In 1987, the total authorized personnel of prefectural police forces was 249,010, of which 218,752 (88 percent) were sworn officers (Keisatsucho, 1988: 302). There are no county or city police. Police stations are under the supervision of the prefectural headquarters, and have no relationship with the municipalities in which they are located. The national and prefectural levels of police officers are recruited separately.

The vast difference in their numerical strength might give the impression that the National Police Agency does not have many meaningful functions as a national police force. As Bayley and Ames indicated, however, the truth is that the National Police Agency controls the prefectural police forces in many ways and can use them as its subordinates. One way is its control over command positions. Executive positions at headquarters of the prefectural police forces are staffed with officers sent from the Agency. Chiefs of the prefectural police forces are all sent from the Agency, and it is rare to find locally recruited officers even at the immediately lower level of division head. Moreover, the status of local officers changes when they reach the rank of senior police superintendent, the sixth rank from the bottom. At that point they become employees of the Central Government. Chiefs of police stations are usually at this rank, and thus the National Police Agency controls command positions at both headquarters and police stations. As we have already seen in the case of the attempted frame-up of a housewife and the case of the death of a juvenile suspect described in chapter 1, one of the main official functions of executive members of prefectural headquarters is to police the locally recruited field officers.

A second mechanism of control is the requirement that the prefectural forces follow various standards established by the National Police Agency. Standards are set for the size of the force, equipment, training, salary, and other matters. Although the prefectural governments are responsible for most of the police expenditures, they do not have much discretion over how their money is spent. In 1987, for instance, the total expenditure on police by the prefectural governments was 2,235 billion yen (approximately $15.4 billions U.S.), compared to 183 billion yen (approximately $1.26 billions U.S.) budgeted for the National Police Agency (Keisatsucho, 1988: 308).

A third control mechanism is through subsidies and special functions provided by the National Police Agency. Twenty-five percent of the agency's budget of 1987 subsidized the prefectural police forces (Keisatsucho, 1988: 302). Functions directly provided by the agency include the nationwide communication network, the centralized identification system, and training of executive police officers. As vividly illustrated by the wiretapping case described in chapter 1, activities in the area of national security are also under the direct control of the agency, which utilizes officers at local police stations through security divisions at prefectural headquarters (Ames, 1981: 142-48).

I shall describe later how control by the headquarters, particularly by those executives sent from the National Police Agency, caused resentment among local officers. I shall also describe how officers assigned to the Security Department of the police station I observed resisted answering my questionnaire despite the support I had from the prefectural headquarters and the executive officers of the station. Except on these and a few other occasions, however, prefectural headquarters was not involved in the everyday activities of general investigation police detectives. Therefore, I will devote the rest of this section to the process of my research at the target police station.

My research was planned in 1973 when I was a research associate at the Faculty of Law of Hokkaido University in Sapporo City of Hokkaido Prefecture, the northernmost island of the four main islands of Japan. The research was divided into seven stages which I will describe in order.

The first stage involved negotiations with the head of the Criminal Division of the Hokkaido Prefectural Police Headquarters in the fall of 1973. These were made in association with my academic supervisor at the Law Faculty of Hokkaido University, Professor Tokuo Kogure, who had introduced me to the head. I explained to the police executive that my purpose was to understand the everyday activities of police detectives and their perceptions about their work environment. As Van Maanen (1978: 335) did in his research, I emphasized that my findings would be useful for managerial purposes.

Negotiations continued through the the head of the Criminal Planning Department within the Criminal Division. With certain conditions attached, I was granted permission to observe and distribute questionnaires at (1) the Hokkaido Police Academy, (2) a police station in Sapporo City, and (3) the Mobile Squad attached to the headquarters. The conditions were: (1) that names of persons, places, and the contents of cases not be specific, and that actual names be held in the strictest confidence; (2) that I not enter the interrogation room because of the risk of a complaint of civil rights violations on the ground that having an additional person on the interrogation team added more pressures on the suspect; and (3) that I not enter the security police sections. The Mobile Squad had just been established at this time and was added to my research plan at the request of the Criminal Planning Department. The second condition was the same as that imposed on Ericson (1981: 34), who in attempting to renegotiate access to interrogations, worsened his relationship with the police. As I shall explain later, this condition did not much affect my chances to learn about what took place in interrogation rooms.

I was told that permission had been granted by the chief of the Hokkaido Police himself. Van Maanen (1978: 327) noted that his access to the target organization was difficult to gain without support from the highest person, and this applied to my case as well. I did not know, however, the reasons that the chief and other executive officers of headquarters allowed my access. This again paralleled Van Maanen's experience (1978: 336). If it is true that the more organized the police force, the less likely it is to grant access to an outsider (Van Maanen, 1978: 324), the distance of the Hokkaido Police from the National Police Agency could be one factor in my success, and I suspect that the Hokkaido Police did not consult the National Police Agency. Another possible factor was that the chief of the Hokkaido Police was about to retire, and would not return to the agency or move to another prefecture. He probably was not much concerned about possible later adverse impacts from my research. Still another factor suggested by other scholars in Japan is that since I was young and unknown to them, the police did not consider me dangerous, but rather thought that I might become a police sympathizer.

The second stage of my research was a study of the Hokkaido Police Academy (on the training system, see Ames, 1981: 168-73). The aim was, (1) to prepare for my study of the police, (2) to make contact with a broad spectrum of police officers from a wide variety of assignments and locations, and (3) to learn about the Police Academy, which I felt was an important aspect of the socialization process for police officers. Between January 1 and February 21 of 1974, I attended the academy for fifteen days. Observations included both formal attendance at lectures and seminars and informal participation in conversations among students during spring break and at other times. The principal subjects of observation were members of the class of just promoted assistant police inspectors and police sergeants. I also attended classes of newly recruited patrolmen and young patrolmen with a few months' experience. Following the concerns already set forth above, I observed classes chiefly in the area of the Criminal Code, the Code of Criminal Procedure, investigation management, and organizational management.

In the third phase, I prepared for the study of a single police station in order to maximize the time I had available and to have sufficient opportunity to gain the trust of the officers. I asked the head of the Criminal Planning Department of the Hokkaido Police Headquarters for access to a large station in Sapporo that had a representative criminal case record and included both

commercial and residential districts in its jurisdiction but not including
Hokkaido University. The head chose a police station on the basis of the reputation of its supervisors there, i.e., a station staffed with the most procedure-
minded supervisors. I refer to this in the study as the Eastern Police Station.
The head thus chose a station which was likely to give me the best impression among the five in Sapporo. In fact, as I will describe later, some detectives expressed resentment of the procedural restraints supervisors imposed
there, and I did not encounter any occasion in which detectives physically
abused a suspect. As a result, I was later criticized by some Japanese scholars for too sympathetic a portrayal of police detectives. I have to emphasize,
however, that less serious yet questionable practices did appear even in a station such as this. We may expect that the same practices occur more often in
stations with lesser degrees of procedural restraint and that the findings concerning the Eastern Police Station apply to other stations as well.

The jurisdiction of the Eastern Police Station was 279 square kilome-
ters (approximately 109 square miles) with a resident population of 310,000
persons. Table 3.1 compares the statistics of this station with those of the
country and the Hokkaido Prefecture for 1973. Most items are from an annual report prepared by the Criminal Planning Department of the Hokkaido
Police Headquarters (Do Keisatsu Honbu, 1974), which featured various
statistics per police detective as indicators of relative work load and productivity. These interesting statistics identify separately all recorded thefts and
all thefts reported by victims before investigation. While unreported thefts
could be found by detectives through confessions of suspects, priority of
investigation is given to reported thefts because of the expressed desire of
victims for apprehension of criminals.

Table 3.1 Crime and Clearance Statistics of the Eastern Police Station
Compared to the National and Prefectural Statistics in 1973

	EASTERN	HOKKAIDO	NATIONAL
A. Recorded Criminal Code Offenses (except traffic-related offenses) (Note 1)	5,690	80,234	1,190,549
B. Overall Crime Rate per 100,000 (Note 2)	1,835	1,517	1,097
C. Number of Recorded Crimes per Detective (Note 3)	129.3	65.4	48.7
D. Overall Clearance Rate	60%	62%	58%
E. Number of Cleared Crimes per Detective	77.8	40.7	28.2
F. Recorded Thefts	4,738	65,364	973,876
G. Recorded Thefts per Detective	107.7	53.3	39.8

Table 3.1 *(Continued)*

	EASTERN	HOKKAIDO	NATIONAL
H. Number of Cleared Thefts per Detective	59.7	29.9	20.1
I. Recorded Thefts Reported by Victims	3,468	51,561	826,204
J. Number of Victim-Reported Thefts per Detective	78.8	42.1	33.8
K. Clearance Rate of Victim-Reported Thefts	35%	45%	42%
L. Number of Cleared Victim-Reported Thefts per Detective	27.9	18.7	14.1

Note 1: source, Do Keisatsu Honbu, 1974; Keisatsucho, 1974: 94.
Note 2: the Eastern Police Station and Hokkaido statistics were estimated from line A and the population statistics; source of the national statistics, Keisatsucho, 1974: 94.
Note 3: source of lines C to L, Do Keisatsu Honbu, 1974.

Statistics in Table 3.1 indicate that the work load for detectives was heavier for Hokkaido than for Japan as a whole, but was even heavier for the Eastern Police Station. The overall crime rate per detective was 2.6 times the national rate, the rate of thefts 2.7 times, and the rate of victim-reported thefts 2.3 times. Line A of Table 3.1 indicates that the rate of major crimes per officer at the Eastern Police Station, with its 267 officers, was approximately twenty-one. This figure is higher than the estimated rate of major crimes per officer in the United States in 1985 (line F of Table 1.1). Although officers at the Eastern Police Station had many fewer serious crimes to solve than American police officers, it is safe to conclude that its detectives were working under probably one of the heaviest work loads in the country.

The Eastern also has some of the most productive detectives in Japan. The number of cleared Criminal Code offenses per detective was 2.8 times the national average, the number of cleared thefts per detective three times, and the number of clearances of victim-reported thefts twice the national average. Because of the extremely heavy work load at Eastern, however, their clearance rate in the category most commonly used to evaluate performance, namely victim-reported thefts, was lower than both the Hokkaido average and the national average. Their rate was second lowest among the five stations in Sapporo, and seventh lowest among the sixty five stations in Hokkaido.

We may assume, therefore, that the Eastern's detectives were under

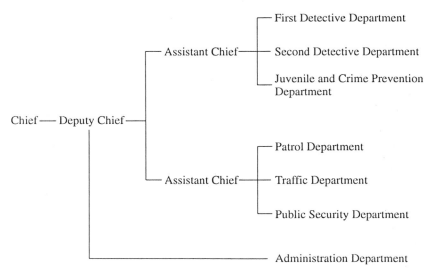

Figure 3.1   Organizational Chart of the Eastern Police Station

strong pressure to improve their statistics, and it became the focus of my research to find situations where the procedure-minded supervisors would deviate from their own principles under this pressure, where the precarious balance of due process and crime control would be broken in favor of the latter.

Including the chief and the deputy chief, the Eastern Police Station had 267 sworn officers. Two assistant chiefs served under the chief and the deputy chief. One assistant chief oversaw the First and Second Detective Departments and the Juvenile and Crime Prevention Department; the other oversaw the Patrol Department, the Traffic Department, and the Public Security Department. The supervisors I dealt with most frequently during my research were the assistant chief in charge of the Detective Departments and the heads of the Detective Departments. The assistant chief was at the rank of superintendent and the department heads were at the rank of inspector.

The Japanese Code of Criminal Procedure gives only inspectors or higher officers the power to apply to the judge for a warrant. This monopoly and the corollary authority to refuse lower-ranking detectives' requests for warrant applications are an important source of their power in the organization. I use the term *supervisor* in the later chapters of this book to refer to these higher-ranking officers, while *detective* refers to officers lacking this authority, persons at the ranks of assistant inspector, sergeant, and patrolman. Sanders (1977: 45) and Ericson (1981: 57-60, 69, 73) emphasized detective sergeants' roles in supervising everyday investigations. Lieutenants and captains in the United States (Sanders, 1977) or inspectors in Canada (Ericson,

1981) were not considered to be directly involved in specific investigative work. The situation is different in Japan. Since cases with any significance need warrants, detective superintendents and inspectors are directly involved in routine activities of criminal investigation. The authority of sergeants and even assistant inspectors is no different from detectives at the rank of patrolman. Bayley (1976: 64) has argued that since the Japanese police have more supervisors, supervision is more extensive in Japan than in America. Bayley has compared ratios of sergeants to patrolmen in Japan and various cities in the United States, but this may be misleading since Japanese and American sergeants are not equivalent.

I shall describe later how this situation places assistant inspectors in a particularly difficult position, facing pressures from both above and below. They were neither real supervisors nor ordinary detectives.

The first negotiations with the station chief took place on February 10, 1974. He showed me great kindness and promised to accommodate me as far as possible. However, as I had been told before, because of the risk of rights violations, I was to be barred not only from the interrogation room, but from the police station detention cell as well. He recommended that I first observe the Patrol Department and then, after I had become accustomed to the ways and atmosphere of the station, the Detective Departments.

The fourth phase was a six-day observational study of the Patrol Department. Of these, four days were spent in twenty-four-hour visits at two police boxes. The Patrol Department had 145 sworn officers and was divided into three sections, first through third, because patrol officers worked in three shifts. Each section was divided into squads of two to five men. At the police box, officers serve in squads. As in other departments, the department head was an inspector, the section heads were assistant inspectors, while the squad heads were sergeants or senior patrolmen. At the police boxes, I accompanied officers on their rounds, as they answered questions for local directions, kept the scene of a crime clear for detectives arriving later, closed bars, searched lost persons feared to be suicidal, and visited elderly citizens living alone. There was little criminal investigation, as has already been reported of patrol activities in Japan (Bayley, 1976: 19-20) and in Canada (Ericson, 1982: 5).

The fifth phase was an observational study in the Detective Departments. At the Eastern Police Station, there were two Detective Departments under the supervision of one assistant chief. The total strength was fifty four officers, including those assigned to station detention cells and identification. The First Department contained the First and Second Theft Crime Sections responsible for theft and burglary, the Forcible Crime Section handling violent crimes, the General Affairs Section responsible for all forms of warrants, documents and records, and the Identification Section. The Second Department contained the Intellectual Crime Section and the Organized Crime Sec-

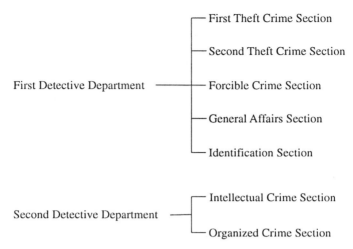

Figure 3.2   Structure of the Detective Departments at the
                 Eastern Police Station

tion. The latter handled cases involving *yakuza* or organized crime figures.
Each section was divided into squads of two or three men. The section chiefs
were assistant inspectors, and the squad chiefs were sergeants. My use of
detectives in this study ordinarily refers to sergeants or patrolmen specializing in investigations.

There were two periods of observation in the detective section. The first
ran from March 11 through April 27, a total of thirty five days. During this
period, at least once a week I attended a duty watch. In the morning, I invariably attended the meeting that took place at 8:30 a.m. During day watch, I had
a desk in the Forcible Crime Section and the Theft Crime Sections. Depending upon circumstances, I would either remain in the station or accompany
officers on outside duty. I simply stayed by them and took notes. I did not
conduct any investigation myself, never provided any assistance to detectives,
and never talked to the suspect, victim, witness, or anyone else the detectives
contacted. Following Van Maanen's typology of participant observers (1978:
344), I was clearly a *fan,* the most common type of observer.

Detectives were generally quite open with and friendly toward me, and
more than a few spoke of their dissatisfaction with the supervisors and the
terms of their duty. They also spoke of their personal experiences and families. Ericson (1981: 31) wrote of his research, "[i]n the early meetings *the*
central concerns of detectives at all levels could be interpreted as one: whose
interests would this research serve, police or some anti-police element?"
Some detectives at the Eastern Police Station also expressed such a concern
to me. However, the dominant suspicion was not whether I was pro-police or

anti-police, but whether I was a spy from the Prefectural Headquarters. After they found that I was not, they were more accepting, and some of them even asked me to report their grievances in my study.

The assistant chief in charge of detectives and crime prevention was extremely kind. He dealt effectively with numerous problems in the course of the observational study and in the distribution of the surveys, and handled all negotiations with the Prefectural Headquarters once I entered the station.

During my observations, in order to be able to see detectives' interactions with suspects and other citizens, I made it a practice to accompany officers on duty outside the station. Since members of each Detective Department worked in a large open space, at the center of which was the department head, it was not too dificult to monitor their activities. By accompanying the detectives on outside duty, I was able to see firsthand voluntary accompaniment and arrest, and search and seizure.

However, I also spent time in the station when a suspect of interest was interrogated, in order to follow the situation. The interrogation room was adjacent to the detectives' office, and in spite of being denied access to the interrogation room, I was able to hear what went on inside as well as the conversations of detectives entering and leaving the room. This also allowed me to learn about detectives' actions and supervisors' attitudes toward them in the investigation process—from arrest, through the detention of the suspect, to indictment. Through observation in the station, I also discovered how applications for warrants were made and how officers dealt with the prosecutor's office.

I did not witness a major investigation in which the station chief himself directs everyday activities of numerous investigators over a long period of time. On the other hand, I was able to learn more about investigations under day-to-day circumstances.

Not all activity observed was meaningful in research terms. Detectives spent a great deal of time in routine work, collecting information and writing reports. Van Maanen (1978: 320) has warned that "the firsthand observation of the police in action can often be a boring and frustrating affair, since there is no assurance that one will see what one came to see." Ericson (1981: 31) too lamented that observing police required a "'wait and see' attitude that subsequently meant more waiting than seeing." My experience was exactly the same. At the National Research Institute of Police Science of the National Police Agency, Uchiyama (1978: 99) surveyed a national sample of cases investigated by detectives and found that only 14.9 percent of a detective's time was spent interrogating the suspect, whether inside or outside the police station. If they had included the time not spent directly on specific crimes, this figure could be still smaller. It is not surprising that I did not have many chances to observe direct encounters between detectives and suspects.

Furthermore, the crime rate seemed to decrease on days I was at the station, and increase on days I was not. I was told, "You aren't around when something good comes up, Professor." Detectives joked when I worked on a night shift, "Ah, Professor is here, so we will be able to sleep soundly." It is possible that my presence influenced detectives' behavior and made them less aggressive in their proactive pursuit of crime. I do not believe, however, that this was the case. Detective work was basically reactive, mostly responding to reports of crime either from victims or patrol officers. Moreover, their work pressure and my continuous presence did not seem to allow them to drastically change their routines on the basis of my presence and absence.

In any event, I had to accept the fact that much of my observation time did not present significant activity. Nonetheless, the value of observation in providing firsthand information on actual circumstances in the field is incomparably superior to archival research and other research methods.

In late April, I interrupted my observations to draft a questionnaire. I needed to know how typical the observed behavior and recorded statements were of the station in general, and among detectives in particular. In early July, in order to gain the necessary advance approval for the survey from the headquarters, I forwarded a copy for inspection through the assistant chief in charge of detectives. Thus I entered the sixth phase—preparation for the survey.

The initial reponse from the headquarters was devastating. It objected to questions regarding terms and conditions of employment, official policies of the Hokkaido Police Department regarding criminal investigation, relationships with ex-convicts, informants, and interference in specific criminal investigation by executive officers at the headquarters. This response was interesting in itself because it told me what areas the headquarters thought most sensitive. I did not want to exclude such questions, and I negotiated directly with the head of the Criminal Planning Department. I again emphasized the value from the managerial perspective of having independent information about detectives. The entire survey was approved two weeks after its initial submission. The approved survey had four parts, two of which were devoted to personality tests, the Maudsley Psychology Inventory and the California Personality Inventory.

The seventh and final stage consisted of a second round of observation, the execution of the survey, and the conclusion of my research. While continuing observation, I discussed how to administer the survey with the assistant chief. Because there was no general meeting of the officers with sufficient time, I decided to distribute and collect the questionnaires in two sets, each with two parts, using the command structure of the station. The two parts of the personality tests were first distributed on July 30 to all 257 officers at the rank of assistant inspector or lower.

At the morning meeting on that day, the assistant chief began by saying, "Word has come in from the Headquarters asking for our cooperation." He proceeded to set forth the plan for the survey and particularly stressed that names would not be required, that responses would not be examined by the supervisors, and that answers would have no impact on personnel policies. Next, I gave an explanation of the contents of the survey, answered several questions, and reviewed the distribution-retrieval method. One detective told me, "Professor, this is a pretty tough questionnaire. What sort of people become detectives—where they are born, what sort of education they have, everything. You could use this for ideological purposes." Another said, "This is a psychological test, isn't it? Aren't you trying to find out that there are a lot of schizophrenics in the police?" Because these detectives were closest to me, I did not feel any element of hostility in these questions. I simply smiled back. These two parts were collected, as planned, one week after distribution. I noted that many officers filled them out on the last day, at the urging of the assistant chief.

The remaining portions were distributed at the morning meeting on August 13, two weeks later, with questions about personal background, perceptions about the environment both inside and outside the police organization, and opinions about proper actions in criminal investigation. Again, aside from my own explanations, there was an explanation from the assistant chief. The following from his comments should be particularly noted:

> There are apparently a lot of objections being made to the Administration Department of the station, but I don't want you to pay attention to that. We [supervisors] will not be looking at these. They are not an examination. They will not be used to evaluate your performance of your duties. This is an academic study, nothing more. It does not matter what your parents' school record, or career, or social status is; I myself am the son of a fisherman. If there is anything you don't want to answer, or anything that you don't understand, it is enough to write that down as your answer. And there has been a lot of talk about whether or not it is permissible for a policeman to respond to this kind of inquiry; on this, we are doing this with the full approval and knowledge of the Hokkaido Prefectural Headquarters, so there is nothing to worry about.

The assistant chief's comments confirmed that there was a widespread suspicion that I might be a spy from the headquarters or in the service of supervisors of the Eastern. One detective said to me:

> It's tough on you, too, isn't it, Professor, asking on bended knee for this one favor? A questionnaire is really a sensitive thing, you know.

When there is a questionnaire, and you answer off-key you could get kicked out, or called on the carpet later on. That is the bad thing about a questionnaire. Me and these guys are answering as we please, but there are some who worry.

This reminded me of an assistant inspector at the Police Academy who told me that "if supervisors are going to look at it, no one will answer a survey." These responses contrasted to the directness and frankness of their statements on the occasions when they criticized or complained about supervisors or headquarters.

In spite of the urging of the assistant chief, officers were slow to return the questionnaire. I continued observation and concluded the research on September 6, 1974. One hundred and ninety-nine officers returned usable questionnaires, with a return rate of 77.4 percent. According to my observations, most were completed at the station immediately before they were turned in. The breakdown of the 199 respondents was as follows: 106 in the Administration and Patrol Departments, 20 in the Traffic Department, 44 in the two Detective Departments, 8 in the Juvenile and Crime Prevention Department, and 12 in the Public Security Department. In 9 cases, the respondent's department could not be determined.

The survey data is used in later chapters of this book primarily to supplement the observational data. The core of the survey is the forty-one questions that deal with the kind of action that should be taken at each stage of a criminal investigation. Since responses to these questions will be cited often in later chapters, the contents of the questions and the distribution of responses are presented in Appendix A.

The data on age from the survey is presented in Table 3.2, while the data on educational level is given in Table 3.3.

Table 3.2   Officer's Age

	20S OR YOUNGER	30S	40S	50S	N.A.
All respondents (199)	38.2%	14.1%	26.1%	12.1%	9.5%
Detectives (44)	15.9%	6.8%	54.5%	18.2%	4.5%

While the youngest category is the largest group in the entire sample, the officers in their forties form the largest group among detectives. On the average, the two Detective Departments have more experienced officers.[1]

Table 3.3   Educational Level of Officers

	JUNIOR HIGH OR LOWER	HIGH SCHOOL	JUNIOR COLLEGE OR COLLEGE	N.A.
All respondents (199)	29.1%	46.7%	13.1%	11.1%
Detectives (44)	36.4%	52.3%	6.8%	4.5%

These statistics include prewar equivalents of each category. The percentage of college or junior college graduates was smaller among detectives, while the percentage of officers with the lowest educational level was larger among them. This probably reflects the older average age of detectives.[2]

---

1. It is difficult to find age distributions of police officers either for the entire country or for Hokkaido Prefecture. For the Tokyo Metropolitan Police in 1976, Murayama (1990: 137) recently reported that 48 percent were thirty years old or younger, 20 percent between thirty-one and forty, 21 percent between forty-one and fifty, and 12 percent between fifty-one and sixty. The percentage of the youngest group of officers was higher at the Tokyo Metropolitan Police than at the Eastern Police Station. This might be explained by the fact that the Tokyo Metropolitan Police had a large number of officers in riot squads, while the Eastern had none. Riot squads do not belong to local police stations, but are under direct control of prefectural police headquarters.

2. Ames (1981: 164) has reported that in 1974, nine percent of the entire police officers was college or junior college graduates. This suggests that in spite of their location in the northernmost island in Japan, the average educational level of officers at the Eastern Police Station was slightly better than the national average.

4

Natural Sequence of
Criminal Investigation in Japan

In this chapter, I will describe how I observed police officers and how I interpreted what I saw and heard. Full quotations of field notes were made for twenty four cases in the original Japanese version of the book, but the same points appeared repeatedly in several cases. Therefore I present here only six cases. These cases will assist readers in evaluating the credibility of my analysis and provide foreign readers in particular with examples of the natural sequence of criminal investigation in Japan. Names of persons, places, and months are all pseudonyms. For instance, detectives with a same pseudonym may appear in different cases, but this does not necessarily mean that they are a same detective. The currency exchange rate was approximately 300 yen for one U.S dollar. Case numbers are same as those in the original Japanese version for the convenience of those readers who may have access to it. When fragments of these field notes are quoted in later chapters, case numbers are provided, so that readers will be able to find the relevant cases in this chapter.

1. Investigation by Patrol Officers

As I have already stated, patrol officers do not play an important role in criminal investigation. Ericson (1981: 89) has reported that in Canada cases involving violence and other bodily harm are screened by patrol officers before they reach the detectives. That is not the case in Japan. Even when patrol officers have a chance to arrest a suspect by themselves, they have to transfer the case immediately to the detectives. In the following case, a suspicious truck overloaded with steel bars is sighted, field questioning is done, voluntary accompaniment is requested, and an emergency arrest is made on the suspicion that the truck is stolen. This case illustrates how cases are transferred to detectives, how patrol officers view this system, and how detectives take advantage of a suspect detained in the police station even after indictment.

Case 3: Emergency Arrest of a Thief by a Patrol Officer

At the Kikusui police box, at 11:15 p.m. on February 23, the squad leader brings in the suspect driver of a truck overloaded with steel bars. The squad leader is tense, his face flushed. The man has not been arrested yet; questions at this stage are merely to identify him, and he needs not be told of his right to remain silent.

- Squad leader: Where do you live, mister? Where's your house?

- Man: Toyohira town.

- Squad leader: Your birth date? Speak up. You know what I am saying. Where did you have your job, mister? A construction company, I guess.

The squad leader decides to make an emergency arrest on the basis of the vehicle. His desire to uncover the existence of prior offenses is clear:

- Squad leader: How many previous offenses? Ah, theft is it? I'll arrest you. Put out your hand.

At 11:23 p.m., after putting handcuffs on the suspect, the leader conducted a body frisk.

- Squad leader: How did you open up the car?

- Man: Pliers.

- Squad leader: Where did you get them?

- Man: They were right there.

The leader immediately called the Eastern Police Station and inquired into previous offenses.

- Squad leader: Where were you caught? How long did you go up for?
- Man: At the Sapporo Prison. A year and a half.
- Squad leader (to the police box staffer): Let's make this an emergency arrest for theft of a vehicle, with the steel bars to be added later.

The suspect is finally informed of his rights, and at 11:27 p.m., the leader requested a car from the Station to transport the suspect. His concern that he meet the deadline for securing an arrest warrant after an emergency arrest becomes apparent.

- Squad leader: (on the phone) It won't make an arrest of flagrant offender. I'm making an emergency arrest. It's an emergency arrest, so we won't have time—please hurry. I can't base the emergency arrest on the steel bars, either. That would be putting arrest before investigation. (To police box staffer) We could add driving without a license, couldn't we? He ran away, so I scolded him, "Why did you run?" He said, "Because I don't have a license." When I went to check out that *yakuza* (organized crime member) that came into the police box a while ago, a car was cruising around. We will seize the truck, and return it to the victim. Cokes and the water heater in the truck were his.

The man sniffles, speaks in a tearful voice.

- Patrolman Abe: Did you buy Cokes?
- Suspect: 960 yen [approximately $3.2 U.S.].
- Patrolman Baba: Where? Today? When? (To another staffer) Will you call the victim company and tell them about the steel rods?

At 11:42 p.m., a car arrives with detectives.

- Detective Ando (to the suspect): Did you stack it yourself? Took a long time, I'll bet. Where did you carry it from? Ah, and this? You used this to open it with, eh? How did you do that?

The police box officers must immediately hand over the case to the detectives. The detectives decide to take statements at the station, but the patrol officers want to retain their control of the case.

- Deputy squad leader (to Detective Abe): What if we hauled the steel bars out, and dragged this guy to the scene for a look? (To the man) Where did you plan to sell the steel?

At 11:50 p.m., the suspect is taken to the station. At midnight, the victim of theft of the vehicle, a company president, arrives at the police box. The officers there decide to send him to the station and have him identify the vehicle. The deputy squad leader of the police box contrasts the skill of this squad leader with the ability of ordinary patrol officers, and expresses discontent that for patrol officers, cases must be sent on to the specialists for more investigation and final disposition. He also says that detectives are not mainly concerned about the offense for which the suspect was arrested, but about the possibility of clearing as many separate offenses as possible by attributing them to this suspect:

- Deputy squad leader: Looks like an emergency arrest, a good case. Our squad leader came from the detectives, so he has a good sixth sense. The detectives want separate offenses, so they took the guy to the station. They are in competition with the Patrol. In the Patrol, we can't get separate offenses, you know. But they didn't arrest him themselves, and that doesn't set too well. Sweating away writing up papers for someone else's case, I don't know what to say.

At 2:00 a.m., the investigation at the police box is concluded. The squad leader does not hide his elation at the opportunity to effect an arrest, which suggests that such opportunities are scarce indeed.

- Squad leader: Professor, you brought a case with you. (Referring to the luck brought by my being there.) The arrest warrant for the truck was accepted over the phone. We'll use the theft of the steel bars as grounds for detention. Today is our day, eh? I'll take care of the paperwork afterwards.

Detectives have been investigating this suspect since then, and on March 14th, at 1:00 p.m., a detective explains what has been going on to me at the station. He hopes to learn of any separate offenses and will use the detention at the station detention cell to investigate this possibility.

- Detective Ando: In the end, he was sent to the prosecutor as a single offender with no accomplice. He's been in three times in ten years, so we decided to charge him as a habitual offender. He's in the station detention cell now because there should be separate offenses.

Detective Ando again informs me of developments on March 20. The suspect is still in the station detention cell and remains there even after he is indicted for the initial charge, although he is now a defendant in the court.

- Detective Ando: Emergency arrest was on the 23rd of February, at 11:20 p.m. Suspect was put into detention by the judge at the station detention cell, and indicted on the 6th of this month. Suspect was charged with habitual theft, including the truck, steel rods, and Cokes. A theft from a warehouse.

It is April 4, now, but the suspect is still in the station detention cell. At 4:10 p.m., the squad leader, now transferred to the First Detective Department, reviews questionable aspects of the case at the station. This implies that the police officers have engaged in questionable behavior while they were clearly aware of its nature.

- Squad leader: The steel rods would not justify an emergency arrest. There was no report from the victim. The vehicle itself is doubtful, too. It happened between 5 and 9 o'clock, the report came in at 10, and he was spotted at 11, which means that it's too spread out both in time and in distance.

Finally on April 11, at 1:00 p.m., more than one and a half months after the emergency arrest, an order comes from the prosecutor to transfer the suspect to the outside detention center. It seems that this is to be done because the defendant-suspect has nothing more to offer to detectives about other offences.

2. Investigation of Theft Crimes

Detectives classify investigations into four categories by the types of crimes they investigate, since each type requires a specific form of investigation. They are thefts, forcible crimes, intellectual crimes, and organized crimes. Intellectual crimes, which involve fraud, embezzlement, election law violation, bribery, and other white-collar crimes, will be excluded from our consideration because I encountered no such case during my observations.

Thefts constitute the largest category of crimes in Japan, excluding traffic-related offences. I will first describe how detectives and supervisors perceive the conditions surrounding theft investigations, and then present three cases.

Sanders (1977: 151, 157, 164) has described the process of theft crime investigation in the United States. Thieves rarely leave clues. For instance, stolen goods are rarely found in pawn shops. Therefore detectives seek a "cop out" or confession from the arrested person about unknown crimes. American detectives consider it a waste to finish an investigation by solving only one crime. They expect to solve as many additional crimes as possible by investigating a single suspect. Similar patterns have also been reported by Ericson (1981: 85-88) for Canada. Crimes in which a suspect has already been taken into custody or is known to the police receive priority in investigation and, thus, are more likely to result in an indictment than otherwise.

The situation is the same in Japan. According to detectives, theft investigations have become more difficult in recent years. One detective said, "From about 1970 onward, the thieves' connections with pawn shops and used goods stores began to stop. This is also true for novice thieves. Unless you catch them in the act, or get them on the fingerprints, you can't catch them." Another detective added, "In recent years, about half of them will deny the offense to start with. It is difficult to get direct evidence of theft. Most of those who deny the offense are habitual offenders. They know from experience that they have rights. In such a case, you cast around for more evidence without revealing what you already have in your hand. It is difficult to get direct evidence of theft. Especially for thefts of cash."

According to detectives, when money is stolen, it is impossible to obtain the money as direct evidence of a crime. Sales of stolen material to used goods dealers and pawn shops have declined. Goods now move through channels which are more difficult for the police to detect. There is no information available on the modus operandi of novice thieves, and so that the only way to catch them is through fingerprints or an arrest of flagrant offender. Finally, even if the offender is arrested and subjected to interrogation, he will usually deny the offense. Since direct evidence of theft is essential and difficult to obtain, the investigation will fail unless the suspect confesses.

These circumstances have an effect upon investigative methods. According to detectives specializing in theft, "Theft crime investigation and forcible crime investigation are totally different. In forcible crime, the focus is upon the quick resolution of the immediate offense. In theft crime, from the substantiation of the reported offense and the investigation of the possibility of separate offenses, to collecting information on unreported offenses by questioning on the street or through house visits, it is a protracted investigation process." "For thief detectives, careful listening and other plodding forms of investigation are the main fare," they say. In a typical investigation, "the men on day shift rush to the scene of the crime. The modus operandi is checked, and names are pulled out of the file of prior offenders. From the reports of witnesses, connections with other cases are sought. When an article has been stolen, its distinguishing features are noted down, and that information is distributed in three steps: prefecture-wide, within the Sapporo district, and within this station." Because of the difficulty of amassing direct evidence, prior offenders are selected from the modus operandi file and other materials, connections with other cases are examined, and upon arrest information about separate offenses other than the one for which the suspect was arrested is sought.

It is difficult to catch first-time offenders, and thus there are many repeat offenders among those who are arrested. Therefore the detectives feel that "most of our [arrested] thieves are habitual offenders," while "the tough one is the first-time offender, the guy who has stolen maybe twenty times or so at his first arrest. There is no record of his fingerprints or modus operandi, so if he doesn't confess, you're through."

Separate offenses uncovered after arrest gain considerable importance. In one theft section of the Eastern Station, for instance, the record of case transfers to the prosecutor for the three months of January through March of 1974 indicated that while there were only twelve cases cleared without arrest and eleven cases cleared with arrest, there were twenty cases of "additional transfer." These separate offenses were uncovered through investigations and interrogation by detectives, and are the true product of detective work. Uncovering as many additional offenses as possible is very important consideration for theft crime detectives.

Because it is difficult to get direct evidence, an investigation does not really get underway until the suspect is confronted directly. The detectives say, "With thieves, it doesn't begin until you have them locked up and get them to confess." Therefore, while cases of forcible crimes can be reassigned from the squad which arrested the suspect to another squad that has fewer matters on its hands, "in theft, we let the squad that has made the first step of investigation [i.e. arresting the suspect] keep the case."

Theft crime investigation is a very laborious and drawn-out process. But it is also true that the vast majority of crimes reported to the police are theft offenses. Therefore, trends in theft are the concern of all detectives. An assistant inspector, a student I met at the Police Academy said, "When the theft clearance record is improving, investigations of all crimes are going well. The actions and the morale of all detectives are going well, and so the results are seen daily in the theft crime area. There is someone in lockup every day. Then when the tide turns, suddenly there will be no one in lockup for half a month." This perception is shared among theft crime detectives.

Finally, because of the large number of theft cases, it is impossible to give the same attention to every case. Thus detectives concentrate on cases in which there is a report from the victim. They focus particularly on breaking and entering offenses, because these could develop into robbery if residents are present.

The policy of the supervisors also is to pursue "newly reported cases, more than unreported cases or reported cases that are stale." However, on other points there exists a subtle difference. Supervisors agree with the detectives that the nature of the crime is changing, but do not agree that the detectives' staffing or skills are inadequate to handle every case carefully. A supervisor said, "Yes, theft is busy, but there is no shortage of staff." "There are officers who stake out, conduct field questioning, and bring thieves in," he added. "A detective with ability makes his own materials." It is important at this point to examine whether the demands of the supervisors, who maintain that improvements in clearance rates are possible, has an effect upon the actions of the detectives, who believe that this is difficult to accomplish.

In terms of these background comments, I present three cases, one involving a male adult suspect, one a male juvenile suspect, and one a female adult suspect. The first case features an emergency arrest, and the other two cases involve ordinary warrant arrests.

Case 9: A Prowler Arrested by the Mobile Squad

At 10:00 a.m. on the 25th of March, we receive a report that a witness saw a prowler enter a temple, but the prowler later fled in his own automobile. Detectives Abe, Baba, and Chiba leave for the scene, but at 10:30 we receive a report that the Mobile Squad of the Prefectural Headquarters has arrested the suspect. The supervisors immediately get involved in the investigation and decide which type of arrest should be made. Detectives at the scene are not allowed to make this decision.

* Supervisor Ando (to the section head): Call them and tell them that we want an emergency arrest, not an arrest in the act.

At 10:47 a.m., word comes that the three detectives have arrived at the scene. The supervisor cannot decide which section should take the case, because he knows there is competition between the sections in charge of theft crimes. He lets the two section heads negotiate among themselves. The section head with the inferior record begs the case from the other, with an air of humiliation about himself. In principle, cases are divided by the two sections according to geographical territory, but in this case the section which was on duty watch and had sent its members to the scene gets priority:

* Supervisor Ando (to the heads of the two Theft Crime Sections): Decide who will handle this among the sections.

- Detective Dando: Let's assign it to the section on duty watch. Otherwise their morale will suffer.

- Detective Endo: That's right. Because you [Detective Dando's section] put two into custody last night, we may take this case over if it's alright. Looks like you're getting someone in every other night, so your record is the only one that gets polished! (laughter)

Another police station also wants this suspect, and now competition between stations appears. Since the Eastern Station took a case away from this station in the past, one supervisor decides to compensate the station by letting it take a portion of the possible multiple offenses of the suspect. The manner in which he explains his decision to the detectives, however, anticipates their unhappiness at sending the case to another station.

- Supervisor Bando (to the section head who took the case): The Southern Station is asking us for permission to interrogate him for extortion, so let them interrogate. They won't ask for the theft offenses as well. And we have gotten cases from their side in the past.

Detectives worry over the possibility that the suspect is a juvenile. If so they will lose the case to the Crime Prevention Department. They want to keep the case to themselves.

- Detective Endo: If he is a juvenile [less than twenty years of age], this is a waste of time. Don't tell me he's even under fourteen [because a thirteen-year old or younger cannot be held responsible for a crime]. If he is employed, he'll come to us, but if he's a student, he'll have to be handled by the Crime Prevention Department.

The supervisors' decision to make this an emergency arrest, instead of a warrantless arrest of a flagrant offender, necessitates additional evidence to support the application for a warrant. A detective in charge of recordkeeping asks the section head for help, but the head expresses his unhapiness with the Mobile Squad, which on the one hand has reduced their chances of arrest while on the other hand has forced them to do more paperwork.

- Detective Fujita: They [supervisors] say it's to be an emergency arrest instead of an arrest of flagrant offender. Could you have Detective Abe take the witnesses' reports for me?

- Detective Endo: It was the Mobile Squad that caught him, and the suspect in custody and the witnesses have all been taken over there, so the Mobile Squad should take statements. They did ask us to take care of the reports on the circumstances and surroundings, though.

- Detective Fujita: Well, please take statements if he comes here.
- Detective Endo: I'll do that.

Interest in separate offenses is apparent from the beginning. The section head assigns this promising case to his best squad.

- Detective Endo: This one surely has separate offenses in him; he broke in in broad daylight. And the Southern Station was about to put out a warrant on him for extortion. This one is for Abe's squad.

At about 11:30 a.m., the Mobile Squad brings in the thief. His statement has not been taken, so work begins there. Detectives are pleased to note that he is an adult. They assign the best squad to this thief who stole only $33 U.S., because their real target is the possibile existence of more serious separate offenses.

- Detective Endo: He is not a juvenile, but an adult. He says, "My father is disabled and in the hospital, my mother works part-time, and I ran away from home two days ago. I just reached for the stuff on the spur of the moment," but these are the most dangerous kind. Trying to buy your sympathy. He stole just a little over 10,000 yen [approximately $33 U.S.] in cash.
- Supervisor Ando: In that case [i.e., his being an adult], it's OK [to arrest him].

The arrest warrant request is being prepared, and I look at it. The time of the offense was about 9:40 a.m. The young man was spotted by the owner, and then ran away. He took only 7,069 yen (approximately $24 U.S.) in cash, and 3,400 yen (approximately $11 U.S.) in canned foods. Yet this case was deemed worthy of the attention of the Mobile Squad, a star unit of the Hokkaido Police, and also was assigned to the best squad of the Eastern Station.

It is already 1:15 p.m. The time limit for applying for a warrant in emergency arrests is about three hours, leaving only a few minutes. The air in the room is tense, and finally, at about 1:30, they go to request a warrant. At 3:15, however, there has been no word that the warrant has been issued. In the meantime, detectives discuss possible ways to developing separate offenses.

- Detective Abe: The guy they just caught a little while ago was carrying these binoculars and this radio-cassette recorder. The money

came out of the cord compartment of the radio, so we had it presented voluntarily and we're checking now to see if it's stolen.

This case is considered so promising that even a theft crime investigator
from the Hokkaido Police Headquarters is here, asking about the situation.
At 4:03 p.m., there is finally word from Detective Endo that the warrant has
been issued, and everyone is relieved.

From 4:30 p.m. to 5:25 p.m., I go with Detectives Abe, Baba, and
Chiba to take the suspect to the spot where he says he threw two savings
boxes. He talks a lot. Fired from his job, he is worried about whether or not
he can get married. Thinking about unresolved cases, the officers ask indi-
rectly, "Have you done anything else?" As one might expect, the binoculars
and the tape recorder are listed as separate offenses, and the suspect will be
taken to the place where the detectives suspect he stole them in a few days.
Detectives also plan to investigate details of his employment. Supervisors
see a danger, however, in overly zealous detectives, and try to restrain them.

- Supervisor Ando: Don't push it too hard. Work on the separate
  offenses after the original offense is pretty much finished.

It is a little after 6:30 p.m. Although the suspect was arrested just this morning, detectives are already working under the direction of the department
head to find grounds for detention. Anticipation of such detention and a prolonged investigation is apparent at this early stage. The plan is to confirm
with the suspect's mother that he ran away from home. Then the police can
argue that the suspect would have fled if not detained. Detectives also want
to know if they can solve another, much larger theft.

- Detective Endo: Detective Baba is out calling on the witness in the
  robbery of 700,000 yen [approximately $2,350 U.S.]. The car used
  in that case was stolen, and there were binoculars inside. The
  physique of the suspect in that case is similar to that of our man, so I
  thought we should have a lineup.

- Supervisor Ando: He [the witness] can't come today. It'll be tomorrow.

- Detective Endo: Looks like he was giving thinner to women to sniff,
  and using a vibrator. There is a lot of sand in the car, so he's been to
  the beach.

- Supervisor Bando: Your typical daytime burglar.

At about 7:00 p.m., we learn that the witness to the theft of 700,000 yen will
not come to the station, and other concerned parties will not be coming in

either, so Detectives Goto and Hata, who have been waiting, go home. On top of all these efforts at the Eastern Station, headquarters joins in. We learn that a call had come to Detective Abe at about 6:00 p.m. from Inspector Yano of headquarters. The department at headquarters in charge of records of stolen goods had asked an investigation department there to check into the binoculars. Inspector Yano also directs Detective Abe to have the witness in the 700,000 yen case confirm the suspect's identity, even though he has not been arrested on that charge. This news infuriates the supervisors of the Eastern Station. They are well aware that this could raise the issue of illegality of the pretext arrest by revealing the real intention to investigate crimes not specified in the warrant application.

- Supervisor Bando: What's he saying, that idiot? There's no need to report something like that to him. We can do that here on our station chief's order. If another call comes in tomorrow, have him call me directly. I'll let him have it. This is different from a rural police force [where Yano used to work].

- Supervisor Ando: Even if we explain it to that idiot, he still won't understand.

- Supervisor Bando: The headquarters have no need to say such a thing. There is always someone who, immediately after assignment to a new job, wants to show off. We are still working on the original charge, you know.

- Detective Endo: If we follow the request from headquarters, it will probably become an illegal arrest for different offenses [not specified in the warrant application].

Case 10: A Juvenile Thief Arrested After Voluntary Appearance

This case involves a juvenile suspect and indicates that juveniles are not necessarily transferred to the Crime Prevention Department. This case also shows the kind of considerations that lead supervisors to choose between ordinary warrant arrest and warrantless emergency arrest.

At 3:20 p.m. on the 18th of March, one of the Theft Crime Sections receives a phone call from a nearby pawnshop. A man carrying a driver's license (for whom there is a call out) sought to pawn a tape recorder. A warrant using his nickname had been issued by the Northern Station for an earlier crime, leading to competition between two stations for a single suspect. I go to the pawn shop with Detectives Abe and Baba.

- Detective Abe: The Northen Station and the Eastern Station are fighting over it.

- Detective Baba: It is not clear whether the tape recorder is stolen, so it will have to be a voluntary appearance.

At 3:40 p.m., we arrive at the pawnshop. Apparently the suspect ran away while the owner was making the call to the station. We borrow the driver's license and the tape recorder and return to the station. The suspect was 165 centimeters (five feet and six inches) high, wore glasses and a sweater. A new photograph has been fastened to the license, but it cannot be confirmed that the photo is actually of the suspect. At about 5:10 p.m., at the station, a detective ponders over the suspect's identity.

- Detective Abe: In that tape recorder case just now, Yamada is the name on an identification card from a trade school that has been left with the driver's license. But earlier a man showing identification from the same school who tried to hock something used the name Yoshida. I wonder if that is him.

At 7:35 p.m., after returning from site management of a fire case, I find that all the detectives of one Theft Crime Section are assembled. It has been established that someone named Yamada received an application form from the trade school mentioned earlier. Detectives cannot decide by themselves whether to arrest him. They have to get approval from a supervisor, so they call their Detective Department head at his home. "We want to make an emergency arrest," they tell him. This action demonstrates that an emergency arrest is not always made in a genuine emergency, where police officers unexpectedly confront a suspect in the field. It can in fact be planned well beforehand. However, the Department head responds, "Wait." He adds, "The station chief would not allow it." The detectives are very displeased by this restraint. About 7:40 the next morning, Supervisor Ando comes in to the station, as supervisors always do when detectives are going to take compulsory investigative measures. Supervisor Ando compromises.

- Supervisor Ando: If we meet the conditions that he has no fixed address, no regular employment, is not under the guidance of his parents, and has a record of criminal conduct, let's do it [make an emergency arrest] tomorrow. In any case, he won't come to us for detention. It will be at the Juvenile Diagnostic Center [It seems the suspect is seventeen years and ten months old]. It would be nice if he were eighteen, though [since he could be detained in the station].

On the following day, at 8:20 a.m., three theft crime detectives are on their way out to make the emergency arrest of Yamada. The First Detective Department head gets permission to arrest him from the assistant station chief in charge of detectives and crime prevention, since decisions on compulsory measures are usually reviewed by more than one supervisor. Detectives do not arrest the suspect, however. Instead, they bring him in on a voluntary appearance. This has an advantage in that they will not exceeed the time limit for detention, which begins only when he is arrested. The suspect is taken into an interrogation room. A supervisor then explains the situation to me. He expresses his hope that this juvenile will be processed according to the adult criminal procedure, not according to the juvenile procedure which restricts arrest of those under twenty years of age.

- Supervisor Bando: The criteria for arrest of a juvenile criminal are whether he is a student or an employed minor, whether he has a prior criminal record, and whether he has committed many separate offenses. Yamada has a record of theft and forcible indecency. In such a case, he will probably be handled by the detectives [rather than by Juvenile Department officers]. (Turning to a Theft Crime Section head) Make a request for an arrest warrant quickly.

At around 11:15 a.m., the investigation report and evidence record is being prepared by a Theft Crime Section. These documents reveal competition between the two Theft Crime Sections. Although it was Detectives Abe and Baba of another section who went to visit the pawn shop, the report uses the name of a detective from this section. At 1:35 p.m., we go out to the scene of a gas explosion, but a message is received over the car radio that the warrant for Yamada's arrest is out. We return to the station. Supervisors had changed their mind and decided to make an ordinary warrant arrest, and detectives had gone to the court to wait for the warrant. At about 3:00 p.m., at the station, a supervisor explains his reason to make an ordinary arrest to me.

- Supervisor Ando: Whether it is an emergency arrest or an ordinary arrest, the time clock runs from the moment of effective custody, so we decided on a straightforward ordinary arrest.

We should note, however, that had they made an emergency arrest immediately after the suspect had been brought in on a voluntary appearance, the time limitation would have started to run at that moment, before application for the warrant. By changing to an ordinary arrest, they effectively delayed the time clock.

At about 6:30 p.m., they have already decided to file for detention of Yamada. A supervisor expresses his hope for detention at the station detention cell.

- Supervisor Ando: His parents can't control him. Outside detention centers lack space. These are the necessary conditions for detention [of a juvenile at the station detention cell]. I am quite sure that he won't be sent to a Juvenile Diagnostic Center.

After the morning meeting on the 20th, I take a look at the papers to be filed with the detention request in the case of Yamada. They are: (1) an ordinary arrest procedure record, (2) record of the suspect's initial pleading, (3) a record of the process by which Yamada was identified, (4) a record of the process by which the owner of the tape recorder, which Yamada left behind when he ran away, was identified, (5) a record of the statement of the pawn-broker to whom Yamada went to dispose of his stolen properties, (6) a record of the process by which Yamada's personal circumstances were examined, and that they satisfy the requirements for detention of a juvenile, (7) a record of the process of investigation of the facts and the necessity for detention, (8) statements of witnesses, (9) a victim's report of lost goods, (10) a list of separate offenses written out by the suspect himself, and (11) the request for detention. They prove effective and the judge permits detention in the station detention cell. The initial concern over the difficulty of detention of a juvenile seems to have been unwarranted. At about 11:30 a.m. on the 22nd, detectives and a supervisor explain the situation to me.

- Detective Chiba: We got detention for Yamada. From the 21st to the 29th of this month.

- Supervisor Ando: If we couldn't get detention in this one, the system would be hopeless.

Case 11: Arrest of a Sick Female Thief

In this case, I was able to observe an ordinary arrest in the greatest detail. Previous studies of the Japanese police suggest that the Japanese police treat their suspects with genuine sympathy. Bayley (1976: 150) wrote, for instance, "a Japanese accepts the accusation and tries to kindle benevolence. In response,...the Japanese policeman is sympathetic and succoring." Ames (1981: 136) reported, "*Keiji* [a detective] can show kindness to a suspect as long as it is 'sincere' and not an attempt to induce a confession. For instance, a *keiji* in Okayama City told me that he brought a *zoni* (a traditional New Year's food treat) [soup with rice cakes in it] from his home to a man in jail during the New Year's holiday to show he respected him as a person." Bayley (1976: 145) also wrote that Japanese policemen devote "much more time to considering appropriate treatment" than American police. Readers may conclude from such reports that the Japanese police are more interested in rehabilitating the suspect than in seeking heavy sentences. But in fact they seek heavy sentences by adding as many charges as possible. They take advantage of the suspect's detention in their police station and of the fact that he cannot refuse to appear before them for interrogation. In the present case, the suspect is a woman, and she is sick. It presents an ideal situation to see how sincerely benevolent detectives actually are.

On the 3rd of April, I negotiate with a Theft Crime Section to accompany them as they make an ordinary arrest of a suspect, a female prowler. They tell me that she is a bar hostess who is under a suspended sentence.

- Detective Abe: We know that she will deny it. She can be violent. No matter how often we call [asking her to come in voluntarily], she doesn't come in, so we took out a warrant.

- Supervisor Ando: If she starts to fight, and you get wrapped up in it and are hurt, it would be bad. So wait in the car.

- Detective Abe: We will confirm her address, and if we are sure that she is there, we will get her and bring her in. We have a warrant.

At 10:05 a.m., we drive from the station. At 10:30, we arrive at her apartment and ask the landlord whether she is in. A detective explains to me how she has outwitted him before. Their frustrated desire to obtain a voluntary appearance before arrest is apparent.

- Landlord: She's not good about paying the rent. Seems that she has been talking about starting her own bar.

- Detective Baba (to me): We're sure of two or three things that she did, but there is no conclusive proof, so we're collecting materials. However many times we ask for a voluntary appearance, she says, "Bring an arrest warrant," and won't come in. She's real dramatic, she cries very readily. A bad apple.... She is a master liar. She said that her child was in school [her child by the man from whom she is divorced is in father's custody]. She has asked me to lend her 300,000 yen [approximately $1,000 U.S.]. Before, when we didn't know that she was using a pseudonym, nothing turned up on a search for a criminal record. We called her up, but she didn't come in. Next, when we figured out her real name, we knew that she had a prior record. It seems she is even thinking of subleasing her place. We have asked her neighbor to let us know if it looks like she is moving out.

At 11:05 a.m., the detectives ask the landlord just to knock at the door. There is no response to the knock. We wait in a classroom of an English language school in the same building. We learn that she goes shopping about noon, so we decide to wait. The detectives do not break in immediately, even though they have a warrant.

At about 1:00 p.m., the curtains are opened, so it appears that the suspect is inside. The detectives express their conviction that once they set out to make an arrest, they must succeed. Yet they hesitate to break in, worrying about possible allegations of misconduct.

- Detective Baba: We, men, have used one of our few cars to come out here, we really have to get her. Footsteps will make noise, so we can't walk up to the door to see if she is in. If we find out she's in, we can go in; you can see inside from the gas station across the street. If we break in without knowing [the situation inside] and there are complaints afterwards, we will have a trouble. If we break in and she isn't there, she'll say that something has disappeared. I would rather catch her when she comes outside.

At 2:10, the landlord comes up, saying "The curtain has been open since morning." At 2:30, a detective makes a call to her apartment, and the woman comes to the phone. Detective Baba says, "Is this Ms. Yoshida?" by making up a name. The detectives still hesitate to break in.

- Detective Baba: If we knock right away, she'll figure it out [that he lied to her, making later interrogations difficult]. So let's wait and then go after she has settled herself a bit. What will we do if she doesn't come out when we knock?
- Detective Chiba: Let's open the door and go in.
- Landlord: After that, I don't know anything.

The detectives decide to arrest her. Even with a warrant in their hands, however, they have to get permission from supervisors to execute it. At 2:33 p.m., Detective Chiba telephones the station for orders, and receives the permission. At 2:35, they knock at the door. The leader gives his name, which she recognizes.

- Detective Baba: Hello? This is Baba of the Eastern Station.

The suspect opens the door herself. The detectives keep things low key. They do not say what they actually expect from her. They say that they want only to ask about the "circumstances."

- Detective Baba: Will you get ready to go?

- Woman: I went to the hospital.

- Detective Chiba: If it's your stomach, you have to take care of yourself. If you resist too long, we will be in trouble; we only want to ask into the circumstances.

- Woman: It is chronic.

- Detective Baba: Well, get your stuff together. You may as well read this for us. This, here. [Produces the warrant.] From the court. For suspicion of this. Because you did this here, we are doing this.

The suspect reads the warrant closely, but the detectives do not want the suspect to know the exact charge written in the warrant. Detective Baba tries to take it from her.

- Woman: Wait a minute [strong voice]. You're not here about Yamashita, are you? About Yamashita?

- Detective Baba: No. It's just as it says there. We'll go over that again later. For now, get your make-up kit together.

The woman becomes thoughtful. The detectives try to persuade her. They do not try to take her forcibly.

- Detective Chiba: However long you stay here, it won't get settled. Let's hurry, eh? Let's go along, now.

- Woman: I have to go there again?

The woman breaks into tears. The detectives try to persuade her, mixing sympathetic words with threats. They are not to be blamed for her arrest, they say. They are merely executing the judge's order.

- Detective Baba: We'll take care of you, and we won't cast you in a bad light. Come on, hurry. There's an arrest warrant out, there's nothing to be done about it. And take along a change of clothes. Yamada, listen to what I am saying to you. Stand up. Hurry up. Listen to me, Yamada. If you tell us, we will understand. If you muddle around, you'll be dragged off to prison and it will be worse. I said it's no use stalling. Quickly, quickly, stand up here. Let's stand up and get moving, Yamada. We can carry you if we have to. Hurry. When we get to the station, we can inquire about the circumstances. Here, you know we can't do that.

Both sides remain silent for a time. The detectives switch to a more sympathetic tone.

- Detective Chiba: You went over before. Were you in [detention] for a month?
- Woman: I was in a long time.
- Detective Baba: That was the detention center. You were probably in throughout trial. We have good weather today, fairly good, don't we?

Detective Baba sighs. The woman cries.

- Detective Baba: Don't break down, you. We'll break down too. You don't want to be cold, so put this on. We'll take care of the rest.
- Woman: Do I have to go in there again?
- Detective Baba: Where? The Sapporo Detention Center? The Central Police Station? We will look out for you as much as we can. Anyway, we really want you to come down. Time being what it is, we can't force you into going, we want your consent. You shouldn't blame us for it; blame yourself. Put this on. Put on your glasses, no one will see you in the car. Fix up your hair, too, eh?
- Woman: I won't be able to come home today?
- Detective Baba: That's right. We will ask you to stay there for forty eight hours.
- Woman: What will happen at the bar?
- Detective Chiba: Call and tell them you won't be coming. You can't have things your way, with a warrant out from a proper judge. You'll need toothpaste, a toothbrush, soap and towels. You're going without them? Take some tissue, too, some tissue. This is a really nice room.

The woman has lost a butane lighter. Detectives Baba and Chiba help to look for it. The woman's voice grows more calm. She thanks detectives for letting her call a friend.

- Detective Chiba: You should take along some gum, too.
- Woman: Let me make a phone call.
- Detective Chiba: Sure.

- Woman (maybe calling to a friend): Atsuko. Can I speak to your mother? Put her on the line, please.... I may be away for two or three days. Where to? Oh, no place special. I will be coming home, though. I want you to come over and borrow a key from the manager, and look the place over. I will leave a key to the door and a key to the stairwell with the manager when I leave. I'll be able to come back sometime this week. Will you leave this week? If I call your place, will you please do what I ask? If something happens to me, please pack up my baggage and send it to Otaru [address of a man with whom she had split up]. I said it was nothing. If you don't hear anything from me in three days, call Otaru. You know his name, right? Otaru. If you can't get in touch with him, call his sister. So if you don't hear from me in three days, gather everything together and send it to Otaru, okay? Thank you.

- Detective Baba: Better take along these strawberries. They'll spoil.

- Woman: I'm so sorry.

- Detective Baba: Not at all. Take them along, the fruit. It's better to take it. Ah, strawberries are already in season again.

At 3:23 p.m., we get into the car, and arrive at the station at 3:45. The Detectives explain to me how difficult it was to get her.

- Detective Abe: Trouble with women is that they will cry on you, if you're not gentle with them. We were sure of two or three offenses, but there wasn't enough to catch her; that's why we gathered our materials together and got a warrant ready. In any case, she wouldn't respond to a request for a voluntary appearance, and told us, "Go take out a warrant." She is under a suspended sentence, so she should not commit the offense again, but she doesn't show any sign of remorse. (Then to the General Affairs Section of the First Detective Department which manages the station detention cell) Can we get dinner [for her]?

- Detective Dando: It [the kitchen] closes at 1:00 p.m. So [she will get only] two pieces of bread, 76 yen [approximately 25 cents' U.S. worth].

Interrogation starts immediately. Detention will prove unnecessary if the detectives limit themselves to the crime that was specified in the warrant, and by 4:10 p.m. she has already admitted to that offense. A detective approaches me and privately says he doubts that arrest or subsequent detention is needed.

- Supervisor Ando: How is it?

- Detective Abe: She admits to the offense.

- Detective Endo (to me): Is it really necessary to arrest a woman like this? If I were a judge, even if I issued a warrant, I wouldn't grant detention in this one.

However, other detectives do not hide their desire to use detention to discover separate offenses. They see detention as a measure which gives them more time to clear separate offenses rather than a measure to prevent the flight of the suspect or the destruction of evidence, as stated in the Code of Criminal Procedure. In the statements below, they explain that an earlier plan to arrest her on another charge was blocked by the supervisors. They deliberately left a known offense out of their application for the warrant in order to justify future detention. They also explain that they wanted her to deny the charges because her denial would have made it easier to get detention. They are annoyed that they must treat a female suspect more gently in spite of their desire for an aggressive investigation in this case.

- Detective Abe: As to why we didn't request a warrant based on the other [earlier] offense, the reason was that we want to be able to get detention. It would have been better if she had made a denial. We had planned to request the warrant based on the other offense, but it was held up from above. The lost article in that case was cash, so it probably can't be found. In that case there won't be direct proof of the charge. That's why we waited for this case. We took out a warrant based on it because she wouldn't respond for a voluntary appearance on the other offense. It really would have been better if she had denied the charge. In that case, it's easier to get detention. Right now, aside from the 10,000 yen [approximately $33 U.S.] that she returned after stealing it, it seems she has borrowed 10,000 yen from her employer. So we are investigating both matters. She has been fired, so we plan to use the risk of flight in our request for detention. She is really quite an actress. On top of that, you have to be gentle with women, so it is a tough case to handle.

On the following day, at about 10:00 a.m., the detectives explain developments in the interrogation. They are excited by the prospect of clearing quite a few separate offenses.

- Detective Baba: We interrogated her until about 7:00 in the evening. She has started to admit another separate offense as well. [An acquaintance asked her to look after the house because the wife of that family was away, and the suspect apparently stole 30,000 yen (approximately $100 U.S.) and a ring.] She has begun to admit to a part of the money, too. We had initially planned to get the warrant on this one, but there was nothing but circumstantial evidence, so we gave it up. The case in which she stole a key and entered later when the place was empty comes next. We will tackle that now.

Two days after the arrest, on the 5th of April, the detectives explain the situation to me. They indicate that the reasons given in the application for detention are different from their real purpose, which is to seek confessions to separate offenses. They expect her to be given detention at the station, which will increase pressure on her to confess.

- Detective Abe: On the woman, we have already requested detention. She has no fixed address, and there is a risk of flight. There is a contradiction between the content of the confession and the report of lost goods by the victim, so we have to work on that question. Nevertheless, we can't write that the detention is to investigate separate offenses. She was under a suspended sentence, so we'll probably get it. Then we have asked that she not be taken away from us to be put into the outside detention center. Her first prosecutor's interrogation will probably be held today.

At 4:10 p.m., the woman comes back from prosecutor's interrogation, and is taken into the interrogation room. The detectives explain to me how they can exploit her, because she has "no brain."

- Detective Baba: She's not the sort of woman that will speak when you just command her to talk. All she is thinking about is going home. If we get detention, she will start to move our way after two or three days. If she were a little smarter woman, we could do nothing, but this one has no brains, you can fool her easily.

On the 8th of April (three days later), I learn how the investigation has developed. They are satisfied by the woman's detention at the station, and the detectives tell me they plan to use this opportunity to clear many separate offenses.

- Supervisor Ando: She was detained. She was not assigned to the outside detention center.
- Detective Abe: We will work on separate offenses a little at a time. We'll take our time with it.

On the 10th of April, I take a look at the ledger of orders from the station chief which is on the desk of a Theft Crime Section head. Reasons for the detention in the ledger are: She has confessed to one part of a separate offense, but there is a contradiction between the amount of money reported lost by the victim and the amount set forth in the confession. She also maintains that she did not steal the ring, thus there is need for further investigation of these issues. This indicates that the purpose of seeking detention is to investigate crimes not specified in the arrest application. But that is not written in the detention application made by the prosecutor to the judge. On the 12th of April, the detectives tell me the situation. The unreliability of the victim's memory is apparent. The detectives are worried about the weakness of the charge used for the arrest, so they want to add more charges. While the detectives are seeking separate offenses, however, they are also aware that the suspect may make a false confession to gain favors from them.

- Detective Abe: We can clearly get an indictment for 20,000 yen [approximately $67 U.S.] stolen from the safe. It does not conform to the report that 30,000 yen [approximately $100 U.S.] and a ring were stolen, but even the victim says, "Now that you mention it, I can't declare certainly that it was put in the safe." Now, the suspect says that "I sent that money to Otaru as day care fees," so we are checking it out. The facts of the theft from the handbag [the offense for which she was arrested] are clear, but she has paid it back. Aside from that, when she was indicted before, she did not make a confession, so there are cases that remain unindicted. We will use these as aggravating circumstances. Aside from that, she says that she "knows about a murder at a certain food and drink place," but there is a chance that she is sweet-talking to curry the favor of the detectives, so we are hurrying to check that out.

On the 15th of April, I learn that the woman has been indicted, but still remains in the station. With the original charge being so weak, the detectives want to attach separate offenses to it.

- Detective Abe: Indictment came out on the 12th. Of course, the facts set forth in the indictment are those of the original offense for which she was arrested, but in fact it is weak on just the original offense. We would like to have two more separate offenses aside from that matter, so we are getting those. We know that it was a lie that she sent the money [to her child].

After 6:15 p.m. on the 18th of April, the suspect complains of abdominal

pain. The detectives say that it is play-acting with the aim of stopping detention or securing a transfer to the outside detention center. Detectives are anxious to continue interrogation in the station, but some of them start to worry.

- Detective Baba: She plays dirty. She has started to talk a little. She
  has a real sense of the bargain. A princess among female thieves.

- Detective Fujita: If it [abdominal pain] takes a turn for the worse,
  we'll take her to the emergency clinic. It's not an act of interrogation, so we will snap the handcuffs on her tight.

- Detective Baba: It's a waste of the opportunity, but I guess, let's
  transfer her.

On the morning of the 19th of April, I learn that the detectives have decided
to transfer her to the outside detention center. However they continue to
interrogate her, and are proud of the number of admissions of separate
offenses they have obtained.

- Detective Baba: We will transfer Yamada. When we had her examined by a physician, he found she had an adhesion where her
  appendix had been operated on. She just admitted another offense.
  That makes eight cases.

- Detective Chiba: Most of Yamada's separate offenses are unreported.
  She gets friendly, then steals from them, then doesn't go there any-
  more. They may suspect, but there is no proof, so they don't report it.

They tell me that victims are not clear on the amount of money stolen and
the places where it was left. I also learn how sick she is.

- Detective Fujita: I was on duty last night, so I'm pretty bushed. On
  the Yamada case, we had the doctor come in, and his examination
  was over at about 9:00 p.m. She has that adhesion in her appendix,
  and besides that, gonorrhea and trichinosis, it's pretty bad.

3. Investigation of Forcible Crimes

Forcible crimes include murder, robbery, rape, injury, and assault. The
basic character of the investigation of these crimes is different from that of
thefts. Pouring energy into a forcible crime case immediately when it arises,
detectives aim to seize the criminal quickly. Ericson (1981: 78) has reported

that in Canada detectives regard those cases which require immediate attention as "serious cases." In this sense, Japanese detectives also regard forcible crimes as "serious cases."

The supervisors explain, "In violent crimes, we have to resolve cases right away, so we move as a team." Therefore, even when their assistance is requested by other sections, the forcible crime detectives are required to reserve their members in the event that a violent crime occurs. In one case, for example, a large number of voluntary appearances occured following a certain unregistered labor union demonstration, and because there were not sufficient staff to handle the burden in the Security Section, the detectives also were mobilized. However, most detectives of the Forcible Crime Section were exempted from this duty. A supervisor told me, "We are assisting with the strike matter, but we also have to be prepared to respond to violent crimes that might come up."

If this degree of haste is required, one might expect procedural constraints to fall by the wayside. According to one supervisor, "[I]n forcible crimes it is easy to find loopholes." To offset the danger of abusing these loopholes, "we have the men work by an orthodox method." In the following pages, we examine how much these "orthodox methods" restrain abuses.

Because of the need for immediate response, emergency arrest is the most common form used by forcible crime detectives. I present below one such case.

Case 17: An Arsonist Who Made False Confessions

Of all the cases which I observed, this is the one in which the detectives had the least confidence in their investigation. Two arson cases arose, and the man subjected to emergency arrest in the second case was interrogated about possible involvement in the first as well, in an effort to solve two crimes at once. Although the suspect was held for the second case, the first arson became the focus of the investigation. The suspect maintained that the first arson had been a conspiracy in which he played only a subsidiary role and was led by two other persons. After long questioning, however, the suspect finally confessed to acting alone. Nonetheless, the detectives were not sure, so he was indicted only for the second arson, and the trial began. During trial, it became clear that the suspect's initial story that he had played only a subsidiary role in the first arson was true.

This case did not attract any attention from the press. It nevertheless indicates that suspects offer confessions that are not true, and further that they may withhold that fact from the prosecutor, the judge, and even their attorneys. Details of this case follow:

On the 11th of March, I first learn from the assistant chief in charge of criminal investigation and the head of a Detective Department that a suspect is in custody for arson. There were two arsons, the first of a noodle shop and the second of an apartment building. The arrest, as stated above, is based on the second case, and the first case is being investigated as a separate crime. Detectives are not sure if the suspect committed the first arson by himself, so that investigation already is focusing on the first case, although arrest and detention was not permitted for that purpose.

According to the statement of Matsuda, the arrested suspect, Wakamatsu, the owner of the barber shop where Matsuda works, asked a third person Yamamoto (whereabouts unknown) to set fire to Wakamatsu's shop. Yamamoto set fire to the noodle shop next to Wakamatsu's shop to disguise their real purpose and with expectation that the fire would also detroy Wakamatsu's shop. At that time Matsuda was in Wakamatsu's shop and had nothing to do with the fire. The First Detective Department head wonders whether Matsuda can be charged for acting as a "screen" (i.e., in helping to cover up a conspiracy). He also is uncertain whether Wakamatsu is the true offender or has some other criminal connection to the case, whether Matsuda's statement is sufficient to investigate Wakamatsu, and whether Wakamatsu is a suspect or a witness. They need proof of the time and place where the conspiracy was formed, of the content of the conspiracy, of the content of the conspiratorial acts, and of Matsuda's state of mind. Supervisor Ando explains the situation. He is not sure about the actual roles of the three possible suspects.

- Supervisor Ando: According to Matsuda's statement, Wakamatsu appealed to Yamamoto, and Yamamoto mentioned the shopowner's request to Matsuda. Matsuda became an accomplice, and Yamamoto set fire to the noodle shop [next to Wakamatsu's shop]. Matsuda himself set fire to the Wakamatsu Apartments [Wakamatsu's parents' apartment building, where Matsuda lived]. Matsuda, borrowing from Wakamatsu, delivered 30,000 yen [approximately $100 U.S.] to Yamamoto. If this were arranged as Matsuda said, Yamamoto should get his money from Wakamatsu, though. According to Matsuda, he committed the second offense [setting fire to the apartment] because after the first offense, Wakamatsu was "acting idle and relaxed." In the first case, Matsuda says that "I left as Yamamoto was making preparations, I don't know anything." But he was a "screen," and he was seen by the owner of the building, so he can be considered a proper criminal.

The detectives have not yet unraveled the facts, and the detention is scheduled to end in only three days. Supervisor Ando is hard pressed to do something, but he cannot decide what.

- Supervisor Ando: On the 15th of March, detention in the second case [for which Matsuda was arrested] will end, so I at least want to do something with Matsuda and Wakamatsu. Perhaps if we can confirm that the 30,000 yen went from Wakamatsu to Matsuda, we can call Wakamatsu a suspect. Our first hypothesis is that Matsuda hated Wakamatsu and that perhaps he set fire to the apartment for that reason. Our second hypothesis is that perhaps Wakamatsu requested Matsuda to do the job. However, it was publicly known that Wakamatsu planned to close the shop soon, so there is the question of whether or not he would still ask an arsonist to burn it anyway. Matsuda says that Yamamoto spread stove oil, but none appears at the scene. He says that the door was opened with a wire, but it can't be opened in that way. Matsuda is in detention for setting fire to the apartment on the 23rd of February. There are no footprints. It was an inside job. You can't get to the second floor [where the fire started] from the first floor. The suspect must have been on the second floor. Matsuda watched the investigation at the scene calmly. His palm print came off of the kerosene can. There was a match [apparently used to set fire]. On the same day, we made an emergency arrest of him. He will reach the end of his detention on the 15th of this month. If things stay as they are, Matsuda is an assisting accomplice to the first offense.

Supervisor Ando is concerned that Matsuda will change his statement at the trial, particularly after the involvement of a state-appointed defense attorney.

- Supervisor Ando: Insofar as Matsuda's statement is to be used as a premise in prosecution, unless the first offense is fully understood, we cannot decide on the motive for the second offense; we cannot indict on just the second offense alone. Wakamatsu owes money for mahjong gambling, so there is at least a possible motive. But without Yamamoto in the case, there is a risk that Matsuda will recant the confession even if we could get one. If an attorney gets mixed up in the case, recantation would be certain. A solo offense [by Matsuda] is a possibility, but because the guy himself says that it was a conspiracy, we can't use that until we have exhausted all other possibilities.

Focusing investigation regarding the first case while having arrested Matsuda for the second also leads Supervisor Ando to worry about the possible allegation of illegal pretext arrest, for investigation of a crime different from the one which was used as grounds for warrant application.

- Supervisor Ando: Unless we persist with the original offense [on which arrest and detention is based], there is a risk that we will be accused of [illegal] arrest for different crimes [not specified in the arrest application]. It may be possible to investigate the first offense after indicting for the second. The tactic favored by the prosecutor may be to indict [Matsuda] for the second offense, using his hatred of Wakamatsu as the motive, then amend the charge once the facts of the first offense become clear. Motive, the circumstances around the arson, the way the fire started, and the extent of the blaze, all need to be drawn up as evidence. Yamamoto himself is not so close to Wakamatsu. Matsuda gave Yamamoto 30,000 yen, so it may be that Matsuda began to hate Wakamatsu, and asked Yamamoto [to set fire].

He laments that the burden of proof on the Japanese police is much more demanding than that on the American police, particularly in regard to the need to prove a motive.

- Supervisor Ando: Under the Japanese Criminal Code, motive is an element in sentencing, and must be proven as a fact. It would be different if, as in America, we might deal only with surface action. Yamamoto was a bartender at a shop that Matsuda used to frequent. He quit as bartender, and took up professional pachinko; now he gets by as a pachinko player. Matsuda goes there [a pachinko parlor] from time to time. Together with Wakamatsu, they form a group for mahjong gambling. If they were after the insurance money, wouldn't Wakamatsu ordinarily have paid his money directly to Matsuda and had him do the job? If you have a vagabond type like Yamamoto do the job, there is risk of trouble later with blackmail.

Supervisor Ando again talks about the danger of being accused of making an illegal arrest for different crimes not specified in arrest warrant, and is proud of his concern for proper procedures.

- Supervisor Ando: We could pick up Wakamatsu for gambling at mahjong, and there are other theft offenses that we could pick up Matsuda on, but that is an [illegal] arrest for different crimes, so we won't do it. Do that, and then there is the chance that everything will be spoiled anyway. It is not that we couldn't stretch things and make such an arrest, but if at all possible, it is better to make it in an orthodox way, although there are those people with a more old-fashioned way of thinking. At the outset, it might have been better to bring in Wakamatsu and have it out with him, but it is more persuasive if we do so only as the last resort after we have followed the primary investigation to its end. Use of the arrest for different crimes may be within the law, but the practice is criticized by the public as irrational and inappropriate. Care is especially important in big cases.

Supervisor Ando is afraid that the prosecutor will release the suspect pending indictment because the detectives have failed to complete investigation of the first arson while the suspect has been in custody for the second. He criticizes the prosecutor for pressing him to hurry the investigation even at the risk of inviting an allegation of an illegal pretext arrest. He resents that prosecutors still treat the police as if they are their subordinates, as before the war. He also finds himself in a dilemma. On the one hand, he does not want to employ a questionable investigation method. On the other, he does not want to see the case thrown out by the prosecutor for insufficient proof.

- Supervisor Ando: The second offense will come to indictment soon, but it is possible that the suspect will be released pending the indictment. There is nothing to be done. It is our policy not to use the different crime arrest [*bekken taiho* in Japanese, meaning, in this case, arresting the suspect on the basis of the second arson in order to obtain a chance to interrogate him for the first arson]. We could have used it long ago if we had wanted to. The prosecutors can stretch things. If there is not proof of guilt, they can go forward without an indictment. As for the police, where there is no proof of guilt, we cannot proceed to arrest. The prosecutors say, "Hurry up and interrogate Wakamatsu," but as a policeman I want to proceed after firming up my primary investigation. The police are no longer an auxiliary unit of the prosecutors as they were under the old Code of Criminal Procedure. Prosecutors [now] do not have direct or distinct powers to command [police officers in individual cases]. As police, it is damaging to our pride to have a case dismissed for "lack of proof." Prosecutors, especially in intellectual crime cases, reason politically. We don't like to see judgments that there is "insufficient proof" for a finding of guilt. We ask them, "Send us the document of the decision of the prosecutor's office," but they don't get around to sending it. Eventually the concerned prosecutor is transferred, and it gets lost in the shuffle.

On the following day, Supervisor Ando decides to proceed on the hypothesis that the suspect acted alone in the first arson as well.

- Supervisor Ando: Of the three hypotheses, we will go with the first.

At about 11:00 a.m., the detectives purchase a plastic bag identical to the one which served as the origin of the fire in the second case. They decide to perform experiments in setting fires and to consult lab specialists. In addition, they continue to interrogate the suspect to obtain a confession which fits the hypothesis of a solo crime. The detectives are tense. In the afternoon, a squad leader comes out from the interrogation room, calling back, "We will make you talk." Supervisor Ando explains that the most desirable confession is one which contains an element of information detectives did not know beforehand. In other words, they consider it preferable to investigate for physical evidence only after they first get a confession, rather than initially searching for physical evidence.

- Supervisor Ando: It looks like we can draw it [the first case] up as a solo offense. He has confessed, "I went inside, but it was dark, so I waited until my eyes adjusted, then I set the fire." He knows the situation inside the room. Even the investigators don't know that, only the arsonist could know. As a motive, we have hatred of the owner, although he has not confessed to that. The story about passing on 30,000 yen is suspicious, too, so we'll check that out.

At 3:35 p.m., Detectives Abe, Baba, I, and an officer from the lab go to the site of the first offense. This is because Matsuda says, "I went in from the back door of the noodle shop, rolled up a white coat that was hanging on the wall, and set fire to it." Like Ando the detectives believe the most desirable confession contains information the police don't know.

- Detective Abe: Even the detectives don't know this, and there has been no report of a white uniform lost. If this is in fact true, it will be something that "only the criminal knows."

At 3:40, we arrive at the noodle shop. The memories of shop workers regarding where they might have left coats when they went home are unclear. Only two shop workers are at the shop. Contrary to Matsuda's confession, there was no place to hang a white uniform, and the detectives look extremely disappointed. At 4:03, Detective Abe telephones Supervisor Ando. But Abe still believes that the suspect really committed this crime.

- Detective Abe: There is no place to hang a white uniform. Please ask Matsuda about it.

At 4:26 p.m., the detectives take statements from the two at the shop. At 4:31, we receive a call from the station. The suspect has apparently changed his story. "He set fire to a white uniform on a shelf inside a closet, he says." But the confession again fails to match the reality: there was no uniform left atop the shelf. Detectives still insist Matsuda must be trying to mislead them.

- Detective Abe: It would have been fine if it had been a towel. When we get back, I'll have to tell him, "Don't you lie to us, dammit. It was a towel, wasn't it?"

The shop employees say they don't know who locked up the shop when they went home. The detectives ask when the shop people came in after the arson. They also ask what was in the closets. Abandoning their view that the most desirable form of investigation starts with confession of an unknown fact and proceeds to confirmation with physical evidence, the detectives now appear to moving toward getting a confession that fits what they have found at the scene.

We return to the station at six o'clock. The detectives decide to interrogate again the suspect. The detectives complain that the right to remain silent impedes their investigation and reaffirm how much investigation depends on confessions.

- Detective Baba: We say first, "You don't have to tell us anything," and then say, "Now talk." It's not like they're going to talk for you.

- Detective Abe: And if they don't say anything, there's nothing you can do. If they don't leave stuff behind at the scene when they leave, there is no proof. And you can't even get their alibi to work on.

Interrogation has apparently proceeded quite well, however, toward confirmation of their hypothesis. On the next day (13th), after the morning meeting, the supervisors call the detectives together. They are pleased that the suspect has finally admitted that they were right. They are aware, however, that confessions which have been changed too often can cause trouble later.

- Supervisor Ando: He acknowledges it exactly like that. Yes, he set fire to a white coat.

- Supervisor Bando: Yesterday, we didn't interrogate him. If the content of the confession wanders too much, its voluntariness comes under suspicion.

The supervisors comment on the progress of the investigation and explain why they have succeeded in solving this difficult case. Yet they remain slightly uncertain, and even admit that there is a possibility of losing the case at the trial.

- Supervisor Bando: There was a confession to serial offenses. They were solo offenses. Immediate protection of the scene by the patrol people was good. Collection of evidence by the specialists was also good. Science was well applied. The basic investigation was well conducted. There have also been problems though. The results of investigations are set forth in announcements and reports, but there is vagueness about the specific distance in time of events from the inception of the offense. Make the fundamental elements more specific. Reports should be comprehensible not only to the detectives in charge, but to third persons as well. There are reports with missing pieces. There are points that were conveyed orally which do not appear in the reports. Why did you trace the footsteps of Yamamoto? There was a call from Iwamizawa City. When? Regarding interrogation methods, let him say everything that he wants, then ferret out contradictions on points relevant to the case. The facts regarding the white uniform and so on are facts which only the criminal could have known, and to which he has confessed. This technique enhances voluntariness in court. What remains is to reinforce the confession. He says that he carried magazines out of the noodle shop; investigate the suspect's room. In any event it is good that you didn't manhandle him. We may lose at the trial, but there will be no doubt about voluntariness; you're doing all right.

- Detective Ando: It is good that we stuck with the original offense [the second arson]. If we hadn't, the original offense could have been spoiled along with everything else.

At 9:00 a.m., Wakamatsu, the barber shop owner and the suspect's employer, comes in. Supervisor Ando, Detectives Abe and Baba go with him into the interrogation room. At 9:45, Wakamatsu goes home. At 10:20, Detectives Abe, Baba, Chiba and Dando, a lab tech, and I go to Wakamatsu's shop. The detectives tell me that they are unsure about the second case too and that they have made the prosecutor angry by their slow-moving investigation.

- Detective Abe: We went to deliver additional papers to the prosecutor in this case [first arson]. Regarding the lid of the kerosene tank in the main case [second arson], the guy [suspect] says that the lid was on it. But when we asked around, we heard that someone found a lid at the site, or that they picked it up and put it in their shirt pocket, and various other things. But in the statement of a witness, there was a pump stuck in the can, without a lid. Even if he [the suspect] is the one [who committed the crime], he doesn't remember very well. The guy made his statement saying, "Now that you mention it, maybe that's the way it was." The prosecutor has gotten angry—"You bring this to us only now," he says. Today we're going to inspect the barber shop. Matsuda says, "I waited until it was time at the barber shop." He says, "I took my own barber's certificate from a drawer [not wanting it burned] and took it back to my apartment." We will see whether the room [in the shop] fits the description in the confession, and whether anyone had seen these papers in the drawer or not.

But the detectives are disappointed again. They are told that rather than a barber's certificate, it was only a postcard notice of Matsuda's licensing. They call back to the station to check. Detectives at the station then apparently questioned the suspect on this point, and we receive a return call from the station. Matsuda adimitted that it was a postcard after all. But the lock on the door differs from the one described in the confession.

At 11:20, we return to the station. In spite of uncertainty in details, the supervisors are already planning a press conference. Supervisor Bando says, "Looks like it will be in the morning papers [tomorrow]." Detective Abe says, "Better if we can make it in time for the evening edition [today]." Reporters are coming and going from the detectives' room. Supervisor Bando is writing the release for the newspapers.

The prosecutor apparently has serious doubts about this case. He asks for more evidence, even for the second arson on which the arrest was based. The detectives begin to suspect Wakamatsu, the owner of the barber shop, as the principal criminal in the first arson.

- Detective Abe: The prosecutor has asked for the clothing worn at the time of the crime. I sent the socks; I'll send the shirt next. I guess the kerosene won't be found, will it?

- Supervisor Ando: Matsuda keeps insisting on his position, so we'll have to speak with Wakamatsu.

- Detective Abe: We should get a "divorce letter" from him saying, "What Matsuda says is a lie." And we should ask about whether it was a license notice or a license certificate.

- Supervisor Ando: Because there was a certificate in the guy's room, rolled up.

- Detective Abe: What! Although he says it was a postcard, I don't think that it was.

- Supervisor Ando: We have to tell him, "That's not right,is it?"

- Detective Abe: This guy is a pain in the neck on the details, isn't he?

- Detective Chiba: We should expect one or two minor errors, otherwise we cannot get anywhere.

At about 12:30 p.m., the Forcible Crime Section head is summarizing the report on the first arson case, concentrating especially on those parts which contradict one another, such as the question of the notice or certificate, and especially how the fire at the noodle shop was set. Detective Chiba says, "I went to the site. If we could have proof just by showing that cloth was burned, I would feel better." At 1:00 p.m., Wakamatsu arrives upon request for his voluntary appearance. Supervisor Ando ridicules him.

- Supervisor Ando: Don't tell me you are going to tell us that you made him do it. Because it is never easy to know about people. Remember you will be a witness at the trial. What connection brought you to hire Matsuda? If we had questioned you just a little earlier, you would have been punished. You were considered a partner in crime, after all. It's not something to laugh about. The circumstances are too ugly. Your insurance was too high, and your conduct is bad.

- Wakamatsu: I gave the 30,000 yen to Matsuda. I lent it to him because he said he would pass it to Yamamoto.

At 1:20 p.m., Supervisor Bando comes to chat with Supervisor Ando. They have not yet transferred the first arson case to the prosecutor, but Bando has told the press that they did.

- Supervisor Bando: I said that we had sent the materials to the prosecutor, but it's okay, isn't it? It will be out on television soon.

However, the prosecutor in charge of these arson cases apparently did not like to receive the first case with only insufficient evidence. At 1:50, he comes to the station. The prosecutor confers with Supervisor Ando and Detectives Abe and Baba, about how the fire was set in the noodle shop case. They decide to remove boards from the inside of the closet of the noodle shop for examination of the ash, athough the shop people are opposed to this instruction. After the prosecutor has left, Supervisor Ando chides Detective Baba.

- Supervisor Ando: I explained it to the prosecutor just as you say. There is nothing I can do about it but trust you.

- Detective Baba: Still seems like you just don't trust me.

An evening edition of a local newspaper carries a report with a photograph: "On the 13th, a man was transferred to the Disrict Prosecutor's Office on suspicion of the arson of a residential building.... At about 12:00 a.m. on the 11th of February, after sneaking into a noodle shop, he set a match to a shelf under the shop counter, which then burned shelves and items on the wall of the shop.... On the 23rd of February, at about 6:45 a.m., he spread kerosene outside the second-floor toilet of the apartment where he lived, and touched a match to it. Approximately 10 square meters of the floor of the apartment hallway were burned.... Irritated about his job, but unable to quit because of a shortage of help, it occurred to him at the time that if he set a fire, he would be able to quit his job freely." But the truth is that the detectives did not know what motivated the suspect to commit the first arson. The papers nevertheless report as if there is no doubt, including the charge that Matsuda committed the crime alone.

On the 14th, at 8:45 a.m., I go to the scene of the first arson (noodle shop) with Detectives Baba and Dando, and lab staffers Akita and Beppu. They decide to remove boards from the closet and take pictures.

- Detective Baba: It is only natural for the shop owner to hesitate.

- Lab staffer Akita: In another case being managed by Chiba, they laid on new mortar right away, and it really caused a problem.

- Detective Dando: They said that they would cover the burned areas at the apartment with boards. We should be sure to have them save it for a year.

From 9:40 to 10:10, I talk with Supervisor Ando and learn that the suspect now is denying again that he acted alone in the noodle shop case.

- Supervisor Ando: He was arrested on the 23rd [of February]. He will probably be indicted on the main offense [the burning of the apartment] sometime this morning. And in the first case [the burning of the noodle shop], he continues to deny it. But in the end he will probably be indicted for that one, too. A criminal's level of living, standard of conduct and sense of values are totally different from those of an ordinary person. Even in that newspaper article, we left out motives. Aside from motivations from mistreatment, he was threatened by the owner with exposure of a theft if he quit his job.

Ando does not appear to have much confidence in his own theory, however.

Investigation on Wakamatsu continues on a voluntary basis. At about 10:40, Detective Endo's squad is interrogating Wakamatsu.

- Detective Fujita: For the moment, he is a witness. Matsuda maintains that it was a conspiracy, and there is a motive. In any case we have to check out these points.

At 11:35, Matsuda is sent to the prosecutor. The detectives plan to interrogate him again after he returns. Matsuda wears summer clothes even now when snow is still on the ground in Hokkaido, and the seat of his pants is torn. The detectives were going to have him change pants, but his other pair was in the same condition. A detective from Detective Chiba's squad is sewing them up. At 11:40 a.m., Supervisor Ando gives an order to Detective Baba. I note that supervisors are involved in the details of investigation throughout the entire process.

- Supervisor Ando (to Detective Baba): Find out whether Matsuda's treatment by the shop owner is normal. Ask at his union and at his school. Also, be sure to find out whether he graduated, and when.

At 12:40 in the afternoon, a detective tells me that Matsuda hates the shop owner.

- Detective Chiba: Matsuda is a strange one. He says, "If I get out, I'll do it to Wakamatsu all over again."

At about 3:30 p.m., Supervisor Ando explains the situation to me. He admits that he is still unable to transfer the first arson case to the prosecutor and his press release was not completely true. The press simply reported what they heard from Ando. He also believes it very likely that at the trial the suspect will recant his confession on the first arson. The supervisor maintains, however, that this uncertainty is an outcome of the very careful investigation, rather than any predisposition to believe that the suspect acted alone.

- Supervisor Ando: The evidence and papers in the main case have pretty much been sent across. Now, we are preparing the evidence and papers in the first case. The prosecutor has doubts about the first case, so as things stand now he probably will not indict. We have no feeling that Wakamatsu was involved. It would be too suspicious if there was an arson immediately after he insured the building. It would be suspicious if there was an arson at the point he appeared ready to close the shop. He was holding back Matsuda, who wanted to quit. If it is a conspiratorial offense, then Matsuda should be threatening him, saying, "If you don't let me quit, I'll expose you." Thus, we can't find a motive for Wakamatsu.

The remaining possibility with the best chance of being proven is that there was a conspiracy between Yamamoto and Matsuda. That may be a subject for continuing investigation. Yamamoto has a prior record for petty fraud. If he has fenced stolen goods for Matsuda, the possibility of conspiracy is strong.

Police investigations are not, as is commonly thought, a simple sprint to the finish. In any case, everyone is acutely conscious of the possibility that a confession will be recanted at trial. Trial will start in two or three months. The [newspaper] report that the suspect has been "transferred to the prosecutor" was not correct, but we had to make the announcement to ease the minds of the people in the neighborhood, and I suppose that it's all right to add some name value [exaggeration] in order to do so.

On the 15th, at about 10:30 a.m., the detectives complain about the prosecutor's demand for more evidence and his reluctance to proceed with the first arson. They also worry over the confession, which is uncharacteristically specific and may look suspicious.

- Detective Abe: The separate offense [the first arson] will not go to indictment right away, so we could follow up some points. (To Detective Chiba) The prosecutor is complaining. Says that the white coat was not in the right place and stuff.

- Detective Chiba: That prosecutor is always making noise about something.

- Detective Baba: Probably he has no confidence in himself.

- Detective Abe: We'll have to get statements from all the staff of the noodle shop about where the white coat was, and whether or not it was burned.

- Detective Chiba: Even if his statement doesn't match the statements of the shop workers, couldn't the prosecutor stand on the voluntariness of Matsuda's confession? It was not easy to see in that place, and I don't think that it's possible to nail down the details the way the prosecutor wants us to. On the contrary, it would be strange to have things established that clearly.

- Detective Abe: If there were something that Matsuda was carrying that was burned in the fire, it would help. We have to ask at the noodle shop again about that.

At about 1:00 p.m., in order to respond to the request from the prosecutor, they conduct a makeshift experiment. The men of Detective Chiba's squad are trying to determine how a cotton shirt burns in an ashtray.

- Lab member Akita: The prosecutor's reputation is on the line if he loses, so he is asking us to do experiments under the same conditions. But that's difficult to do even at the research lab at the headquarters.

On the 18th of March, about 8:20 a.m., I learn that the suspect had been indicted on the 15th for the second arson—the one on which the arrest and detention was based—but he still remains in the station because investigation of the first arson has not yet been completed. At around 1 p.m. that same day, interrrogation of Matsuda starts yet again.

On the 19th, at around 8:20 a.m., they tell me that they are still investigating the first arson. The squad has changed, and the new squad repeats the same questions. In spite of their preference for avoiding arrest on the basis of a crime different from the real target, they are so desperate that they plan to arrest Wakamatsu on a totally unrelated petty fraud charge, just to detain him in the station for interrogation.

- Detective Chiba: I plan to end the investigation on the arson today and turn to corroboration of the suspect's statement. This came to us from Endo's squad, so we'll have to take statements again starting with the motive problem.

- Supervisor Baba: Whatever we do, we have to thoroughly investigate Wakamatsu. In the first case, there is no proof, after all. We are thinking of taking out an arrest warrant for petty fraud.

At about 10:30 a.m., the detectives are still investigating the license notice. They do not appear to consider that the suspect's original denial of acting alone in the first arson might be true and that this might explain why his confessions are unreliable as a basis for searching for physical evidence. They cannot conceive that they have unintentionally forced the suspect to make constantly changing, useless confessions, which in turn have produced all their confusion.

- Detective Abe: In Matsuda's statement, he says that he took the notice postcard from a drawer at the barber shop and then took it to the supervising agency, received his certificate there and went home. Therefore, the notice postcard should be at the agency, and the certificate should be at his residence.

At about 1:50, I learn that the prosecutor still refuses to accept the police conclusions about the first arson. The detectives' morale in this case is visibly low.

- Detective Abe: There was a call from the prosecutor. He said, "If you plan to send the first arson case across, let me know first." Seems he does not want the case sent to him in the current form of investigation. Sounds like we have to get Yamamoto to save the case.

On the 22nd, the suspect still remains in the station. A detective explains the detention system to me.

- Detective Goto: Matsuda has been indicted in the second case, but he is still in the station detention cell. A suspect doesn't automatically go to the outside detention center upon indictment. The prosecutor puts out a transfer order saying, "Transfer the suspect." Even when the suspect has been moved to the outside detention center, we can have him brought back on the prosecutor's order.

At about 1:00 p.m., the detectives admit that the first case is still confusing. They maintain, however, that there was nothing wrong with their investigation, since a more complete investigation of the crime scene at the beginning should be avoided and because it is better for them not to present complete evidence on the first date of trial. The detectives firmly believe that the first priority in an investigation is to get a confession and that they should start real investigation only after that. They do not consider that each time they got an erroneous confession, they had to repeat the process, and that this pattern of investigation has produced a vicious cycle in which a false confession caused a longer investigation, and a longer investigation produced yet another false confession. In the meantime, the detectives lost the opportunity to recover evidence from the scene of the crime and to explore other possibilities.

- Detective Chiba: He says that the back door was open [in the first arson], but wasn't the door actually locked? Matsuda says that he didn't turn on the lights inside the room, but wouldn't he then be unable to see the numbers on the keys? So didn't he turn them on? Matsuda says, "I rolled up a white coat that was hanging to the left immediately inside the door, and set fire to it," but was it actually hanging there? There are pictures of matches believed to have been used in starting the blaze, but judging from the way they lie, are these not simply dropped matches? There are continuous footprints from rubber boots leading away from the back door of the shop, but

Matsuda's shoes were lightweight summer shoes. If the case is hit in these places, what will happen?

And we have Matsuda's parents coming after the first case, asking that he be allowed to quit his job. If that is so, wasn't it unlikely that Matsuda was at the point of setting fire to the place? Wakamatsu's alibi for the first case is vague. The insurance that Wakamatsu put on the place just before the fire is fishy, too. Even if he had quit the business and sold out, he couldn't have gotten much. But in all of this, if we run a complete investigation at the scene, there will be a question of whether we have gotten a statement that conforms to our own preconceived ideas. Then again, if we submit airtight proof at the first trial, there will be suspicion that we might have constructed the evidence. And so we would lose the capacity to defend our position and expand our proof.

On the 29th of March, at about 2:00 p.m., the detectives are trying to conclude the investigation of this troublesome case, although the prosecutor still refuses to accept it. The detectives are worried about the trial, but they also express the hope that the defense attorney will be a state-appointed one.

- Detective Baba: There has been an indictment on the apartment fire only. Soon we will send the noodle shop fire across, too. Prosecutors may point out that we haven't gotten Yamamoto, so we'll put out a call for him on the fraud charge. We'll request a warrant. If the case is run by a state-appointed defender, there won't be much of a problem. Detective Chiba will be called [to the trial], though.

After more than a week, however, they have been unable to conclude the investigation. On the 8th of April, at 4:10 p.m., a supervisor tries to justify his decision to send the case to the prosecutor, partly on the basis of the suspect's interest to avoid double jeopardy. This case now is nothing more than an annoyance to them.

- Supervisor Ando: We are discussing our plan to put Matsuda's first case together and send it to the prosecutor. The lighting [in the noodle shop] is just according to the confession of the suspect. On whether there was a white uniform hanging up in the corner, they say that they sometimes hang one up to wash their hands, and it is confirmed that two uniforms have disappeared, so this at least does not conflict with the confession. We experimented with combustion and burning. In the end, he has confessed, and since there is nothing to back up a denial of the confession, we should send the case across.

The prosecutor still maintains that he wants us to wait until we have Yamamoto before giving him the case. Probably the prosecutor has a suspended disposition and a continuing investigation in mind. But withholding the case is a detriment to the suspect. Even if there is no indictment in the case, if it is sent across he will not be indicted again for the same crime. To the judge, the first case will be on record as having gone to the prosecutor, who failed to bring an indictment. He [the judge] would make his decision in the second case in light of that knowledge as well.

One full month after the suspect's arrest, on the 11th of April at 1:00 p.m., an order is issued to transfer Matsuda to the outside detention center. While theoretically the maximum length of detention after arrest is 23 days, the existence of crimes other than the one for the arrest provides the police with an opportunity for a longer detention at the police station.

Although Matsuda is no longer in the station, the detectives have not completed the investigation. They are waiting for the arrest of Yamamoto on an unrelated charge. On the 16th of April, a supervisor explains the situation to me.

- Supervisor Ando: As for Yamamoto, there is a call out for him for fraud. After he is arrested, if suspicion of him in the arson case grows stronger, we will arrest him at that point for arson.

The detectives are all concerned with the trial. They express the hope that the state-appointed attorney will not challenge the prosecution, while at the same time they complain about the prosecutor's doubts about their construction of the cases. On the 23rd of April, they discuss the situation. They still believe that Matsuda committed the first crime by himself, but the prosecutor still refuses to accept this explanation. It is noteworthy, though, that the prosecutor has not opted for a suspended indictment of the first arson, which is well within his authority, but is simply demanding more information which in turn has caused a lengthier detention of the suspect.

- Detective Endo: Looks like the trial of Matsuda comes tomorrow. Looks like the prosecutor will recommend sentencing only after one hearing. I heard that the state-appointed defender consented to [the introduction] of the record of the suspect's statement [as evidence]. The decision will probably be handed down at the second hearing. I think that the first case will go across today, although the prosecutor keeps picking at this and that aspect of it. Supervisor Bando says to send it across today, so we are working on it.

Matsuda admits to the first offense as his solo action. He says that his motive for [originally] pleading a conspiracy was to involve Wakamatsu and Yamamoto. The main motive relates to Wakamatsu. He also hated Yamamoto for taking 30,000 yen from him. The prosecutor's problem is that with that earlier statement on the record, he can't rest easy until he nails Yamamoto. Also, this problem of his setting fire to the white uniform is not clear. The employees are vague about whether maybe they hung white uniforms up there or didn't. If we had sent this case across together with the main offense [the second arson at the apartment], the main offense might have not been cleared on a single hearing. Supervisor Bando says, "Send it across anyway, and transfer any stuff that we get afterward."

- Supervisor Ando: The prosecutor is trying to slow us down with obstructive requests.

Detective Endo's squad still wrestles with the problem of whether there was a white coat hanging in the corner. At 4:30 p.m., we go to the noodle shop, because the detectives have lost the diagram showing the exact location of the hook that held the door curtain. Detective Bando says, "We can send it over later."

On the 24th of April, at 1:00 p.m., I arrive at the Sapporo District Court to observe the first hearing of Matsuda's case. As the detectives had hoped, the state-appointed attorney apparently has not reviewed the evidence much in advance.

- Attorney (to the prosecutor): I didn't have time to look at the psychiatric medical examination. Do you have it?

He goes over to the prosecutor, who then shows him the medical report, which the prosecutor has not submitted as evidence. Matsuda remains at his place.

- Attorney: Ah, in regard to this [the medical report], this is a problem.... I consent to the rest.

At 1:07, the hearing convenes with three judges. The chief judge confirms the attendance of the parties and reads aloud the alleged facts. Matsuda stands. The prosecutor's indictment is then read aloud. The offense is arson and the theft of an electric fan, a pot, skis and sticks, a heater, records, and an electric plane, worth a total of 100,000 yen [approximately $330 U.S.]. The chief judge informs the suspect of his right to remain silent. "What you say may be used both in your favor and against you." I start to take notes which I knew violates the court regulations in those days.

- Chief Judge: Are there any mistakes in the facts?

- Matsuda: There are no mistakes.

- Attorney: There are no mistakes.

- Chief Judge: Do you have anything to say...nothing?

- Matsuda: Nothing.

- Chief Judge: I will write this into the record of evidence.

- Prosecutor: I will make my opening statement.

The prosecutor refers to the unindicted first offense at the noodle shop. He says that after Matsuda's voluntary appearance, a polygraph was administered and an emergency arrest followed. The defense attorney does not challenge the statements that were taken from the suspect.

- Attorney: We consent to all the records of statement.

- Chief Judge: I will add this to the register of evidence consented to. Please display the evidence.

The prosecutor displays the evidence.

- Prosecutor: Matches.

- Chief Judge: Attorney for the accused, approach and examine the evidence.

- Attorney (to Matsuda): Do you remember these? Are these the ones?

- Matsuda: The name [inscribed on the matches] is the same, but I am not sure whether this is the same box.

- Prosecutor (to Matsuda): The kerosene can. This is it, correct?

The court clerk finds me taking notes at this moment, and says, "No note taking." The following material is reconstructed from my memory, and was written down immediately after the close of the hearing.

- Matsuda: The color is the same, but I can't be sure whether this is the same one.

The judge begins reading Matsuda's statement aloud. The one regarding the unindicted noodle shop case is quite long, and changes and contradictions are clear. The defense attorney does not appear to have recognized this, nor does Matsuda appear to have explained this case to the attorney. Part of the statement reads that "The master [Wakamatsu] called upon Yamamoto to set fire to the place." The attorney does not comment on the statements, instead he makes request for the psychiatric examination that was not submitted by the prosecutor as evidence because it was favorable to Matsuda, and he himself also requests a psychiatric examination.

Then the attorney asserts that there was a difference in the reported volume of thinner sniffed by the defendant during the second offense. The detectives have not told me that Matsuda sniffed paint thinner during the second offense. The attorney takes the position that "the burden of proving the lack of exculpatory conditions lies with the prosecutor." This is contrary to the established view that the defense has to prove the existence of exculpatory conditions. This question is discussed by the judges for about twenty minutes in the back room. The judicial trainees go to listen to the discussion. The judges reappear and the chief judge questions Matsuda, asking about the general circumstances of sniffing thinner and the circumstances at the time of the offense. He also probes contradictions in earlier statement.

- Matsuda (regarding the general circumstances of thinner sniffing): I put thinner into a plastic bag, and put it to my mouth. I can see colors on the things around me. It seems like I am in a dream. My head gets warm inside. I get sleepy. At some point, the plastic bag comes away from my mouth, and I go to sleep. When I regain consciousness, it is early in the morning. I don't remember anything about the time between when I got sleepy and when I went to sleep. [regarding the circumstances at the time of the offense] I began to sniff thinner. I looked into the room of two girls on the second floor. They called me, and I went to their room. When I came back, I sniffed some more. After awhile, the window began to look like it was surrounded by flowers. My head got warm. I began to get angry about the boss. I felt like setting a fire, and I set it.

The prosecutor questions Matsuda, attempting to confirm the statement taken by the detectives. The problem with taking no verbatim records during interrogation becomes apparent.

- Matsuda: I don't know how much time passed after I came back to the third floor and started sniffing again, until I started the fire. I don't know what the detectives put down, but I told them, "I am not sure."

The chief judge seriously questions the contradiction between the statement just made regarding the ordinary circumstances of the suspect's sniffing of thinner, and the statement produced by the prosecutor that the fire was set while the suspect sniffed thinner. The problem of the absence of verbatim records of interrogation is again apparent.

- Matsuda: I felt that it really was true that I was called to their room [of the two women on the second floor]. I am not clear about the time that I set the fire. About how much I sniffed before setting the fire, it looks like the detectives wrote it down like I had sniffed for "about twenty or thirty minutes," but I told them, "I don't remember clearly." I am fuzzy about what the matches and the kerosene would have looked like. I hazily remember that there was a kerosene can that I saw through a glass pane on the way down to the second floor. I bought a 200 yen [approximately 67 cents U.S.] bottle of thinner, and I sniffed about two centimeters out of the bottle.

At 2:41, the judges retire for another conference. During the recess, the attorney says to the prosecutor, "If he spread nine liters of kerosene, is that all the fire you would get?" The prosecutor says to the clerk, "When we break, I want to see today's record. Where it says that he spread nine liters of kerosene."

- Chief Judge (to the prosecutor): Why don't you submit that [the psychiatric report] into evidence?

- Prosecutor: As material connected with another crime [the first arson], it is based upon different premises, and I have decided not to submit it.

- Judge: And what about the attorney's demand [to produce it as evidence] ?

- Prosecutor: I consent.

- Judge: You consent, do you!

The prosecutor acts uncertain. He says, "I just took over the case." In practice, prosecutors are divided into two teams, investigation and trial. A single case is investigated and tried by different prosecutors.

- Judge: The next hearing will be on the 15th of May. We will schedule it for 10:00 a.m. As is my right, I will order another psychiatric test. The issue set down by the attorney—"concerning state of mind after sniffing of thinner for two to three hours"—is of itself illegal, and cannot be the aim of test, so I will make it "psychological state at the time of the criminal act, especially the circumstance of sniffing of thinner, and other items of concern." The doctor will probably cooperate with us, but if it should happen that he cannot come to be [in court] with us, we will go to visit him.

I was not able to follow the development of this continuing trial and the outcome of the investigation of the first arson at the noodle shop due to the limitation of research period and because I wished to follow other cases of investigation. On the 1st of August, however, I note that a morning edition of a local paper has reported on this case. Matsuda's first statement was evidently true. The crime was planned by his boss, Wakamatsu. Wakamatsu asked Yamamoto to join in carrying out the arson, and Yamamoto asked Matsuda to help him.

> The Eastern Police Station, which had been investigating the arson case which occurred in February of this year at a noodle shop in the Toyohira district of Sapporo City, learned that neighboring shop owner Wakamatsu asked his friends to set the fire with the aim of collecting the insurance money. These two friends were arrested by the 30th of July. Arrested were Wakamatsu (30 years old) and Yamamoto (30 years old). Matsuda (20 years old), arrested on the 23rd of February on suspicion of another arson, is currently in custody under indictment in the Sapporo District Court. It has been learned that the arson at the noodle shop was done by Matsuda and Yamamoto, and it has been revealed that Yamamoto acted at the request of Wakamatsu. Yamamoto hired Matsuda, and together they committed the arson. In setting fire to the noodle shop, they sought to avoid detection of the plan to destroy Wakamatsu's shop. They assumed that the fire would also destroy the aging structure of Wakamatsu's shop. Matsuda, in setting fire to the Wakamatsu apartments, acted because Wakamatsu lived in the same apartments, because his salary was only 12,000 yen [approximately $40 U.S. a month], because it had been discovered that he had stolen kerosene from the shop, and because he was constantly being scolded and was dissatisfied. Therefore, he set a fire in front of Wakamatsu's room.

This newspaper article, which must have been based on a press release from the station, does not mention that the police had not believed Matsuda's initial statement, nor does it tell of the tortuous process by which police had changed the direction of the investigation.

There is a significant difference between the incidents of false accusations I described in chapter 1 and this case, where Matsuda was at least an accomplice. The whole process of the Matsuda case, nonetheless, demonstrates how easy it is for a suspect to confess to a false charge, and how difficult it is not only for the press, but also for insiders in the criminal justice system such as judges, prosecutors, and defense attorneys to detect that fact. It is also clear that detectives can be caught in a vicious cycle that they themselves create, in which their emphasis on obtaining confessions rather than on gathering other evidence at the beginning of an investigation can lead to false statements, which in turn causes further delay in investigation.

4. Investigation of Organized Crimes

Organized crime investigations cover cases in which the suspects are members of gang organizations, regardless of the crime (see, generally, Ames: 1981, chapter 6). Certain types of crimes are stressed in these investigations, however, and their special character generates the particular style of investigations in this area.

According to a supervisor in charge of the Organized Crime Section, the district covered by the Eastern Police Station contained seven organized gangs, with some 375 individual members. Of these, 25 persons were "bosses," 80 "whips" and other supervisors, 221 "gang members," and 49 "associate members."

The detectives are shorthanded. A detective says, "Although we can generally follow their movements, they move in and out a lot, and we are short-staffed." Thus, the Organized Crime detective asks Theft Crime and Forcible Crime Sections, "If a matter is being handled by the Forcible Crime or Theft Crime Sections, but there is a suspicion that the suspect might be a gang member or an associate member, would you circle 'gang' [on all investigation report papers] for us please? There doesn't have to be a clear foundation for the classification [of the suspect as a gangster]. You can just tell us in person if you want."

The detectives think that interrogation of a gang member may be a harsher one than for other types of interrogation. According to one supervisor, "The suspects in intellectual crime cases, and suspects who have gang connections, are clearly different from thieves and others. They know a bit of law, and at least know that they do not have to comply with voluntary measures."

Thus, the detectives think, "the first principle in dealing with gangs is always to use compulsory measures." In interrogation as well, they think it necessary to treat the suspect more severely. For example, in a case in which a victim was threatened with a homemade pistol, one detective speaks sharply to the suspect, "No one would get in my way if I sent you up on attempted murder," but a supervisor comments, "He is not angry there, he is using persuasion." Another detective also explains that some level of aggression by police is tolerated because, "in the organized crime area, they figure that most of the guys they're dealing with are basically rotten" and also because they believe that ordinary people support such actions.

A type of crime which is particularly stressed is the sale of amphetamines, the bread and butter of the gangs in Japan (Ames, 1981: 117). Illegal use of stimulants is covered by the Stimulants Regulation Act, and direct proof of possession, sale, or use is desirable in order to obtain conviction. According to one supervisor, "The strategy on our side is to use a 'break-in warrant' [a search warrant] to create an opportunity to find them committing a different crime [on the spot], and then carry out a warrantless arrest, converting a search to an arrest." Detectives utilize this tactic as their most important investigative technique.

A search warrant typically is issued to search for materials connected with a specific crime, but given the lapse of time required to obtain information and the warrant, the detectives do not expect to find the materials specified in their warrant application. They know that "stimulants are the toughest thing [to locate]. They can be washed away, and they don't open up the door for you when you knock." Thus, obtaining information of past possession, sale, or use, they then apply for a search warrant for drug and equipment pertaining to that past crime, and use it to make a warrantless arrest for a new offense at the site of the search.

Thus organized crime investigations use tactics not found in theft and forcible crime investigations—tactics which are legally more questionable. In a study of vice investigations, Skolnick (1966: 144-49) has reported that American detectives more often take practically rational behavior than constitutionally acceptable behavior. The same may be said with regard to organized crime investigations in Japan.

Supervisors and detectives express different opinions about such tactics. One supervisor is more supportive, saying, "I think it is hard for people to understand how hard we work to stay inside the boundaries of the law. And the opponent is a professional criminal." But another supervisor says, "That may be true in the Organized Crime Section, but on our side, we put especially heavy restraint on search and seizure. There is more than one way to skin a cat."

The 1974 "Criminal Case Management Register" of the Organized Crime Section of the Eastern Police Station indicates that in the first three months of that year there were twenty cases handled without use of compulsory methods, twenty one warrantless arrests, four emergency arrests, fifty one ordinary arrests with warrants, and forty eight cases resolved as separate offenses. Thus, the record confirms that compulsory investigations are the rule.

I would also like to call attention to the relative importance of separate offenses (other than those used as grounds for arrest and detention) in organized crime cases . Given the difficulty of arresting organized crime members, the clearance of separate offenses, and post-arrest interrogation to that end, particularly during detention, is an important part of organized crime investigations.

I chose to analyze the following case here because it included the highest-ranking gangster among the cases I observed. In this case, a boss was arrested on a bail forfeiture, and some separate offenses were subsequently uncovered.

Case 24: Bail Forfeiture of a Crime Syndicate Boss

On the 10th of February in the Organized Crime Section, Yoshida, a crime syndicate boss, has been caught. When a traffic squad went to seize an underling for a traffic offense, the boss leapt from a window of his apartment in his housedress, thinking that they had come to arrest him. Upon checking the record, a warrant for arrest for forfeited bail was discovered, so the traffic squad picked him up and brought him in. Observe from the comment below that the detectives are going to use a search warrant exactly for the purpose I have just described. Also note that the detectives could force the suspect to present urine for testing through his ostensibly voluntary cooperation.

- Detective Abe: Looking at his arms, there were needle marks. When I asked him about it, he admitted using stimulants. We had him take a urine test, and it came up positive. Anyway, now we get a warrant [search warrant] and break in. Aside from that, without us asking anything, he says, "In Tokyo, I did a 20,000,000 yen [approximately $66,700 U.S.] extortion, isn't that why you're here? If that's it, send me to Tokyo."

- Yoshida: I'll tell you what I've done, but I'll tell you nothing about anyone else. Even if I do know, I know nothing. Amnesia, you know. [To me] The reporter [thinking I am a newspaper reporter] will probably paint this one with a wide brush, won't you?

The detectives do not want any publicity in this case because of what they plan to do.

- Detective Abe: If the papers write about it a lot, breaking in [search] will become more difficult.

- Supervisor Ando: That's a real animal in there. Even so, he responded well to voluntary accompaniment, didn't he?

On the 12th, the detectives are interrogating Yoshida. His common-law wife is sitting together with him in the interrogation room. I have never before seen this kind of situation where any person other than police officers is allowed to be present at an interrogation. It reminds me of reports of apparently cordial relationships between the police and gangsters (Ames, 1981: 107).

- Yoshida: I will cooperate with you, Mr. Detectives, so call Tokyo on the phone. I have underlings working for me, I need to talk with them about the materials. Construction materials, but not stimulants, no.

This response from the suspect makes the detectives uncomfortable, because detention is easier to get when the suspect refuses to cooperate.

- Detective Baba: What will we do about a cause for detention? Even if he does say he'll cooperate...[we want to detain him.]

The judge issues a search warrant for Yoshida's apartment, but the detectives do not believe that they can find the materials they described in the warrant application. Judges generally appear to either pretend unfamiliarity with this tactic, or deliberately cooperate with the detectives.

- Detective Abe: The order for a break-in is out.
- Detective Chiba: It's [the stimulants] probably already gone, though.

On the 15th, we go to the suspect's apartment, a break-in on suspicion of stimulants at Yoshida's residence. Detectives Abe, Baba, Chiba, and I meet Yoshida's wife at the door at 2 p.m. Detective Abe immediately reads the warrant to the wife. This procedure is quite different from the way the detectives showed the arrest warrant to the female thief in Case 11 described above in this chapter.

- Detective Abe: Take a close look at this, ma'am.

We finish the search at 2:55. In the end, there was nothing that was subject to search. No stimulants surfaced. The suspect himself had said that he had porn films, so these were expected, but there are only clippings of the title and leader of a movie film. There is an announcement for a formal event to be held by a gangster group, so that is taken. To the wife, "We'll take this, o.k.?" and it is shown to her. Her husband does not know about this search, and the detectives ask her not to tell him.

- Detective Abe: It's over, but it would be best not to mention anything to the boss. For us, there is nothing special in it, nothing turned up.

- Detective Baba: Sorry to have messed things up. We tried to put things back the way we found them.

Upon leaving, a detective tells me how he let the wife take them through the apartment. He did not tell her that they were going to search there.

- Detective Abe (on being admitted to the apartment): I deceived the wife. She let us in and so on.

The wife had come to the station to meet the suspect, so she was taken directly from the station to the entry way of the apartment. She does not know that they may at any time retain an attorney.

- Wife: Can't we call for an attorney yet?
- Detective Baba: You can call for one any time.

The objective of the entry was to locate syringes. Papers, memos, telephone logs, formal announcements, and so on were also scrupulously searched for.

- Detective Chiba: He will lose an 800,000 yen [approximately $2,670 U.S.] bail, and on top of that there are the stimulants, battery with injury charges, and extortion. If he has twenty prior cases, he could be put away for five years. If he hadn't run away, it would have been about eight months. [If he had not run away] The court's decision would be out in February [this month], so he would probably have had [the next] New Year's at home [after release from the prison term].

Yoshida was out on bail at the time of the trial for battery with injury but did not appear for trial, so bail was forfeited and the imprisonment warrant issued. Aside from this, he is wanted at the Iwamizawa Station for battery with injury, and at the Aomori Station [outside Hokkaido] for extortion.

- Detective Abe: He had been in a hospital, so he should have acquired and sent his medical records [to the court for postponing a trial, instead of fleeing].

The detectives have found that the suspect extorted a checkbook from a bank and let his men use it. This case is reported in the press, and the detectives explain the situation to me on the 18th (three days after the search).

• Detective Abe: Yoshida is a rotten one. The personal check was extorted from the head of a branch office of the Sapporo Bank. Yoshida says, "Even if I had dropped it, if someone else used it, I would pay for it myself," but in fact, it's the sort of thing that you would get upset about, isn't it? Looks like he is trying to cover an extortion. Even though it was just a small mistake, the head of the office didn't come on strong [when Yoshida called the bank], but went to meet him carrying beer with him, so you can see the beginnings of it. Even though he only has savings of a few tens of thousands of yen, on the head's order he borrows money unsecured using another's name. That's strange. I heard that Yoshida asked the head to lend the overdrawn money to him [without collateral]. The Tokyo case, too, was bad. He extorted 20,000,000 yen from a real estate man, and when he [Yoshida] gave a ride [to the real estate man] in his car, he started clicking a lighter in his pocket and said, "I wonder which is faster, my pistol, or you jumping out the door." He told him, "I'll kill you," and the guy was plastered up against the wall [side of the car], they say. The reason no call was put out on that one was probably because they didn't know his real name. He has used so many fake names that he has forgotten which was which himself. Yoshida is the boss of a "vagrant youth gang," and has about thirty members under him. A "vagrant youth gang" is not one made up of juvenile delinquents, but one that doesn't run gambling operations or sell protection at festivals, but runs other businesses exclusively. Rotten characters.

Today's morning edition of a local newspaper reports on this bank case. Eight personal checks from the Sapporo Bank were used on the 13th and 14th of this month. When the checks were presented to the bank on the 16th, there were only a few tens of thousands of yen on deposit, but the account was already overdrawn to the extent of 1,600,000 yen [approximately $5,300 U.S.]. Including subsequent withdrawals by the deposit holder [the arrested boss], the overdraft ran to two million and some thousands of yen. More than half of the checks remain unaccounted for, and there is fear that they may yet be used. The checks were printed by gang member Yoshida with a pseudonym, but they were being used by members of the gang. Yoshida claims that the checks were lost, but because the account had just been opened with little money in it, and because the withdrawals were made on Saturday and Sunday when the account balance could not be checked, this is being viewed as a large-scale fraud. The paper does not say that the check book was given by the bank branch manager to Yoshida.

On the following morning, the newspaper follows up the first story:

There has been a total loss of 2,820,000 yen [approximately $9,400 U.S.] on 20 checks. A call has been put out for Uno, a 28-year old gang supervisor. On the 10th, Uno had picked up two checkbooks by the roadside, and at the Susukino Jewelers' he bought two foreign-made watches, and two foreign lighters, purchases totalling 700,000 yen. The checks had been printed by a gang member Yoshida (40 years old) using a pseudonym. However, judging from talk at the store which suffered the loss, aside from Uno, many others in the gang used the checks for purchases on a day when the balance could not be checked. Yoshida's opening of the account came immediately before the offense, and the balance in the account was only 35,000 yen [approximately $117 U.S.]. Therefore, the police are viewing Uno and Yoshida as co-conspirators, and trying to identify all of the other members of the gang involved in this fraud.

As in the earlier newspaper article, the involvement of the bank branch manager still is not reported.

5. Summary

I conclude this part by indicating the basic patterns in the processes of investigation carried out by the detectives.

First of all, at the stage preceding arrest in theft and forcible crime investigations, there are voluntary accompaniments and voluntary appearances. There are quite a large number of cases in which such cooperation is requested of the suspect, even when the detectives already have an arrest warrant in their hands. In forcible crime investigations, the focus upon a quick resolution of cases makes field questioning particularly important in situations where neither a warrantless arrest nor an emergency arrest is reasonable. In such a case, field questioning may lead to a voluntary accompaniment, and this is converted to a voluntary appearance for purposes of interrogation when a certain amount of evidence surfaces.

In organized crime investigations, although it does not necessarily precede all arrests, search and seizure plays a particularly important role. The main purpose of such tactics is to discover evidence for separate offenses which have not been specified in the warrant.

At the arrest stage in theft crime investigations, I find ordinary arrests as well as emergency arrests that closely resemble ordinary arrest. In forcible crime investigations, I find both ordinary and warrantless arrests, and emergency arrests that closely resemble the warrantless arrest of flagrant offenders.

In either field of investigations, emergency arrest appears to play a large role.

At the interrogation stage, there is a common pattern of interrogation throughout detention at the police station, and a concern for solving offenses other than those specified in the arrest and detention applications. These patterns are most pronounced in the theft crime area, but they also are found in the forcible crime and organized crime areas. In my observations, there was no case of an arrest that was not followed by detention and all detentions were in the police station detention cells. Concerning differences at the interrogation stage, compared with interrogation for theft crime and forcible crime, organized crime interrogation is more severe. It appears that this greater severity is backed by a detective's sense of social approval of what he does.

In short, Japanese police officers not only fully utilize their enormous advantage over the suspect which is provided by the very enabling legal framework, but they also try to expand that advantage.

With this background on the natural sequence of criminal investigation by types of crime in Japan, I will proceed to part 2, the main part of this book. I draw upon observational materials from across different areas of investigation and supplement these with the results of a questionnaire survey, indicating first the attitudes and behaviors of detectives with more details through each step of an investigation. I then explain their attitudes and behaviors in part 3. The six cases presented above will guide the reader in evaluating the credibility of my analysis in the following chapters.

Part II

Description of Investigative Activity:
How Do They Think and Behave?

5

Investigative Efficiency and Procedural Compliance

This part of the book describes the attitudes and behavior of Japanese police detectives at each stage in their investigative activities. The investigative process in Japan can be divided into five stages: (1) voluntary investigation; (2) search and seizure; (3) arrest; (4) detention; and (5) interrogation in which there is an emphasis on separate offenses (i.e., other than the charge used for arrest). Search and seizure may occur after arrest as well as before, but searches on a warrant also create an opportunity to make an arrest for a crime in commission. Below, I discuss search and seizure prior to arrest. In the interrogation process, investigation of separate offenses may take place throughout the duration of voluntary and compulsory investigation, although this basically occurs after arrest, particularly after detention. Detectives need to investigate separate offenses to justify their demand for detention. Separate offenses often are solved when aggressive interrogation extracts a confession from a suspect. In this view, I will discuss detention and interrogation for investigation of separate offenses in that order.

I combine here observational materials with additional survey data. Firsthand observation provides a description of the attitudes and behavior of police in the field, while survey data are used to examine the prevalence of the observed views and behaviors.

Before looking to the attitudes and behavior of the detectives themselves, I first review materials relating to the police academy and to the attitudes and behavior of the supervisors within the Eastern Police Station. Discussion of the police academy reveals internal guidelines and the prevalence of the observed attitudes and behavior in Hokkaido as a whole. In addition, the attitudes and behavior of supervisors are important influences over detectives' conduct.

I pay the most attention to the interplay between aggressiveness of investigation and procedural restraints. The reason for this special focus is that the investigative activities of the police have conflicting behavioral expectations—the expectation of aggressiveness to efficiently solve a crime and the expectation of caution not to violate the rights of suspects and other citizens.

The law, then, contains these contradictory expectations of the police. The police are first of all supposed to "prevent and suppress crime, conduct investigations, and arrest suspects," but at the same time they must avoid interfering with "the freedoms and individual rights guaranteed by the Japanese Constitution" (Police Act, Article 2). In other words, while "bringing forth the actual facts, and swiftly carrying out the penal laws and regulations," they are to preserve "guarantees of basic human rights" (Code of Criminal Procedure, Article 1; see also Criminal Investigation Standards, Article 2).

These contraditory expectations are manifested within functional provisions as well. The police are allowed to question the suspect while in custody (Code of Criminal Procedure, Article 198, Section 1), but also are required to advise the suspect to exercise the right to remain silent and the right to retain counsel (Code of Criminal Procedure, Article 198, Section 2; Article 203).

Thus the problem directly confronting the police is that, unless there is eminent danger of post hoc judicial control protecting the rights of the suspect, it is more efficient to use actions that are questionable from the perspective of protection of individual rights. The purpose of this part of the book is to determine the extent to which such questionable actions actually occur.

To begin with, how do we rate the degree of aggressiveness in police behavior and attitudes? The standards I will use for this purpose are (1) judicial interpretations of the law up until the point of the research, (2) the guiding policy within the force, and (3) the evaluation of the supervisors and detectives themselves.

A problem of precision remains, of course. For example, where there has been no judicial opinion in a given action, it is difficult to assay the exact level of the action's questionability. We are limited to characterizations such as "actions which, reasoning from trends of judicial interpretation, may not be clearly viewed as illegal, but which, depending upon circumstances, are thought to be debatably questionable" or "actions which are of such degree of questionability that the detectives themselves harbor some doubt about them." Since it is normal for interpretative judgments—policies in the police organization and evaluations by the judiciary, police supervisors, or detectives—to exhibit diversity, I wish to make the standard of questionability quite low and concentrate on whether an action arouses even slight debate or doubt.

One point must be considered before proceeding: whether or not officers themselves really recognize an incompatibility between efficient investigation and respect for the rights of the citizen accused. I will present empirical evidence of the validity of my general assumption that efficient investigation and procedural compliance are perceived to be incompatible by police officers.

In the American context, Skolnick (1966) has most strongly emphasized the incompatibility of order and legality. He has argued that "the police is *the* institution best exemplifying the strain between the two ideas" (Skolnick, 1966: 9). According to Skolnick (1966: 181, 186, 202-3), the clearance rate as the standard of efficiency employed in police departments may in fact undermine due process of law, where constitutional protections for the suspect come to be regarded by the police primarily as administrative obstacles, and due process of law is seen as a set of working conditions that are becoming increasingly more arduous. Skolnick concluded his book (1966: chapter 11) with the pessimistic observation that police professionalization stressing efficiency might worsen the conflict between order and legality. I have observed that Japanese police officers share this perspective with American officers.

Evidence clearly shows that Japanese officers believe that the two ends of efficient investigation and procedural compliance are in conflict. This certainly is the position expressed at the police academy. For example, a teacher said to me, "If you want to talk about protection of civil rights, let's also think about their by-products," and a student in a class of assistant inspectors said, "In practice police work doesn't work out according to the textbook."

The observed attitudes of field supervisors are more complicated. On the one hand, there are supervisors who clearly state that the two aims cannot be achieved simultaneously, saying "Investigation is different from procedure, you see. We don't catch the criminal through procedure, do we?" On the other hand, there are supervisors who say, "The most effective way is the most legal way," "It's no good to say 'We can't catch the criminal following procedure' and play it freehand," or "If [by following procedure] arrest rates drop for a short period, that's okay." In the end, it appears that the average attitude among supervisors is "Efficiency and procedure are not in harmony, but it is not acceptable to say so and not to protect procedure."

Among the detectives, thoughts like those expressed by the second group of supervisors are not to be found.

Some detectives deny any compatibility. For example, a theft offense detective said, "By following the law just exactly so, you don't catch the thief and can't solve the crime." To detectives taking this position, knowledge of procedural law is little better than an obstacle: "Study is necessary, but if you know too much, you can't get started on an investigation" (theft crime officer).

There were also detectives who felt ambivalent. They believed "due process in investigation made it difficult to arrest criminals in a proper investigation, but that is probably the right course."

The data shows that supervisors and detectives share the majority view that pursuit of efficiency and respect for procedure are in conflict, and that my basic understanding is confirmed.

Let us proceed to analyze the material regarding the relative weight placed upon pursuit of efficiency and respect for procedure. I also will look at how questionable respondents view their own aggressive tactics in the pursuit of efficiency. This analysis in turn suggests what factors cause changes in aggressiveness.

6

Voluntary Investigation

I first examine the conduct, or attitude toward conduct, of detectives regarding voluntary accompaniment or voluntary appearance. Bayley (1976: 146) has reported that "over four-fifths of all suspects are handled without arrest on an 'at home' basis" in Japan and that "the vast majority of suspects cooperate voluntarily in their own prosecution." This chapter describes police actions to secure such "voluntary" cooperation.

The Police Duties Execution Act allows the police to ask a suspicious person to accompany them to a police station or a police box. The act does not treat requests of *voluntary accompaniment* as investigative activities because the police encounter the suspicious person by accident and no specific charge has yet been established. At the same time, the Code of Criminal Procedure permits the police to ask a suspect to appear at a police station or a police box, and defines such requests of *voluntary appearance* as investigative measures because there are specific charges when the police ask the suspect to appear. Voluntary accompaniment and voluntary appearance are indistinguishable in reality since voluntary accompaniment can also develop into interrogation about specific charges. In fact, police officers usually call both actions voluntary "accompaniment." Therefore I will often use the two terms interchangeably in this chapter.

1. Police Academy

First let us see how the matter is taught at the police academy, in order to determine the policies that are formally permitted or promoted within the force. One lecture I attended was designed for entering supervisors and police patrolmen and was on the subject of voluntary appearance under the Code of Criminal Procedure. The lecturer stated, "When you are going for a voluntary appearance, you must first prepare thoroughly; it requires sound preparation and careful examination. Then, when your subject shows an attitude of refusal, one is expected to use persuasion toward the end."

When the subject responds to persuasion, the question of where to escort him arises. Students are taught to "avoid distant places which, because of time and place considerations, might erode the voluntariness of the accompaniment." When you have to take him to a distant place, the instruction is to "opt for a forcible arrest." And cautions are given that "if, after going to a *chuzaisho* [residential police box where an officer lives with family] or *hashutsusho* [nonresidential police box to which officers commute], you further ask the suspect to accompany you to the main station, voluntariness can easily be denied." Here, we should note that officers are aware of the possibility of criticism by the court on the voluntariness of an appearance, and that at the point of requesting a voluntary appearance they may essentially be making an arrest.

The lecturer also cautioned about the danger that the voluntary appearance may be interpreted by the court essentially as an arrest and the time limit for filing a request for detention will run from that point. For example, the notion is that "basically, if you have the requirements for arrest, you should go ahead and make the arrest. Otherwise, on the execution of the warrant a long time later, detention is often rejected." From this warning, it can be supposed that even when they already have an arrest warrant, officers sometimes do not use it immediately and request voluntary appearance first.

The reason for requesting a voluntary appearance while holding an arrest warrant is to avoid mistaken arrests. On this point, the instructor speaks of his experiences:

> Since it might be mistaken, I didn't execute the warrant until he confessed, and in the meantime I worked up the materials. However, I found that the material wasn't sound; the warrant had been issued, but it [evidence] wasn't good enough to go beyond that, and so I released him.

In another case:

> We filed for a warrant on the basis of the statements of the victim and a detective. It didn't look right. Because of that [questionable] background of the warrant, we brought him in on voluntary appearance, with the intention of holding the warrant until he confessed. At that point, we discovered it was a mistaken arrest.

Confessions are pursued without moving beyond the voluntary investigation stage because it is thought that arrest is for the guilty.

However, while concern is focused on the confession, it is critical that the voluntary appearance or accompaniment is truly voluntary. The police academy stresses that voluntary measures must be truly just that. This command implicitly acknowledges that abuses happen:

> Interrogation after voluntary accompaniment may raise a question of whether voluntary accompaniment was sought in order to evade time limitations after arrest. This is the most important problem.

On this point, students are instructed as follows:

> Suppose we have voluntary accompaniment at eight o'clock, confession at eleven. The detainment filing is likely to be rejected by the court if you send the case to the prosecutor forty eight hours after eleven o'clock. It is best to count your time from eight o'clock.

Detectives must also be careful about the length of the interrogation:

- A lot of confessions are taken at eight or nine in the evening after voluntary accompaniment at eight or nine in the morning. But if you used eight to eleven hours for interrogation, the court is likely to decide that you tried to evade the time limitation after arrest and to deny the voluntariness of the confession. Therefore, if they don't confess in six or seven hours, file for a warrant.

- If there isn't a confession within six or seven hours of voluntary accompaniment, file for a warrant. Try to get a confession and prepare for filing for an arrest warrant at once.

- Once you have confirmed facts and the suspect's profile, it is time to finish it up. The problem is not whether or not he confesses. Where there is a warrant, or preparations for a warrant, you should make the arrest.

We can imply from the length of interrogation that confessions are sometimes sought before a filing is made for an ordinary arrest warrant.

However, according to the instructors' talk of their experiences, not that much attention actually is paid to the possibility of judicial criticism. The situation was described as follows by instructors:

- The greatest number [of suspects] break down at about nine in the evening. You get him on a voluntary accompaniment at about eight in the morning, and he breaks down at about nine in the evening. When I was out there, we wouldn't let him do anything; your suspect is 99 percent guilty, and is likely to injure himself and others. After all, when it comes to the actual judgment, we take things into account.

• In a certain case, we didn't let him call out until the warrant was issued at around midnight. It didn't cause any problem at trial.

What is being "taken into account" here by instructors are the circumstances of interrogation. First of all, "it is too late to warn the suspect of his right to remain silent at the point of making out his statement. Give the warning immediately after the voluntary accompaniment." On the number of interrogators, it is thought that "one is the best principle. At most, two. If you have three, it is likely to be called psychological force, or coercion." Regarding dress, the instruction is that "civilian clothes are best. If there are uniforms, it is easy for others to misunderstand." Where there is a request by the suspect to leave, it is thought that "there is no way but persuasion. Voluntary accompaniment is sought when there is substantial suspicion, and so words to the effect that 'It's to clear you of suspicion' are good. Outside contact must not be refused because young judges, in particular, ask if it was freely allowed during interrogation at the detention hearing." With regard to attorneys' requests to see the suspect, students are taught that "there is no statute that you must follow, but you must respond with consideration of the right to a defense, particularly when the suspect requests to meet with the attorney. For instance, ask the attorney to wait [rather than to simply refuse]."

In conclusion, while there is a strong awareness of judicial evaluation of the voluntariness of appearances and confessions, and there is guidance in conformity with that awareness, there is a perception that the chances of actually incurring judicial criticism are low.

2. Supervisors

Supervisors do not believe that it is difficult to obtain a voluntary appearance:

A telephone call is enough for a voluntary accompaniment; you can prepare well before asking, and many will offer to come whenever you give them a time, without causing a fuss or denying the request. If there is much trouble, I tell officers to repeat the request, and in the meantime to get a warrant.

In investigating organized crime: "The thing that encourages a voluntary accompaniment is the personal influence of the organized crime detective." This strategy suggests that strength of suspicion at the stage of the voluntary appearance is close to that at arrest.

Furthermore, supervisors acknowledge that voluntary appearances may be requested while the arrest warrant filing is being prepared. Once a warrant already has been issued, a request for voluntary accompaniment is frowned upon. For example, when I asked about this, one supervisor responded by asking with a disturbed frown, "Is there someone in the Patrol Department who brings men in voluntarily even when the warrant has issued?"

There is a strong perception of the time limits that exist before sending the suspect to the prosecutor and detainment:

- Calculation of time is done from the voluntary appearance. We do not think about stretching out the time. In case of an arrested suspect, I myself calculate the time from the point where he enters the control of the police. It goes without saying that I do so even when the suspect is brought in as a voluntary appearance if he is taken in the same way as by arrest. It is good enough to send him to the prosecutor without confession and to prove it at trial. The accused will be detained for testing and so forth, and he will just suffer disadvantages.

- If you say, "We catch you for such and such facts," it is clearly an arrest. But even when we don't say it, we always distinguish between voluntary accompaniment and arrest. Do you understand this?

Naturally, despite the supervisors' intentions, there is room for doubt whether or not this kind of management—of looking back to the starting point for calculating time—ends in approval of a voluntary accompaniment that scarcely differs from an arrest. Even though the beliefs of the supervisors are as set forth above, they themselves acknowledge that there are subordinates who think differently, and that they cannot completely control the actions of their subordinates.

Finally, regarding interrogation, and the time within which it is to be completed, the policy is to let the suspect go home at the time ordinary people go to bed—at about nine to ten o'clock. But there is no hesitation to ignore this policy when the occasion demands.

To sum up, the supervisors' policy is to place the time from which the transferral or detention clock begins to run at the point of actual duress, or "voluntary appearance." We may suppose, quite naturally, that this indicates an awareness of possible judicial criticism at the detention hearing. However, supervisors are conscious of the fact that control over subordinates is imperfect. They allow detectives to seek voluntary appearance at the same time they are preparing for an arrest warrant filing. With regard to the length of interrogation, although they are cautious in principle, they can become aggressive in response to necessity.

3. Detectives

How do the detectives incorporate their police academy training and the directions from their supervisors into their behavior?

They understand that they must not use force against suspects. A theft crime detective relates the following experience:

> In a case I handled three years ago, a detention filing was denied by District Court Judge Abe. There was a report from a pawn shop that a guy pawned a tape deck that looked stolen. Two of us went immediately by car, questioned him, asked him to come in on voluntary appearance and opened the car door. Then the suspect says, "I don't want to go!" and runs away. A mechanic at a nearby shop trips him and knocks him down. We ran up, and grabbed his arm. He said, "I won't run now," so we brought him into the station sandwiched between us in the car. At this point, we didn't know where the goods had been stolen from. If we had known, we would have booked him then as an emergency arrest. During rapid questioning at the station, he confessed to stealing it from a friend. We booked him. The arrest warrant was issued. On filing for detention, I was called before the judge. He said that grabbing his arm was a compulsory measure. Because it was an illegal arrest, detention filing was denied. The judge said that counting from the point we grabbed his arm, more than seventy two hours had passed. Asserting that the arrest warrant came out after that, the prosecutor appealed. Dismissed. Released. Although, with another warrant, we arrested him right away after that....

But if the only effect of resorting to force is to push back the starting point from which detention filing time is counted, and serious consideration is given by the courts only to the time calculation, this leads to the conclusion that there is no need to change the methods used in voluntary accompaniments. Some detectives claim that the method of boxing in suspects between two or more detectives is not used. However, in actual voluntary accompaniments, suspects are boxed in, seated in the back seat of a two-door auto with detectives on either side, exactly as in the case of a "rear of car" arrest in Canada reported by Ericson (1981: 140). When there is neither arrest nor detention while a voluntary investigation is conducted, there will be no chance for the time limitation to become an issue, and consequently no danger that the method of the voluntary accompaniment will be criticized.

Furthermore, even if there is a voluntary appearance, if this isn't made clear on the record, there is no fear that the starting point will be recalculated. For example, a detective told his colleague, "Don't write down that it was a voluntary accompaniment." Then to me, he said, "Because we'll be told that the voluntary accompaniment was an arrest, we don't write it down on purpose, see." There is a strong awareness that if force was present, there may be criticism based on the starting time for the transfer to the prosecutor and detainment filing. However, detectives do not necessarily believe that they must change their methods of voluntary accompaniment, nor correct those methods. The paperwork can be done to show that there was no voluntary appearance, even when a voluntary appearance is requested with a warrant in hand.

Behind the aggressive actions in voluntary appearances, there is an attitude that "one must not fail on a voluntary appearance," or "it is a disgrace to fail on voluntary appearance." This is exemplified in statements such as, "However much you call it *voluntary* questioning and accompaniment, the fact is that as a police officer you can't let them run away" (theft crime detective).

Some of the voluntary appearances which are thought to be so easy by the supervisors actually are accomplished by the "persuasion" of officers who are motivated by the thought that they "can't let him get away," and may involve actions which are problematic, if not clearly illegal.

Why, despite the stress placed upon "voluntary character" of accompaniments by the police academy education and the supervisors, do detectives develop the attitude that they "can't let him get away"? The survey data allows us to examine the detectives' attitudes toward proper conduct during investigations.

The first items in Table 6.1 deal with questioning and voluntary accompaniment under the Police Duty Execution Act. Since duty questioning leading to a voluntary accompaniment is the first step in the investigation, it is appropriate to consider both together.

Table 6.1 shows that the great majority of detectives (84 percent) see duty questioning not only as a means of crime prevention, but also as an important link in investigations (items 1 and 2). According to item 3, the majority opinion among detectives (63 percent) is that frequent duty questioning is counted in evaluating an officer's performance.

Duty questioning is not always successful. In items 4 and 5, a majority of detectives feel that the number of citizens who refuse to cooperate in duty questioning and voluntary accompaniment is increasing.

Table 6.1   Attitudes about Voluntary Investigation

SIGNIFICANCE OF DUTY QUESTIONING

---

1. Do you believe that duty questioning is useful for the *prevention of crime*?

Yes	Undecided	No	Total Respondents
83.7	14.0	2.3	(43)

2. Do you believe that it is useful as a link in investigations?

Yes	Undecided	No	Total Respondents
92.9	4.8	2.4	(42)

DUTY QUESTIONING AND PERFORMANCE

---

3. Do you believe that frequent duty questioning *enhances a policeman's reputation*?

Yes	Undecided	No	Total Respondents
62.8	18.6	18.6	(43)

REFUSAL OF DUTY QUESTIONING AND VOLUNTARY ACCOMPANIMENT

---

4. Do you believe that the number of people who *refuse to cooperate in duty questioning* has been increasing?

Yes	Undecided	No	Total Respondents
65.1	16.3	18.6	(43)

5. Do you believe that the number of people who *refuse to cooperate in voluntary accompaniment* has been increasing?

Yes	Undecided	No	Total Respondents
72.1	16.3	11.6	(43)

DUTY TO COOPERATE IN DUTY QUESTIONING
AND VOLUNTARY ACCOMPANIMENT

---

6. Do you believe that *a duty to cooperate with the police* should be recognized by the citizen of Hokkaido to at least respond to duty questioning?

Yes	Undecided	No	Total Respondents
69.8	20.9	9.3	(43)

7. Do you believe that *a duty to cooperate with the police* should be recognized by the citizen of Hokkaido to at least cooperate with a voluntary accompaniment?

Yes	Undecided	No	Total Respondents
53.5	27.9	18.6	(43)

Table 6.1 *(Continued)*

DUTY QUESTIONING AND VOLUNTARY ACCOMPANIMENT; OFFICIAL POLICY
AND PUBLIC OPINION (SEE NOTE)

---

8. Do you believe that the statements contained in quotations in items 62 through 67
regarding voluntary investigation are in accordance with the official policy of the
Hokkaido Police?

Yes	Undecided	No	Total Respondents
57.1	19.0	23.8	(42)

9. Do you believe that the statements contained in quotations in items 62 through 67
regarding voluntary investigation are in accordance with the thoughts of the supervisor at the police station with which you are connected?

Yes	Undecided	No	Total Respondents
57.1	19.0	23.8	(42)

ILLEGAL DUTY QUESTIONING AND VOLUNTARY ACCOMPANIMENT
AND ONE'S SERVICE RECORD

---

10. When an officer is later told by a judge that "the duty questioning was illegal," do
you believe that this is a negative commentary affecting his reputation as an officer?

Yes	Undecided	No	Total Respondents
31.0	33.3	35.7	(42)

11. Do you believe it has this effect if it is held that "the voluntary accompaniment
was illegal"?

Yes	Undecided	No	Total Respondents
32.6	32.6	34.8	(43)

REFUSAL OF VOLUNTARY APPEARANCE

---

12. Do you believe that the number of persons who refuse to cooperate with a voluntary appearance requested over the telephone has been increasing?

Yes	Undecided	No	Total Respondents
58.1	32.6	9.3	(43)

DUTY TO COOPERATE IN VOLUNTARY APPEARANCE

---

13. Do you believe that a duty should be recognized by the citizen of Hokkaido to
cooperate in a voluntary appearance even when merely requested by telephone?

Yes	Undecided	No	Total Respondents
52.4	31.0	16.7	(42)

Table 6.1   *(Continued)*

VOLUNTARY ACCOMPANIMENT AND VOLUNTARY APPEARANCE
WHERE THERE IS AN ARREST WARRANT.

---

14. Do you think that there are quite a large number of cases in which, although holding an arrest warrant, an officer, without promptly executing the warrant, requests a voluntary accompaniment or a voluntary appearance?

Yes	Undecided	No	Total Respondents
48.8	30.2	20.9	(43)

15. Do you believe that such cases are becoming more common?

Yes	Undecided	No	Total Respondents
39.5	37.2	23.3	(43)

VOLUNTARY ACCOMPANIMENT AND VOLUNTARY APPEARANCE
WHERE THERE IS AN ARREST WARRANT; OFFICIAL POLICY.

---

16. Do you believe that such cases are in accordance with the official policy of the Hokkaido Police?

Yes	Undecided	No	Total Respondents
50.0	38.1	11.9	(42)

17. Do you believe that such cases are in accordance with the beliefs of the supervisor at the station to which you are attached?

Yes	Undecided	No	Total Respondents
52.4	35.7	11.9	(42)

THE PURPOSE OF VOLUNTARY ACCOMPANIMENT AND VOLUNTARY
APPEARANCE WHERE THERE IS AN ARREST WARRANT.

---

18. Do you believe that the purpose is to *make sure that this will not be a false arrest*?

Yes	Undecided	No	Total Respondents
53.5	27.9	18.6	(43)

REFUSAL TO ANSWER QUESTIONS FOLLOWING VOLUNTARY ACCOMPANIMENT
OR VOLUNTARY APPEARANCE

---

19. Do you believe that the number of persons who, although going to the effort of cooperating with voluntary appearance or voluntary accompaniment, will *not answer your main question*, has increased?

Yes	Undecided	No	Total Respondents
55.8	25.6	18.6	(43)

Table 6.1   *(Continued)*

DUTY TO RESPOND TO QUESTIONS FOLLOWING A VOLUNTARY
ACCOMPANIMENT OR VOLUNTARY APPEARANCE

20. Do you believe that *a duty* should be recognized by the ordinary citizen of Hokkaido *to respond to questions* once he has cooperated in a voluntary accompaniment or voluntary appearance?

Yes	Undecided	No	Total Respondents
54.8	26.2	19.0	(42)

DELAY IN INVESTIGATIONS RESULTING FROM RESPECTING
THE WILL OF THE SUSPECT: PUBLIC OPINION

21. Assume the following case: "An officer gives up on duty questioning, voluntary accompaniment and voluntary appearance in response to the will of the contact. The contact later resurfaces as an important suspect, and due to the delay in the initial investigation no effective evidence can be gotten against this suspect. In the end, the criminal could not be found." In such a case, do you believe that the mass media would criticize such a "*giving up*?"

Yes	Undecided	No	Total Respondents
52.4	33.3	14.3	(42)

RESPONSIBILITY FOR PROOFS OF INNOCENCE AT THE TIME
OF VOLUNTARY APPEARANCE.

22. Do you think that we should give the suspect responsibility to prove his innocence? First, with respect to the voluntary appearance stage.

Yes	Undecided	No	Total Respondents
51.2	23.3	25.6	(43)

Note: see items 62–67 of Appendix A.

In spite of this difficulty, we see in Appendix A (items 62-67) that many detectives disapproved of the action of taking the arm of a person who refused voluntary accompaniment. However, about half of the detectives said that once they started duty questioning, they had to accomplish their objective, and most of them supported the action of grabbing a suspect. Here in items 6 and 7, we see that the majority of detectives believe that citizens have a duty to cooperate with the police in duty questioning.

In connection with this information, let us look to items 8 and 9. I asked whether the generally aggressive direction as evidenced in responses to items 62 to 67 in Appendix A regarding methods of voluntary investigation is in accordance with the internal policy of the police force and the policy of the supervisors. Half respond that it is. Moreover, according to the next responses (items 10 and 11), even if a given duty questioning is held to be illegal, this fact is not thought to have a negative effect on one's record.

The above survey data suggests several things about the attitude of the majority of detectives. To wit, duty questioning is a link in investigations; performing this task frequently enhances one's reputation. However, the number of citizens who refuse to cooperate in the voluntary accompaniment is increasing; therefore, even if it is not proper to take the arm of a person who refuses to cooperate in a voluntary accompaniment and lead him in, it is still approved by official policy and by the supervisors to chase after someone who runs away and to lay hands on him. Once duty questioning is begun, the object must be accomplished. Even if a duty questioning is held illegal, this is not thought to have a negative effect on one's reputation. Of course, there is no assurance that the detectives' perception is accurate and actually accords with the official policy within the force, or with the policy of the supervisors. However, there is merit in examining this perception on its own terms.

Most detectives approved of physically detaining suspects who attempted to run away during duty questioning. A Supreme Court ruling (Supreme Court, July 15, 1954, *Keishu* 8, 1137) has approved an analogous behavior. A police officer had questioned a man on the road at night and had brought him to a police box on voluntary accompaniment. He ran away, however, when officers started to question him about his personal effects. Then one of the officers grabbed him from behind and stopped him in order to continue questioning. The Court held that the officer did not exceed the boundaries of proper execution of his duties. However, there was a subsequent and contrary lower court decision in which the subject of a duty questioning ran, while the detectives were giving warnings such as "Stop, or I'll arrest you!" and "Run and I'll shoot!" At the end the suspect was stopped. The restraining hold on the suspect's shoulder was held to be an illegal act of force (Osaka District Court, September 20, 1968, *Hanta* 228, 229). Depending upon the circumstances, then, there is a possibility that similar actions will be held illegal. To the extent that the above-described actions are approved by detectives, we may conclude that many detectives condone problematic behavior that is not conclusively within the law.

Next, I examine police attitudes toward the voluntary appearance under the Code of Criminal Procedure.

In item 12 of Table 6.1, more than half of the detectives report their belief that the number of persons who refuse to make a voluntary appearance in response to a telephone request has increased. This contrasts sharply with the opinion of the supervisors as we have seen in the observational data.

How should an officer deal with this increasingly more difficult voluntary appearance?

Now let us refer to Appendix A again, items 84 through 86. Although by far the majority of detectives denied taking the arm of a vacillating person and leading him in, the majority believed that once one set out to obtain a voluntary appearance, one must certainly accomplish that objective. Furthermore, half of the detectives approved of chasing after a fleeing person, and laying hands on him. Item 13 here shows that a majority of detectives want to make it a citizen's duty to cooperate in a voluntary appearance even if requested only by telephone.

There is greater reserve with respect to voluntary appearance than to duty questioning. However, it is important to note that, as a general attitude, in both cases detectives believe that they must accomplish their objective. This finding conforms to the expressions of the detectives in the observational data.

In this connection, regarding situations in which an officer goes to see the suspect and requests a voluntary appearance, there have been lower court decisions criticizing the method of sandwiching the suspect between detectives on the street or in a car (e.g., Kobe District Court, July 9, 1968, *Kakeishu* 10, 801; Takamatsu District Court, November 20, 1968, *Kakeishu* 10, 1159). If one also considers the lower court decisions quoted above in regard to duty questionings, it cannot be said that actions like those referred to in Appendix A, item 85 are absolutely permitted.

There is a similar attitude toward the voluntary appearance under the Code of Criminal Procedure as there is toward duty questioning. Aware that their rapport with the objects of the voluntary appearance may have deteriorated, many detectives feel that in order to attain their objective, they must engage in actions which can be somewhat questionable from a legal standpoint. They do things that fit with that attitude.

The next issue is the attitudes of detectives in cases in which voluntary accompaniment under the Police Duty Execution Act or the voluntary appearance under the Code of Criminal Procedure are involved after the police have obtained an arrest warrant. Ericson (1981: 141) has reported that among the Canadian police, arrest warrants rarely are used even when they have been secured. Voluntary accompaniments in Japan resemble such warrantless arrests and it follows from the observational data discussed earlier that cases definitely exist in Japan where a voluntary accompaniment is sought in spite of the fact that an arrest warrant is in hand. In items 14 through 17, most detectives in my survey do not believe that this practice is so common as to be quite widespread or increasing. However, a majority of the detectives are aware that the practice is approved within the police organization.

Some of the questions inquire about the reasons for the use of this method and the responses are presented in item 18. A majority of detectives assert that the purpose of voluntary appearance is to confirm that there will not be a false arrest, which suggests detectives believe that suspects must clearly impress the officer of their guilt at the time of an arrest.

The detectives' methods I am examining here are not considered so problematic as far as caution is exercised by them in order to assure that the arrest is not a false one. However, if prior receipt of an arrest warrant generates a more determined approach by the officer requesting a voluntary accompaniment or appearance, this could later lead to rather sensitive problems concerning the issue of "voluntariness" at the time of judicial examination. Even if the final objective itself is justifiable, these may be termed at least "problematic" investigations, which is further suggested by the denial of supervisors that this method is ever used.

When, as a result of the attitudes and consequent actions outlined above, there has been a voluntary accompaniment under the Police Duty Execution Act or a voluntary appearance under the Code of Criminal Procedure, this is followed by questioning or interrogation. I will now turn to an examination of the attitudes of the detectives conducting such questioning or investigations. As a prefatory note, from the detective's perspective there is no question that even the duty questioning under the Police Duty Execution Act is part of a criminal investigation; for this reason, and because the duty questioning is often considered interchangeable with the questioning for investigation of a specific crime, I made no distinction between the two in the survey questions.

First of all, from a survey question about the degree of rapport with suspects questioned, in item 19 (Table 6.1) I find that half of the detectives recognized a worsening of this relationship. How do they respond to this worsening situation?

Looking to Item 101 from Appendix A, we can make the following observation. A majority of the detectives disapproved of actions such as grabbing the arm of a person who makes as if to leave in the middle of a question; boxing a person in and taking him along; continuing questioning into the middle of the night; attending a person at meals, in the toilet, and during breaks; denying food, use of the toilet, or breaks during interrogation; or chasing after and grabbing a person who has run away while being taken in. However, far more than a mere majority approve of the most general idea that necessary information must be drawn out without fail.

Next, in item 20, half of the detectives want to place a duty upon citizens to respond to questions. There is restraint in regard to actions described in concrete terms, but the more generalized attitude is that a police officer absolutely must accomplish his purpose, and that the citizenry owe a duty of cooperation to the police.

Above, I have described the attitudes of the police at each stage of action in voluntary investigations, as revealed by the survey data. Looking back over the ground I have covered, the following common patterns emerge. Most or a majority of the detectives recognize a worsening of their relations with citizens who are subject to investigation. They feel that at each stage of investigation they are bound to accomplish their objectives, and they want to have citizens compelled to cooperate with the police. A trend exists for more detectives to deny more concrete, problematic acts at later points in the investigation, but this does overcome this basic general pattern.

The important point here is the belief on the part of detectives that they must succeed in their actions. When voluntary investigations are conducted in this frame of mind, and the object of the investigation is not inclined to cooperate, or changes his mind about cooperation, the officer must take some action in order to assure success.

In this connection, it is interesting to note the officers' awareness of criticism leveled at their fellows when, out of respect or sympathy for the person under suspicion, they ultimately fail to clear the case. According to item 21 (Table 6.1), a majority of detectives feel they will be criticized by the media, at the very least. This finding, combined with the fact that a court ruling that a duty questioning was illegal will not mar one's reputation within the force, is suggestive of the nature of the sanctions under which the detectives operate; lower efficiency will be punished, while illegal investigative actions will not.

Item 22 in Table 6.1 relates to the citizen's duty of cooperation. Not only do a majority of detectives demand a citizen's duty to cooperate, but a majority also believe that the suspect must establish his own innocence.

The central discovery from the survey is that detectives feel a need to accomplish their ends and expect the cooperation of the citizen, who should make those ends easier to accomplish. We can only conjecture about actions taken in the event a contact refuses to cooperate.

4. Summary

Both the survey and the observational material has shown that in voluntary investigations failure to accomplish the objective is unacceptable to the detectives. We must of course consider why this attitude arises despite the emphasis placed upon "voluntariness" by police academy instruction and by the supervisors. When a goal must be accomplished, it is considered necessary to overcome any opposition; the persuasive methods used to this end thus already bear a problematic relationship to "voluntariness."

Ericson (1981: 136) explains that in Canada the general test to decide if an arrest has occurred is "whether the suspect perceives he is at liberty to depart from the presence of the police officer if he wishes to do so." Police detectives in Japan believe that they have to prevent the departure of the suspect. Some of their actions might be judged as virtual arrest if put to the Canadian test. Ericson (1981: 139) reports that in Canada "when the decision was made to take the suspect into custody,...[t]he most common strategy...was to have the suspect apparently 'consent' to being questioned in controlled circumstances." Detectives in Japan adopt similar strategies when they decide to bring the suspect to their station and question him without formally arresting him. They control circumstances around the suspect so that he will "voluntarily" accompany them to the station, stay there, and admit to the charge. McBarnet (1981: 36) writes that in Scotland while detention for questioning is in theory impossible, it is nonetheless perfectly possible in practice, because its "voluntary" nature has been interpreted very broadly in law. Japanese courts have taken similar positions regarding the limits of voluntary investigation.

7

Search and Seizure

Search and seizure pursuant to a warrant are forcible methods of investigation which do not involve taking custody of the person. Where there has been an arrest, search and seizure may also be conducted without a warrant.

The most significant point revealed by my observation was the unusual use of search and seizure pursuant to a warrant in organized crime cases. These are the relevant details.

1. Police Academy

The police academy training regarding the Code of Criminal Procedure explains the meaning of the phrase "at the time of arrest" in Article 220 of the code in a more restricted sense than used by the Supreme Court. In the words of the instructor, "Let us look to Articles 33 and 35 of the Constitution. In a majority decision of the Supreme Court in 1961 [June 7, 1961, *Keishu* 15, 915], it was held that a search and seizure is acceptable if there is unity of place regardless of whether it is before or after the arrest; and that, in an emergency arrest, it is acceptable to search before the arrest even when the suspect is not present. However, this holding is unreasonable." A student presenter added, "The Supreme Court decision of 1961 is limited to actual exigent circumstances. An actual act of arrest should be taken as a precondition to a search incident to arrest."

Reservations of this sort manifest themselves in other areas as well. One student stated, "When there is evidence in a place other than the place of the arrest, even if the suspect says, 'I will go and get it myself,' you should file for a warrant and conduct a search and seizure." In response to a student who asked, "Can you only seize material with a clear connection to the crime? Or is the officer's judgment sufficient?" the instructor responded, "There must be 'reasonable grounds for suspicion.' The officer's subjective opinion is not sufficient."

It is important to note these reservations which question Supreme Court precedents. They indicate that the official policy of the Hokkaido police is quite conservative.

2. Supervisors

My observations of the supervisors regarding search and seizure concentrated upon special use of such procedures pursuant to a warrant in the investigation of organized crime. This involves the use of a search warrant based upon a past crime to allow the possibility of a warrantless arrest of a flagrant offender at the time of the search for a different crime. This method is used often in investigations involving illegal stimulants.

Why do officers not try to arrest the suspect for the past, known crime, without first spending time on a search? Supervisors say that "even if the stuff [stimulants] is there, if he [the suspect] says, 'It's not mine,' we can't get an indictment. In that case, we don't want to be told that it is a pointless arrest." In addition, gathering sufficient material to apply for an arrest warrant is sometimes difficult.

At this point, the search warrant, easier to obtain than an arrest warrant, is used. According to one supervisor, "The search permit can be had on the statement of a single person." Ericson (1981: 152) notes in the Canadian situation that "obtaining a search warrant never proved to be difficult." It is no different in Japan.

It is difficult to decide upon the time in which a search warrant should be exercised. As one supervisor stated, "The effective period for a search warrant is only seven days, and so it has to be executed with excellent timing, in such a way that the warrantless arrest of a flagrant offender can be carried out." The use of the search warrant is determined by its purpose, to create an opportunity for a warrantless arrest.

In fact, such warrants do not always lead to arrest. Supervisors say that if the evidence is hidden or if it is washed down the drain, it's hands off. If the officer breaks in, and the suspect denies that the evidence is his, the officer cannot carry out a warrantless arrest.

It is very important to move faster than the suspect if officers want to use a search warrant to make a warrantless arrest at the scene. A supervisor, in showing me a search and seizure warrant, said in regard to a successful arrest, "It was a great thing to forestall them in advance."

However, judicial control over search and seizure warrants is becoming stricter. One supervisor moaned that "it is difficult to get an extension [of the expiration of a search warrant] out of some young judges."

I was also able to see memoranda from a judge regarding the specificity of the object of the search. One memorandum read:

> In the petition, the things to be searched for are listed without any concrete connection with suspect facts. Those things which are connected by possession or transfer need to be set forth respectively. A rigorous connection is to be made between the suspected facts and the things to be searched for. In "transfer" crimes, one expects that the goods will no longer be at hand; things like expended syringes have no connection in the first place. Even with "possession" crimes, it is hoped that one will think twice.

According to the supervisor who showed me this memorandum:

> In this case, a person told us that he had bought it from [the suspect], and so we thought we would seize what he actually had in his possession. But the foundation for the petition in this case was "transfer," and so we were told as follows. "In this case, you may only seize that which was passed." We should have written down "possession" as well.

This supervisor said, "We want to write as broadly as possible. Of course, words like 'everything and anything connected with this case' are from the distant past, though." Supervisors seem to think that it is impossible today to define the object of the search as broadly as would be needed under the circumstances. There is distinct criticism of this restrictive trend in procedural law. When an organized crime detective said with dissatisfaction that "there are judges who will tell you to go in through a fifth story window, or break down an iron door; but you can't do these things in the real world. We don't even have the money to maintain wrecking tools," a supervisor responded, "They [judges] know nothing about the hard truth of investigations."

Since this is the situation, it is necessary to make the most productive use possible of opportunities for search. Ericson (1981: 150) writes that in Canada searches enable detectives "to uncover evidence for criminal charges in relation to matters that were not part of the primary matter under investigation." In the use of a search warrant I describe above there is no "primary matter" at all. A search is carried out to uncover a totally different and new crime.

It is clear from entries in investigative reports that supervisors approve the use of a warrant issued on the basis of past actions, with an expectation of a warrantless arrest on the basis of other, new facts. For example, regarding the possession and use of stimulants, one directive in a station chief's book of orders reads, "Obtain search and seizure permission, and conduct a forcible search of the suspect's home," and for the circumstances of disposition, "Request a search and seizure warrant, and upon seeing the item, carry out the [warrantless] arrest."

However, supervisors who approve this method do not deny its problematic nature. Their approval does not presuppose that the method is legitimate, and it is not the result of their own interpretation of the law or of a value judgment. Rather they see the behavior as an appropriate technical response to effect an arrest in a particularly difficult field. This use of a search warrant is not considered totally legitimate, but nonetheless considered "administratively reasonable" (Skolnick, 1966: 223). In the investigation of organized crime, the supervisors are predisposed to approve the use of search and seizure in the manner described above. This is in striking contrast to the way in which the subject of search incident to arrest was taught at the police academy.

3. Detectives

The first point to consider in discussing organized crime investigations from the perspective of the detectives is that arrest warrants are difficult to obtain. As one detective said, "In the old days, you could get a search warrant on an anonymous phone call, and so if you wanted to go for it, you could just say that there had been a call. Because the evidence would turn up, you see. And if it did turn up, naturally it turned out that there had been a call." Search warrants are still easier to secure than arrest warrants. For this reason, attempts are made to use the search warrant to create the opportunity for a warrantless arrest. I was told, "The purpose of a search warrant is more to effect a warrantless arrest than to obtain proof of an act." Detectives believe that the supervisors approve of this practice, and therefore they act accordingly.

However, there is no prospect that a search warrant will be issued if such a purpose is plainly evident to the judge. In order to persuade the judge of the connection between the thing sought and the facts of the past crime, detectives must create the impression that the search warrant is necessary and appropriate. For example, as one detective said, "We take the statement [from the informant] that 'it [stimulant] was used today,' and then request a warrant by saying, 'Stimulants believed to remain' in the petition."

Regarding the judicial demand for specificity in describing the object of the search, one hears disgruntled complaints such as, "We set out the suspect facts in the petition, and it seems to me that that is being specific." But judges will not issue a search warrant for general items such as stimulants that "were possessed or transferred several days before." As one detective went on to explain:

> It would be just as well not to attach the separate fact sheet to the issued warrant, but for the sake of specificity, we have to attach it. Do that, and the informant's name will be spread around. One technique for dealing with this is to drop the case on which the search warrant was founded at the point of the execution of the warrant, and carry forward only the crime witnessed at the time of the search. Our principal purpose is to get the guy. Although, I suppose that it is almost an illegal arrest for a separate case [not specified in the warrant].

Thus, the arrest for which the search warrant was used is both the real purpose of the warrant and a means of protecting the informant.

Because there is not always an opportunity for arrest during the period of the warrant's effectiveness, detectives devise excuses to extend the warrant. For example, one told me:

> A search warrant is just for one week, and so if there is no chance for an arrest in that period, it's over. If we try to get information from a bookie's client, the client becomes a suspect as well, so there is no reason he should cooperate. And so, by making up things to say like 'the condominium manager is afraid of trouble, and so won't lend us a key,' we will petition for an extension.

Effective use must be made of a warrant which has been acquired with such effort. Just as was noted in regard to voluntary investigations, it seems that "failure is unacceptable." In addition, it is clear from investigative documents that search warrants are used to effect arrests for current act. For example, in a gambling case involving a bookie, the search was conducted on racing day, when numerous calls placing bets came in to the suspect during the search which was made on the basis of a different, past crime. The officer was able to intercept an incoming call, confirm that it was a betting operation, and effect a warrantless arrest.

In a case related to stimulants, two separate search and seizure reports were filed. The first report stated, "None of the articles to be searched for was found." The arrest was based on new facts discovered at the time of the search, and the second search and seizure report described how the police found different stimulants at the scene. The suspects admitted their purchase, and they were taken to the station and tested for drug use. The tests were positive and they were placed under emergency arrest.

In organized crime investigations, the use of search warrants to create an opportunity for a warrantless arrest is supported by detectives and used in the field. These beliefs and actions are based upon the perceived difficulty of obtaining an arrest warrant, coupled with the conviction that there are crimes and suspects for whom they do not expect to easily find the evidence necessary to prove past violations of the law and the need to protect informants.

Whereas my direct observation concentrated upon the special use of search and seizure in organized crime investigation, the survey material represented in Tables 7.1 and 7.2 reveals general attitudes toward search and seizure.

The first issue is the perception of judicial control over search and seizure. Table 7.1 covers warrants. Most, or a majority, of detectives believe that the requirements for issuance of a warrant have become more strict, while at the same time they do not believe that a large number of warrants are refused, nor that the number refused has been rising. Still, a majority of detectives do not feel that a large number of searches and seizures are declared illegal after the fact or that the number of such decisions is increasing.

Table 7.1   Situation Surrounding the Issuance of Search and Seizure Warrant

1. Do you believe that the number of cases in which the warrant is denied is large?

Yes	Undecided	No	Total Respondents
14.0	30.2	55.8	(43)

2. Do you believe that such cases are increasing in number?

Yes	Undecided	No	Total Respondents
11.6	34.9	53.5	(43)

3. Do you believe that even in cases in which a warrant is ultimately issued, that the conditions and reporting requirements are becoming more stringent?

Yes	Undecided	No	Total Respondents
59.5	21.4	19.0	(42)

4. Do you feel that the requirements of specificity regarding the object of the search and seizure have become particularly stringent?

Yes	Undecided	No	Total Respondents
71.4	11.9	16.7	(42)

5. Do you believe that the requirements of specificity regarding the place of the search have become particularly stringent?

Yes	Undecided	No	Total Respondents
69.0	16.7	14.3	(42)

6. Do you believe that a judgment of the necessity of the search has become particularly stringent?

Yes	Undecided	No	Total Respondents
59.5	21.4	19.0	(42)

7. Do you believe that even in regard to searches and seizures pursuant to a warrant, that the number of cases in which the search is held to have been illegal after the fact is large?

Yes	Undecided	No	Total Respondents
2.4	28.6	69.0	(42)

8. Do you believe that the number of such cases has been progressively increasing?

Yes	Undecided	No	Total Respondents
2.4	28.6	69.0	(42)

Table 7.2 concerns judicial regulation of search and seizure incident to arrest. As with search and seizure pursuant to a warrant, most detectives do not feel that a large number of cases have been held to be illegal by the courts, or that the number of such cases is rising. However, in contrast, most or a majority feel that rulings regarding the scope of the things searched for and the contemporaneity of the search have become more stringent.

Table 7.2   Situation Regarding Search and Seizure at the Time of Arrest

1. Do you believe that in searches and seizures at the scene of the arrest not pursuant to a warrant, a large number are held to have been illegal by the judge?

Yes	Undecided	No	Total Respondents
2.4	21.4	76.2	(42)

2. Do you believe that such cases have been increasing?

Yes	Undecided	No	Total Respondents
2.4	23.8	73.8	(42)

3. Do you believe that the requirement that the search be conducted immediately following the arrest has become particularly stringent?

Yes	Undecided	No	Total Respondents
58.1	20.9	20.9	(43)

4. Do you believe that the scope of items which may be subjected to seizure has become particularly narrow?

Yes	Undecided	No	Total Respondents
60.5	20.9	18.6	(43)

Regarding judicial control, there is no significant difference between the officers' attitudes regarding searches pursuant to warrant and searches at the time of arrest. There is a general consensus that while post hoc rulings that an arrest was illegal are not numerous, control has become more strict.

The ways in which these attitudes affect behavior are shown in items 197 through 201 in Appendix A. Although most detectives deny conducting searches incident to arrest out of the presence of the suspect and attempting to conceal the suspected facts from the suspect, a majority believe that they absolutely must succeed.

Detectives express caution with regard to concrete action, but in general discussions an aggressive view prevails, a pattern consistent with the attitude toward voluntary investigations.

8

Arrest

As a result of arrest, investigation and interrogation are possible while the suspect is at the station, at least during the time of confinement pursuant to arrest. I will discuss the actual conduct and attitude of officers at the time of arrest.

The most unexpected information ascertained through observation is that emergency arrest is used with unexpectedly great frequency. Below I focus my observational material on emergency arrests.

1. Police Academy

During field work, I was able to sit in on discussions in a course on the Code of Criminal Procedure for police sergeants. Arrests other than emergency arrests were one topic of discussion.

At the time I was there, the academy instructors taught that issues relevant to each type of arrest are to be considered in light of post-arrest confinement. For example, in an ordinary arrest with a warrant, the officer should check whether or not the arrest warrant was displayed, as required by Article 201, Section 1 of the Code of Criminal Procedure. When there is an arrest without a warrant in hand, the officer should determine if there was an emergency, as required by Section 2 of the same article, and discover whether the reason for not displaying a warrant was announced as well as if the warrant was displayed promptly after the arrest was made.

It was pointed out that "in order to prevent the rehashing of arrests, the fact that a filing for an arrest warrant is founded on identical facts as a previous filing should be honestly indicated according to Article 199, Section 3 of the Code of Criminal Procedure."

Immediately following arrest, the officer takes a *benkai* or pleading from the suspect. The academy taught that "taking the suspect's pleading is not an interrogation; it is not necessary to inform the suspect of the right to remain silent. It is enough if the pleading is of two or three lines. It is not a full recorded statement. Where it appears that the suspect has used the opportunity of the pleading to make a confession, ask him again after informing him of the right to remain silent. You must not interrogate under the guise of recording a pleading." From the perspective of the supervisors, there is room for questionable activity.

After the recording of the initial pleading, it is time to decide whether or not confinement is appropriate. The law allows the police to *ryuchi* or confine the suspect for forty eight hours before bringing him to the prosecutor. According to the instructor, the purpose of this confinement "is to prevent the destruction of evidence of guilt, conspiracy, and flight; it is not to be used for the convenience of investigations by demanding confessions, interrogation about other crimes, or to save time and trouble in requesting an appearance, nor is it to be used as a form of discipline or punishment for crime." In deciding to continue confinement one must give consideration to "the legality of the arrest, the appropriateness of the arrest, the risk of flight, the risk of destruction of evidence of guilt, and other considerations." In the training on arrest and detention, heavy stress is laid upon respect for procedure.

However, the instructor who taught that post-arrest confinement was not to be used for the convenience of investigation said of his own experience:

> When he [a suspect] was caught on a stolen goods charge different from the case on which I wanted him, he was locked up at the Sapporo prison for the term of his detention [contrary to his expectation that the suspect would be detained in his own station]. Therefore we released him on the stolen goods charge, and because the judge was a leftist, we arranged the formalities, filed for a warrant in this case [i.e., the case on which the detective actually wanted the suspect], made the arrest, and had him detained in the substitute prison [the station detention cell] again.

Detention or *koryu* is different from post-arrest confinement or *ryuchi* in that the former is based on a judicial approval. However, confinement creates a situation similar to detention at the police station. Given this conduct on the part of instructors, it is doubtful whether the students will act according to the official policy which they have been taught.

The same stance is taught with regard to emergency arrest. According to the instructor, the decision to proceed with confinement following emergency arrest depends upon the following conditions:

> Whether it is one of the specified crimes for which emergency arrest is allowed, whether there is reason enough to cause suspicion, whether due to the need for haste an arrest warrant cannot be sought from a judge, whether there is adequate proof that an arrest warrant cannot be sought, whether there is adequate proof that there is risk of flight or of destruction of evidence of guilt, whether the notice required under law was given regarding all the above reasons for arrest, whether the suspect was swiftly brought in, whether the arrest was effected within the jurisdiction of the arresting person.

Furthermore, the academy taught that "the Sapporo District Court will not give you an arrest warrant if three hours pass following emergency arrest. The policy of the National Police Agency is the same."

The basic policy of the police academy requires at least the appearance of procedural compliance. This conforms with statements such as the directive from the headquarters in a case I observed: "Avoid emergency arrest if at all possible."

What are the attitudes and the conduct of the first-line officers who operate under this general policy?

2. Supervisors

In contrast with the stress laid on respect for procedure at the police academy, the words and actions of the supervisors in the field are a mixture of aggressiveness and reserve vis-à-vis arrest and confinement.

For example, regarding an injury case related to a mob war that started with a refusal of payment for labor, a supervisor said, "We arrested him just for coercion [for laying a Japanese sword against another person when refusing payment]. We were afraid of a mistaken arrest," and saying this, he stressed that the arrest had to be for only the precise facts shown by the evidence. The supervisor also said, "It is not good just to ask whether we've got a warrant, and execute it mechanically. There are cases which support *not* executing the warrant, depending upon the actual circumstances." He advised that voluntary investigations be used to the greatest extent possible.

However, there is evidence to show that initial restraint is used to justify subsequent aggressive investigative action. For example, in Case 17 it was said that "at the outset, it might have been better to bring in Wakamatsu [a suspect] [for a different charge] and have it out with him [question him about the crime they really want to investigate], but it is more persuasive if we do so only as the last resort after the primary investigation [of the crime specified in the arrest warrant] is finished."

This aggressiveness is especially apparent in orders for emergency arrest. In Case 9, when news came that the Mobile Squad had made the arrest, it was ordered to make "an emergency arrest, not an arrest in the act." There is a tendency to substitute the relatively easily accomplished seizure by emergency arrest for the "troublesome" and "difficult" ordinary or warrantless arrest.

3. Detectives

It is not the detective's function to apply for arrest warrants, so we cannot identify a standard for the decision to file for an arrest warrant from the detectives' words and acts. The detectives prepare the materials for the application. Statements about this function provide a basis for understanding the filing process. The actual arrest, recording of the pleading, and interrogation during post-arrest confinement are the responsibility of the detectives and formed the basis of my observations.

Regarding the ease of obtaining a warrant, detectives believe that a history of past criminal activity is an advantage. It is also better if the suspect's location is unknown, which may even lead to detectives stretching the facts to fit their needs. A detective told me, "Contrary to what you might think, it is actually better if his [the suspect's] location has been unknown. Our men know where he is, but like I say, it's better if his location is unknown."

In holding out for a voluntary investigation before finally making an arrest, some detectives believe that resistance or opposition to the voluntary investigation will make an arrest easier. For example, two intellectual crime detectives investigating a bribery case for violation of the Public Elections Act had the following conversation:

* Abe: That old lady was shouting, "Bastards!" at the Prosecutor's Office.
* Baba: Hm, she shouted the same thing when she was here. Has she admitted to the charge?
* Abe: She has.
* Baba: She's shouting like that even though she admits it?

- Abe: Um. They're asking her where the money came from.

- Baba: That old lady's rich; 10 or 50 thousand yen [$33 or $167 U.S.] could be her own, couldn't it?

- Abe: Hey, she's fighting back, so we can get an arrest. If she had taken it easy from the start, we could never arrest her.

Once the detectives have prepared the materials, the supervisors file for the warrant; the arrest warrant is issued; and the detectives go out to make the arrest. At this point, their attitude is that they must succeed, as we have noted in regard to other stages in the process. We need to examine whether this attitudes exists at the post-arrest stages as well.

Once the arrest is completed, the arrest report must be put together. It is important to fix the arrest time because of the time limit for referring the suspect to the prosecutor and requesting detention. In describing a fight where the roles of the participants were confused, a detective said, "By the appearance of the fight, you couldn't tell who was a criminal and who not. [So the detectives brought both to the station without arrest.] At the station, we can question them and figure out what we will do.... But in fact we write it up as a warrantless arrest at the scene of the fight one hour before." This statement suggests a problem that must be taken into account in the post hoc evaluation and analysis of investigative papers, because these papers do not necessarily indicate the actual time of arrest.

Warrantless emergency arrest frequently is used by theft crime detectives. There are also instances when emergency arrest is proposed to their supervisors by the detectives. For example, in Case 10, calling the chief of the First Detective Department from the pawnshop site, the detective said, "We want to make an emergency arrest," when seeking an order.

However, there was some criticism among the detectives of the supervisors' frequent use of emergency arrest. For example, a detective expressed his doubts:

> The way that our Detective Department chief operates now, what I don't like is that he uses emergency arrest more than is normal. It is best if you get a warrant in accordance with procedure. And you can hold it if you want to, and bring the guy in on voluntary appearance, and check him out to confirm it if you want.

Thus the aggressiveness of the detectives' conduct regarding emergency arrest is not necessarily based upon a conviction about the legitimacy of their position, whether through legal interpretation or value judgment. It is, in part, a response to the perceived permission or demand from supervisors, and an awareness that this is a technically appropriate way to resolve cases efficiently.

A similarity exists between the positions occupied by emergency arrest in theft crime and forcible crime investigations, and the special use of search and seizure in organized crime investigations. Both are aggressive ways of seizing the person. But more specifically, because voluntary investigation can provide an opportunity for interrogation, there is a progression from confession to emergency arrest in theft and forcible crimes. In organized crime investigation, it is difficult to induce cooperation in interrogation and the aim is to make a warrantless arrest by means of conducting a search. Whether or not the supervisors and detectives are aware of it, aggressiveness is manifested at this turning point of investigation in both cases, with the seizure of the person.

Let us review one final point in discussing attitudes and behavior regarding arrest. Ordinary arrest or emergency arrest cannot be carried out solely by the decision of the detectives themselves. The events which the detectives themselves carry out are the act of arrest, the trip to the station, the recording of the pleading, and other specific steps within this process. They cannot, however, make the decision whether or not to effect an arrest.

This has an impact upon detectives. On the one hand, even when they are critical of the supervisors' policy regarding emergency arrest, detectives do not oppose supervisors who order aggressive investigative actions. On the other hand, even if detectives have an aggressive attitude toward an investigation, they cannot make an ordinary arrest if the supervisors do not secure a warrant for them. When acting beyond the sphere of the supervisors' direct control, the aggressive tendencies of the detectives can amplify the aggressiveness of the supervisors and overcome their reserve. Regarding arrest in general, this last point is demonstrated by the fact that while there were elements of reserve in the supervisors, the detectives more plainly expressed aggressiveness.

As I have just said, the detectives do not make the decision to file for a warrant, and the situations in which they themselves must decide whether or not to arrest are limited; therefore, in most of the survey questions below I ask for perceptions and evaluations respecting the circumstances of arrest. We can infer the attitude of the detectives regarding the appropriate actions at the stages of arrest based on their estimates of the undesirable effects of a tightening of judicial controls and from their perception of the function that arrest should serve. The responses to the survey questions cover the stages from arrest through the referral of the suspect to the prosecutor.

The first issue concerns the function served by arrest. According to Table 8.1, items 1 through 3, most detectives acknowledge as a matter of course that the legal functions of arrest are to prevent flight and to prevent the destruction of evidence. It should be noted, however, that at the same time most detectives also maintain that a function of arrest is to create an opportunity for interrogation of the suspect. This contrasts markedly with the emphasis placed at the police academy upon the fact that arrest is not an investigative convenience.

Table 8.1   Attitudes about Arrest

THE NEED FOR ARREST

---

1. Generally speaking, in actual fact for what reason is arrest necessary? First of all, is it necessary to prevent flight?

Yes	Undecided	No	Total Respondents
79.1	16.3	4.7	(43)

2. Is it necessary for the personal interrogation of the suspect?

Yes	Undecided	No	Total Respondents
62.8	16.3	20.9	(43)

3. Is it necessary to prevent destruction of evidence?

Yes	Undecided	No	Total Respondents
81.4	14.0	4.7	(43)

SITUATION CONCERNING WARRANTLESS ARREST OF FLAGRANT OFFENDER

---

4. Do you feel that there are a large number of cases in which, after a warrantless arrest is effected, the court holds that "this was not a proper warrantless arrest"?

Yes	Undecided	No	Total Respondents
7.0	20.9	72.1	(43)

5. Do you believe that such cases are increasing in number?

Yes	Undecided	No	Total Respondents
18.6	16.3	65.1	(43)

6. Do you believe that the requirement that there has been a clear criminal behavior, in particular, has become more strict?

Yes	Undecided	No	Total Respondents
61.0	4.9	34.1	(41)

7. Do you believe that the requirement of a close connection in time with the criminal event, in particular, has become more strict?

Yes	Undecided	No	Total Respondents
54.8	16.7	28.6	(42)

Table 8.1   *(Continued)*

SITUATION CONCERNING WARRANTLESS ARREST OF FLAGRANT OFFENDER

8. Do you believe that the requirement of a close proximity to the site of the crime, in particular, has become more strict?

Yes	Undecided	No	Total Respondents
52.4	19.0	28.6	(42)

9. Do you believe that the requirement that arrest be necessary, in particular, has become more strict?

Yes	Undecided	No	Total Respondents
58.1	16.3	25.6	(43)

SITUATION CONCERNING EMERGENCY ARREST

10. Do you feel that there are a large number of cases in which, after an emergency arrest is effected, the court holds that "this was not a proper emergency arrest"?

Yes	Undecided	No	Total Respondents
15.0	35.0	50.0	(40)

11. Do you believe that the number of such cases has increased?

Yes	Undecided	No	Total Respondents
14.3	23.8	61.9	(42)

12. Do you believe that the requirement of adequate suspicion, in particular, has become more strict?

Yes	Undecided	No	Total Respondents
58.1	16.3	25.6	(43)

13. Do you believe that the requirement of an emergency situation, in particular, has become more strict?

Yes	Undecided	No	Total Respondents
55.8	18.6	25.6	(43)

14. Do you believe that the requirement of a need for arrest, in particular, has become more strict?

Yes	Undecided	No	Total Respondents
62.8	14.0	23.3	(43)

15. Do you believe that the requirement of a quick filing for an arrest warrant after arrest, in particular, has become more strict?

Yes	Undecided	No	Total Respondents
64.3	16.7	19.0	(42)

Table 8.1 *(Continued)*

SITUATION CONCERNING ORDINARY ARREST

16. Do you feel that there are a large number of cases in which the court denied the warrant?

Yes	Undecided	No	Total Respondents
9.3	32.6	58.1	(43)

17. Do you believe that such cases are increasing?

Yes	Undecided	No	Total Respondents
14.0	34.9	51.2	(43)

18. Do you believe that the requirement of a need for arrest, in particular, has become more strict?

Yes	Undecided	No	Total Respondents
51.2	23.3	25.6	(43)

EXERCISE OF RIGHTS BY SUSPECTS

19. Do you believe that the number of cases in which an attorney is brought in by the suspect before indictment is increasing?

Yes	Undecided	No	Total Respondents
60.5	30.2	9.3	(43)

20. Do you believe that in such cases requests to meet or communicate with an attorney have been becoming more frequent?

Yes	Undecided	No	Total Respondents
53.5	32.6	14.0	(43)

INVESTIGATIVE EFFICIENCY AND THE SUSPECT'S ATTORNEY

21. Do you believe that the efficiency with which crimes are solved is significantly reduced by the introduction of an attorney at the suspect stage?

Yes	Undecided	No	Total Respondents
9.5	35.7	54.8	(42)

22. Do you believe that contact with an attorney should be forbidden at least during the 72 hours of confinement pursuant to arrest?

Yes	Undecided	No	Total Respondents
11.6	32.6	55.8	(43)

23. Do you believe that you will have to accept the reform in the future that an attorney is appointed by the state at the suspect stage in certain cases, as they are now for defendants in public trial?

Yes	Undecided	No	Total Respondents
51.2	30.2	18.6	(43)

24. Do you believe that, even if the right to retain an attorney is good, the duty to inform the suspect of that right should be abolished?

Yes	Undecided	No	Total Respondents
3.6	14.3	82.1	(28)

ATTORNEY'S PRESENCE AT INTERROGATION

25. Do you believe that if a rule were made that no confession may be admitted into evidence unless the suspect's attorney was present at the interrogation, this would seriously affect the efficiency with which crimes are solved?

Yes	Undecided	No	Total Respondents
56.1	31.7	12.2	(41)

26. Do you believe that you will have to accept the reform introducing such a system?

Yes	Undecided	No	Total Respondents
10.0	32.5	57.5	(40)

PRESENT STATE OF TRANSFER OF THE SUSPECT TO THE PROSECUTOR

27. Do you believe that even the current system of transfer interferes with the efficiency with which crimes are solved?

Yes	Undecided	No	Total Respondents
21.4	42.9	35.7	(42)

EFFECT OF A REVISED TRANSFER SYSTEM AND EVALUATION THEREOF

28. Next, if a system were instituted under which the person of the suspect were transferred automatically to the custody of the Prosecutor's Office at the time of transfer, do you believe that this would seriously interfere with the efficiency with which crimes are solved?

Yes	Undecided	No	Total Respondents
58.1	23.3	18.6	(43)

29. Next, if the time for transfer were reduced to 24 hours, do you believe that this would seriously interfere with the efficiency with which crimes are solved?

Yes	Undecided	No	Total Respondents
74.4	14.0	11.6	(43)

If arrest is seen as making interrogation possible, what is the perception of the judicial controls in this area? Awareness of such controls in regard to warrantless arrest of the flagrant offender is covered in items 4 through 9. Most, or a majority, of detectives believe that the requirements of clear criminal behavior, of a close time connection with the criminal event, of a close proximity to the site of the crime, and of a need for arrest have become more stringent. There is obviously an awareness that the requirements for warrantless arrest generally are becoming stricter.

This same pattern is manifested in regard to emergency arrest, as shown in items 10 through 15. Most detectives do not believe that emergency arrests often are overturned, nor do most believe that the number of such cases is increasing. Neither do they think that the requirements generally are becoming more strict. However, when the question concerns specific requirements, most or a majority of detectives felt that judicial rulings on the noted requirements have become more strict.

The pattern is somewhat different, however, regarding ordinary arrest, treated in items 16 through 18. While most detectives believe that there is not a large number of cases in which arrest warrants are refused and that such cases are not increasing in number, a majority believes that the requirement that the arrest be necessary has become more strict in regard to the requirements for issuance of a warrant.

The predominant perception of the detectives, in differing degrees, is that judicial control has become more strict for each type of arrest. A common perception among many detectives is that there is a trend in judicial decisions to make the requirements of an arrest more stringent for the convenience of investigation and interrogation, albeit the trend is gradual and differs with the type of arrest.

After a successful arrest, the pleading is recorded, and the suspect must be informed of the right to retain an attorney. Items 19 and 20 provide responses to questions regarding detectives' perception of the effect of informing the suspect of the right to retain an attorney and the consequent attachment of an attorney to the case. Most or a majority of detectives believe that the number of suspects retaining an attorney, or asking to meet or communicate with an attorney, has increased.

However, according to items 21 through 24, these developments are believed not to have interfered with the efficiency with which cases are solved. Moreover, as was seen in item 311 of Appendix A, most detectives have a reserved attitude regarding informing suspects of the right to select an attorney.

A majority of detectives oppose extension of the right to retain an attorney to include a right to have one's attorney present at interrogation, as shown in items 25 and 26. Such an extension is opposed because it is anticipated that it would reduce the efficiency of crime solving.

We may summarize the above information regarding the retention of an attorney and informing the suspect of his right to do so as follows. The positive attitude many detectives take toward these mechanisms is based upon the fact that the requirements have no direct effect upon the central tool of investigation, i.e., interrogation. For many detectives the chief function of arrest is to make interrogation possible.

Finally, let us review the attitude of detectives respecting transfer of the suspect to the prosecutor. Under the current system, the suspect must be transferred to the prosecutor within forty eight hours of arrest. According to item 27, most detectives neither agree nor disagree with the proposition that the current system interferes with the efficient solution of crimes. However, according to items 28 and 29, a majority of them are opposed to automatic transfer to the prosecutor's custody or shortening the time limit for transfer. The responses make clear the detectives' basic attitude that arrest should provide an opportunity for interrogation.

Most detectives believe that judicial controls over arrest have become more strict and that an attorney more often is retained by the suspect, although they do not believe that these factors have reduced the efficiency with which crimes are solved, and they do not oppose the introduction of state-appointed attorneys at the suspect stage. But, these latter views are held only to the extent that what is done does not interfere with interrogation, which they see as the chief function of arrest.

4. Summary

The Hokkaido Police Department puts forward a quite restrained arrest policy at its academy. This restraint also is manifested in orders by the Hokkaido Police Headquarters to the police stations. However, observing the field supervisors in action, it is clear that their attitudes and actions display a mixture of aggressiveness and restraint. Moreover, many detectives have a more directly aggressive attitude toward arrest. Detectives' aggressiveness is manifest in actions at the site of the arrest, in the recording of the pleading, and in interrogation following arrest, and their actions tends to amplify the aggressive aspect of the supervisors.

This aggressiveness certainly is not rooted in a conviction of its legitimacy. It is instead a utilitarian convenience. When detectives feel that there will be criticism from the judge, their doubts arise not from skepticism about the legitimacy of the supervisors' orders, but rather from fear of practical adverse consequences. Nevertheless, this does not lead the detectives to oppose the aggressiveness of their supervisors' orders.

In the next part of the book I will investigate the reasons why detectives as a group have a more aggressive attitude than supervisors, and why supervisors come to direct the use of questionable investigative methods.

9

Detention

The police must transfer evidence and the person of the suspect to the prosecutor within forty eight hours of arrest. Otherwise, the suspect will be released. If the prosecutor feels detention is necessary after the confinement pursuant to arrest, he must request it from a judge within twenty four hours. Therefore, police officers do no more than request that the prosecutor seek detention.

However, police investigations may continue after detention. Because the suspect will be secured by detention for ten days, with possible extension for another ten days, the police are quite anxious to secure such detention. Under Article 1, Section 3 of the Code of Prisons, in which police station detention cells may be substituted for prisons, there is a chance that the suspect will continue to be held at the police station during detention. In that case detectives, to whom the primary function of arrest is interrogation, can continue to question the suspect while he or she is held at their own station.

Below I review the use of detention and the attitude and conduct of detectives with respect to it.

1. Supervisors

It is clear that detention is used for interrogation in regard to separate offenses extraneous to the case which originally justified arrest and detention. For example, Case 17 shows that the detention period was spent largely in investigation and interrogation relating to the separate offense.

Because the police regard the primary purpose of detention to be the

141

continuation of investigation and interrogation, they speak of detention almost as if it were their right to secure it, as in Case 10, "We got detention." Nevertheless, the right to request it resides with the prosecutor. The police, for their part, must prepare the papers and request that the prosecutor file for detention. Detectives will be involved in the preparation of materials, but the process takes place under the direction of the supervisors. For example, in Case 9, the supervisors directed detectives to obtain corroboration from the suspect's mother that he was not living at his home.

The way in which the supervisors view the utility of detention is reflected in reports from the supervisors to the station chief and in memoranda from the supervisors to the prosecutor requesting a filing for detention. For example, after an ordinary arrest of a nineteen-year-old driver for theft of a television, the supervisors requested detention for the following reasons: The suspect "has confessed to two other separate offenses [and therefore]...it is necessary that he be detained at this station for the need to take him to confirm the place where the stolen goods were sold.... [S]ince it will be conceded that there is a risk of destruction of evidence and flight, it is required to detain him and carry out interrogations and investigations to corroborate the statements." Similarly, the request "relating to the location of the suspect's detention" stated, "since continuing interrogation and investigations are necessary, we would prefer that the suspect undergo detention at the current station." Although in acknowledging the legal requirements for detention, supervisors reported that there is "a risk of destruction of evidence and flight." It should be noted that this statement is considered secondary to the primary "need for interrogation and corroboration of the statements." The supervisors believe that detention exists for the convenience of investigations and interrogation, particularly in connection with separate offenses, and they use this device accordingly. However, it is unclear to what extent the prosecutor discloses this aim to the judge when he files for detention.

From the concern voiced above about investigation and interrogation, particularly in regard to separate offenses, we may infer that detention at the police station detention cell is desired. On this point, there was a supervisor who stressed that station cell detention was beneficial to the suspect, saying, "If you can make it clear that the substitute prison is comparatively beneficial to the suspect, this should be recognized by the judge. Look at the disadvantages of the outside detention house to the suspect." However, this same supervisor, in Case 10, said about a juvenile suspect, "In any case, he won't come to us for detention. It will be at the Juvenile Diagnostic Center. It would be nice if he were eighteen, though [since he could be detained in the station]." No attempt is made here to conceal the fact that detention is seen from the standpoint of convenience in investigations.

2. Detectives

The detectives also speak as if detention existed for the benefit of the police. "They'll think it over for half a month [during detention before indictment]. After the indictment, we will still have one more month to cook them [because detention may be repeated for each unindicted charge even after indictment for one charge]," a theft crime detective said of detained suspects. "Two or three days in detention, you'd think they would start to see things our way," another said, although he did not write in the investigation report that "the reason for requesting a filing for detention was to investigate separate offenses."

It is useful to inquire, in light of the observational material, what reasons the detectives believe they must give in order to ask the prosecutor to file for detention on their behalf. In Case 3, detectives treated a known fact as a separate offense and used it as the grounds for filing for detention. In Case 11, a detective said, "She has been fired, so we plan to use the risk of flight in our request for detention, " and "She was under a suspended sentence, so we'll probably get it." In the same case, a detective said, "We would have been better off if she had denied the facts on which the arrest was based. In that case it's easier to get detention." In another case, a detective indicated that it would be easy to secure detention if the suspect denied his guilt. "Generally, if you finish with interrogation right away, you can't get detention,...so they will purposefully let the statement-taking go, and say 'There is need for investigation.'" It is understandable that "risk of flight" is used as one of the justifications for detention. But beyond this, detectives offered the suspect's denial of guilt, separate offenses, and the need for continuing investigation as grounds upon which a detention filing may be successfully pursued. In some cases, investigations and interrogations are delayed deliberately in order to gain a justification for filing for detention, the need for continuing investigations is fabricated, some part of the facts already known from the time of the arrest are covered up, and a need for investigation of separate offenses is created. Rather than seeking to complete all investigations and interrogations within the period of voluntary investigation and the forty-eight-hour period of confinement following arrest, from the outset the police policy is for investigations and interrogation to go forward with an eye to the detention period.

The detectives who believe that they may be granted the requested detention when such reasons are offered must believe that the prosecutors also expect detention to be used primarily for interrogations. For example, in one case the prosecutor told a detective, "Keep at it another week," because "the guy's not being clear about the motive." In order to clarify the motive for the crime, the prosecutor expected the detective to seek a confession during the renewal term of detention.

Detention is most useful if the suspect is fully in the hands of the police. For example, in Case 11, theft crime detectives expressed satisfaction when they heard that the suspect had been detained and assigned to their station detention cell.

The detectives do not hide the fact that this preference is for the convenience of investigation and interrogation and for the pursuit of separate offenses. For example, in speaking of his own experience, a theft crime detective recalled, "I firmly asked that the place of detention be made the station detention cell, and they took him to the outside detention center on me. The detention center is tough to deal with, too. At the substitute prison [station detention cell], you can take him out and put him away at any time, but not there." In the opinions of the detectives, these conveniences for investigation and interrogation should not be lost following indictment. For example, in Case 17, the suspect was kept in detention at the station after having been indicted for the crime which led to his arrest.

The words and acts of the detectives reveal a remarkable emphasis on pursuit of the suspect's statement. Survey responses also reveal this pattern.

Table 9.1   Attitudes about Detention

NEED FOR DETENTION

1. In fact, why do you think detention is necessary, generally speaking? First, do you believe that it is necessary to fully complete investigation?

Yes	Undecided	No	Total Respondents
76.7	14.0	9.3	(43)

2. Next, do you believe that it is necessary to investigate separate offenses?

Yes	Undecided	No	Total Respondents
62.8	20.9	16.3	(43)

3. Next, do you believe that it is necessary to prevent destruction of evidence?

Yes	Undecided	No	Total Respondents
79.1	18.6	2.3	(43)

4. Next, do you believe that it is necessary to conduct personal interrogation of the suspect?

Yes	Undecided	No	Total Respondents
67.4	23.3	9.3	(43)

5. Next, do you believe that it is necessary to prevent flight?

Yes	Undecided	No	Total Respondents
81.4	16.3	2.3	(43)

Table 9.1 *(Continued)*

NEED FOR DETENTION

---

6. Do you believe that it is at the point of detention that true investigation really begins?

Yes	Undecided	No	Total Respondents
20.9	27.9	51.2	(43)

PROBLEMS RELATING TO DETENTION AT THE OUTSIDE DETENTION CENTER

---

7. What problems do you see arising when "the place of detention will be the outside detention center"? First, do you believe one problem is that "it becomes difficult to establish a human relationship with the suspect"?

Yes	Undecided	No	Total Respondents
53.5	32.6	14.0	(43)

8. Do you believe that one problem is that "one cannot bring out the suspect and conduct interrogation whenever desired"?

Yes	Undecided	No	Total Respondents
76.7	23.3	0	(43)

IMPACT OF CHANGES IN THE DETENTION SYSTEM

---

9. If the deadline for detention filings were moved back to 12 hours, do you believe that this would significantly interfere with the efficiency with which cases are cleared?

Yes	Undecided	No	Total Respondents
51.2	27.9	21.0	(43)

10. If a system were imposed under which the period of detention were reduced to 5 days, with no possibility of extension, do you believe that this would significantly interfere with the efficiency with which cases are cleared?

Yes	Undecided	No	Total Respondents
67.4	23.3	9.3	(43)

11. If a system were imposed under which the place of detention were fixed as the outside detention center, do you believe that this would significantly interfere with the efficiency with which cases are cleared?

Yes	Undecided	No	Total Respondents
53.5	30.2	16.3	(43)

Table 9.1   *(Continued)*

DEMAND FOR AND EVALUATION OF REFORM IN THE DETENTION SYSTEM

---

12. Do you believe that you will have to accept the reform to move back the deadline for detention filings to 12 hours?

Yes	Undecided	No	Total Respondents
11.6	34.9	53.5	(43)

13. Do you believe that, in cases in which there is need for investigation of separate offenses, detention, and its extension and re-extension should be granted as a matter of course?

Yes	Undecided	No	Total Respondents
60.5	18.6	20.9	(43)

14. Do you believe that, in cases in which the suspect maintains silence, detention, and its extension and re-extension should be granted as a matter of course?

Yes	Undecided	No	Total Respondents
74.4	16.3	9.3	(43)

DEMAND FOR AND EVALUATION OF REFORM IN THE PLACE OF DETENTION

---

15. Do you believe that detention at the police station detention cell should be granted as a matter of course when the suspect maintains silence?

Yes	Undecided	No	Total Respondents
62.8	27.9	9.3	(43)

16. Do you believe that detention at the police station detention cell should be granted as a matter of course when there is need to investigate separate offenses?

Yes	Undecided	No	Total Respondents
67.4	23.3	9.3	(43)

DEMAND FOR POLICE POWER IN DETENTION (SEE NOTE)

Note: Questions 17 and 18 followed the question, "Do you believe that 'The decisions of the officers responsible for the suspect should have a more direct authoritative force'?"

17. What is your opinion in regard to the decision whether or not to impose detention?

Yes	Undecided	No	Total Respondents
51.2	23.3	25.6	(43)

Table 9.1   *(Continued)*

DEMAND FOR POLICE POWER IN DETENTION

---

18. What is you opinion in regard to the decision over where the place of detention should be?

Yes	Undecided	No	Total Respondents
69.0	19.0	11.9	(42)

According to items 1 through 6, most detectives justify detention in preventing the destruction of evidence and of flight, allowing completion of thorough investigation, permitting personal interrogation of the suspect, and enhancing investigation of separate offenses. As expected, they cite the legal requirements of a risk of destruction of evidence and flight, and one suspects that most detectives, while setting forth such justifications, have as their true purpose the furtherance of investigation and interrogation, particularly in regard to separate offenses. A majority do not see this as the point at which true investigation commences, but even so there is no doubt that at this point they wish to solve additional offenses through pursuit of confessions.

Similarly, items 7 and 8 present the responses to inquiry about the function of detention at the police station detention cell. Here, most detectives believe that detention at the police station is necessary for the establishment of a "human relationship" with the suspect for smooth interrogation, for the use of interrogation facilities, and for easy access to the suspect. According to many detectives, greater use of detention at the station detention cell is a desirable measure and enhances the efficiency of investigative activity.

When asked to predict the effects of a shorter deadline for filings for detention, a foreshortened period of detention, or absolute refusal to allow detention at the police station detention cell, most detectives fear a negative effect on the efficiency with which cases are cleared. This is shown by items 9 through 11.

In items 12 through 14, most detectives not only demonstrate opposition to the foreshortening of the detention filing deadline, but also would seek detention as a matter of course in cases in which there is a need for investigation of separate offenses or in which the suspect denies the offense.

In regard to the police station detention cell, as shown in items 15 and 16, although a majority of detectives may not be opposed to a ban on its use, most would press for its employment as a matter of course in order to investigate separate offenses and pursue confessions.

A similar opinion is held regarding the voice of the police in decisions bearing on detention and the place detention held (see items 17 and 18). Supervisors and detectives agree that the detention system exists for the purpose of forwarding investigations and interrogation. However, the detectives express more clearly than the supervisors their aim to develop a "human relationship" with suspects during prolonged confinement and to soften their resistance, ultimately producing the desired confession that will solve separate offenses.

3. Legal Implications of the Detention Practice

Where do detention practices lie on the spectrum of legal theories?

First of all, is the need for investigation and interrogation of separate offenses recognized as adequate justification for detention? Judicial practices indicate that if the reasons legally justifying arrest are fixed as "A," but the real purpose of detention is "B," there will be no opposition to detention if both "A" and "B" are set forth; however, there will be refusal of detention if only "B" is presented. In my field observations, detention was granted in most of the cases. This suggests that even when the prosecutor was motivated essentially by the desire to investigate separate offenses, he still must have filed either upon technical reasons for arrest or upon both these and the real reasons confided by the police.

No matter how the prosecutor files for detention, there are surely cases that will be questionable. I observed incidents where the real reason the police asked the prosecutor to file for detention was clearly through a desire to interrogate the suspect regarding separate offenses. Even where this was not apparent from the start, in the end detention usually was used for the purpose of investigating separate offenses.

The same is true of requests to extend detention. Under Article 208, Section 2 of the Code of Criminal Procedure, extension of detention may be acquired where there is "unavoidable cause." The Supreme Court has held that this requirement is met when investigations are complicated and if there will be delay and difficulties in collecting evidence. The Court has further held that a desire to investigate connected cases is permissible in the determination of whether the detention period should be extended (July 3, 1962, *Minshu* 16, 1408). Furthermore, in practice, when information concerning separate offenses is necessary in order to decide whether or not to indict on the original offense (e.g., to prove criminal intent or a plan of criminal action, or to make the original offense worth indicting by adding the weight of separate offenses), an extension will be granted. However, should the original reasons justifying detention disappear, detention must end, even if it cripples the investigation of separate offenses. Detention cannot be extended solely to interrogate the suspect about separate offenses.

Nonetheless, during my observations no filing for an extension of detention was rejected. It must be inferred that either the prosecutor asserted information concerning separate offenses was necessary to the decision of whether to indict, or that he asserted the difficulty of investigating the original charge justified extension of detention, whether this was true or not. It is difficult to reconcile the realities of filings for detention and its extension with the general doctrines in the field.

The identical situation exists in regard to requests that detention be at the police station detention cell on the ground that separate offenses require investigations.

Precedent and legal theory say that substitution of the regular detention center with the police station detention cell should be the exception and must be exercised with moderation. In pratice, however, detention at the station detention cell is granted as long as the judge finds that there are no abuses of the suspect by officers and no denial of the suspect's rights to defend himself, that there is no room in the detention center, or that detention at the outside detention center will seriously hinder the investigation. Reviewing judicial decisions in which detention at the police station detention cell has been approved, one finds it is granted when several suspects have been placed in separate detention at the police station detention cell to prevent conspiratorial communication; when the complicated nature of the crime necessitates ready access to suspects for interrogation and transportation to the scene of the crime; when conflicting statements make it necessary to use lineup and confrontation techniques; and, finally, when interrogation involves multiple exhibits of evidence. Detention at the police station detention cell has not been granted in cases where there is no urgent need for a lineup or confrontation or where detention at the outside detention center caused no practical difficulty.

I have no record that police cited the above mentioned special circumstances when they asked prosecutors to petition for detention at the police station detention cell. Perhaps the prosecutor nonetheless asserted the presence of such circumstance, because I did not encounter any case in which detention at the station detention cell was denied. However, even if this were so, there have been incidents questionable in light of the judicial decisions. This is especially so in cases in which the investigation of separate offenses was the central reason for requesting detention at the station detention cell. According to judicial doctrine, detention at the police station detention cell should be refused when interrogation regarding separate offenses is the overriding reason for requesting it. Many cases that I observed included this element, but detention was refused in none of them. Apparently the Sapporo judges did not make much effort to find the facts of these cases. They consistently granted police the opportunities to aggressively pursue confessions and to discover additional offenses by holding the suspect in their own detention facilities.

10

Interrogation, Confession, and Separate Offense

In the review of detention in the preceding chapter, the importance of interrogation as an investigative method becomes quite clear. Separate offenses often are disclosed by a confession obtained through interrogation and then later are confirmed by an investigation which corroborates such a confession. In order to use interrogation effectively, officers must have control over the suspect. For this purpose detention, especially at the police station detention cell, is necessary.

1. Police Academy

The offense used as the ground for arrest is called *honken* or main offense. Police do not stop their investigation by simply solving *honken*. They always want to solve as many separate offenses as possible.

There are two types of separate offenses. One is *bekken* or a different crime. A *bekken* is a specific crime the police believe that the suspect committed, but about which they lack sufficient evidence to apply for a warrant.[1] The other is *yozai* or an additional crime, a crime the police discover in the process of investigating the main offense. In reality, however, the two types

---

1. This usage of the terms of *honken* and *bekken* follows the one used among the officers I observed at the Eastern Police Station. The more common usage, particularly the one adopted by the mass media, reverses the meaning. When a person is arrested on a minor charge while the police expect to interrogate him for a different major crime, the media call the minor one as *bekken* and the major one as *honken*.

151

of separate offenses often are difficult to distinguish. Even when they do not have a specific *bekken* in mind, the police usually expect at least a *yozai* while still working on the main offense. Either can increase the productivity of criminal investigation since a single arrest solves more than one offense.

Even at the police academy, one witnesses a tremendous concern over the discovery and solution of separate offenses. For example, one instructor stated, by way of criticism, "Old sergeants and such will ask for detention because they are after separate offenses." A student in an assistant inspector class said, "In the main case [used as the ground for arrest and detention], the facts used as grounds for arrest added up to airtight proof. [There was no need to continue investigation in that case.] Why do we want detention? Naturally, we are concerned over separate offenses." Further, in a lecture for sergeants:

> When I told him "Piss!" and he turned up positive for amphetamine, I could have arrested him. But you can't get detention for a juvenile. So I contacted the family court and had him sent to a Juvenile Diagnostic Center. Then you check out separate offenses at the Center. The longest period you can get there is four weeks.

The importance of solving separate offenses also is taught at the police academy. For example, in a class of recruits, an instructor stated, "Investigation of stolen goods is to discover separate offenses. Securing a complaint from the victim [for the unreported separate offense] is fundamental. If at all possible, let the victim write it himself." The sergeants are taught, "[When using a tape recorder] bring out for the record facts, circumstances, and explanations which are beneficial to the criminal. This can also be used to bring out separate offenses."

The primary aspect of interrogation is the confession. Confession is necessary in order to assure that the arrest is not a false one. For example, the instructor of a class for sergeants spoke of a case in which he had participated, "Policy was that the warrant would be executed when doubt over whether it might be a false arrest was dispelled by the confession." Even when an arrest warrant had been issued, this meant calling the party in on voluntary appearance, conducting interrogation, awaiting confession, then carrying out the arrest.

Furthermore, confession is necessary to uncover evidence and prove guilt in those crimes for which evidence is scarce. For example, an instructor in a class for sergeants responded to my question about the need for confession by saying, "Depending upon the crime, we may not have any physical evidence. And in fact, confession by itself is not sufficient; there must be a thorough corroboration...confession is necessary to the discovery of physical evidence."

There is an awareness that confession is necessary to indictment, conviction, and obtaining a more severe sentence. The same instructor quoted above stated, "Prosecutors demand pursuit of confessions. Without a confession, they won't indict," "Sometimes they can't win at the trial without a confession," and, "If they request six years, and the decision comes in for three, the police will be criticized for inadequate corroborating investigations."

The possibility of doubt regarding the voluntariness of the confession is stressed in advance at the police academy. In teaching the method for tape-recording a statement, the instructor of a sergeants' class stated:

> Have an observer. Just one is enough. This is to counter any exclusion [of statements at the trial] on grounds of psychological pressure. Short questions, long answers. This refutes defensive arguments that questions are leading. Get down the record of situations, explanations, circumstances favorable to the criminal. This is to forestall suspicion that the tape is a creative or edited production. The purpose of tape recording when taking of the statement is to illustrate the voluntary nature of the statement.

An instructor in an assistant inspector class described the ideal interrogation room as "a room which does not arouse suspicions of human rights violations. Seat the suspect with his back to the window in order that his expression can be clearly seen. No knives in the detectives' room. Do not leave nightsticks or bamboo swords in the interrogation room."

Then, how can detectives get confessions from suspects? According to the students, whether interrogation takes place smoothly depends upon whether a "human relationship" with the suspect is established. For example, one assistant inspector said:

> If the human relationship is pleasant, interrogation becomes easy. After release, there is communication and support. The detective takes care of the suspect's problems with his own money. Drop in on him after release, and he's happy. There is a confession even in cases involving radical students because a detective is able to establish a good human relationship with the suspect. There are cases, too, in which the suspect will give his confession to no one but detective so and so.

If all of this is so, one should find that a kind of ongoing relationship develops between detectives and repeat offenders. As we have already seen, detention at the police station detention cell is requested for the sake of developing this pleasant "human relationship."

Judging from the content of the instruction at the police academy, it appears that the significance of voluntariness in the statement is adequately stressed in the official policy within the police force. However, I will show that field officers do not believe in the legitimacy of this commitment to propriety and that only superficial observance of the law will be prevalent.

2. Supervisors

The supervisors are quite concerned about the solution of separate offenses. For example, in Case 9, a supervisor said, "Don't push it too hard. Work on the separate offenses after the main case is more or less finished." In this expression we see an attempt to contain excesses by the detectives. However, even in such a case the supervisor is not prohibiting pursuit of separate offenses, but merely providing guidance about how to proceed. When the supervisor believes it necessary, he does not hesitate to order investigations which stress separate offenses. For example, in Case 17, "The evidence and papers in the main case [the offense used as the basis for arrest and detention] have pretty much been sent across [to the prosecutor]. Now, we are preparing the evidence and papers in the first case [separate offense]."

One important problem bearing upon interrogation is the degree to which strict proof must be obtained. A comment from Case 17, the arson investigation, suggests that proof requirements affect the entire investigation: "Motive, the circumstances around the arson, the way the fire started, and the extent of the blaze, all need to be drawn up as evidence." Another comment in the same case:

> He carried a kerosene can in from the entry, spread it on the floor and set fire to it; but because he was sniffing thinner, he is not clear about whether or not the lid was opened. He set fire to a garbage bag, but there is a question of whether there was only one bag or two. Two people put out garbage bags. The contents of only one person's bag remain. Was it burned up, or was it not there in the first place? We can't write in the indictment papers "He committed arson somehow or other."

A supervisor said, "Above all else, I detest the expression 'Sometime around a certain day in a certain month.' Let's work at getting out the supporting facts." According to the supervisors, the standard of proof is quite strict.

The difficulty of proving motives and the belief that such proof is indispensable encourages pursuit of confessions. For example, again in Case 17, a supervisor said:

Under the Japanese Criminal Code, motive is an element in sentencing, and must be proven as a fact. It would be different if, as in America, we might deal only with surface action.

However, there is a definite awareness that too much can be made of a confession. In the words of one supervisor, "Naturally, it is hazardous to go forward with just the statements of the suspect and those connected with him. Let's have concrete corroborating investigations." But, there is no denial of the general importance of the confession.

Supervisors are very aware that once there is a confession, they can justify the arrest. For example, a supervisor stated, "There is reasonable cause for arrest [in this case] because there is both testimony and circumstantial evidence. It is a case in which, if there is a confession, we can make an emergency arrest."

Supervisors believe that without a confession, there can be no indictment. One supervisor said that generally, "Even if you say you have complete proof, if there is no confession, the prosecutor will probably not indict."

A good confession is "a statement that could be made by no one but the criminal." For example, in Case 17, a supervisor explained;

He has confessed, "I went inside, but it was dark, so I waited until my eyes adjusted. Then I set the fire." He knows the situation inside the room. Even the investigators dont't know that, only the arsonist could know.... The facts regarding the white uniform and so on are facts which only the criminal could have known, and to which he has confessed.

In other words, this is a fact unknown before the confession, but which upon corroborating investigation turn out to be true.

When a confession like this is forthcoming, it carries decisive weight in the supervisors' convictions that the suspect has truly committed the crime. Confession is superior to other forms of evidence. However, a confession also must be corroborated with other evidence.

Supervisors also emphasize a proper way of interrogation to secure voluntary confession. A supervisor said, in Case 17, "Let him [the suspect] say everything that he wants, then ferret out contradictions on points relevant to the case.... This technique enhances voluntariness [of the confession] in the court." It is ironic that, because of this concern over voluntariness, long confinement of the person becomes necessary.

Supervisors generally display a conservatism in their statements about weighing confession too heavily and regarding the problem of voluntariness. Nevertheless, in actual cases, they occasionally give quite aggressive orders to the detectives. In one case, for example, a supervisor shouted at the detectives, "Tell them [suspects] 'You tell us exactly what you did, or we won't let you go.'" We have to find the reasons that supervisors take such questionable actions contrary to their general policies.

3. Detectives

Sanders (1977: 151, 164) has described the situation of theft crime investigation in the United States. "Burglaries are difficult crimes to solve, and were it not for...multiple clearances on cop outs...even fewer would be 'solved.'" Thus detectives "hope not only of solving this one case but also, if the burgler is caught, of being able to clear several other burglaries at the same time." About Canada, Ericson (1981: 170) has reported that generally "multiple charging was the norm." Theft crime detectives in Japan think and behave in a similar manner. They are particularly conscious that there is no effective method to improve their clearance rate except to find separate offenses by those persons they are able to arrest from time to time. For example, detectives say:

- The best thing is for there to be discovery, an immediate sprint to the scene, and an arrest in the area. Unfortunately, this is not possible in reality. Thus, you must make the gems [suspects who appear to be connected to numerous separate offenses] the center of your attention, and work at your investigation. If you catch a couple of gems worth forty or fifty offenses apiece in a month, you'll wipe out the unsolved cases right away.

- In theft investigations, after you catch them you have to use the *taguri* method—first get the confession to separate offenses, then find supporting evidence.

These expressions reveal the importance of improving clearance rates and demonstrate the use of the method of collecting evidence of separate offenses after the pursuit of confession.

In the United States police say, "It's a waste of time to work any single burglary" (Sanders, 1977: 164). Likewise, I heard Japanese detectives make statements such as, "It's a waste to end it with the main offense," and, "We can add X number of charges." A theft crime detective said on the telephone to the assistant prosecutor in charge of the case, "Besides trespass to a structure, with the theft of a pipe wrench and iron bar, and the knife as illegal possession of a sword, it increases to three offenses." There was also the statement by a theft crime detective in another case, "I ordinarily anticipate multiple separate offenses. We have numerous crimes to clear; we can't let it end with trespass to a residence." It is clear that this aggressiveness in pursuing separate offenses is closely tied to the detectives' awareness of the need to enhance clearance rates. And the desire to bring out as many separate offenses as possible is not limited to investigation specialists. A police box officer remarked, for example, "It is trespass to a structure, but it would be a waste to stop there."

Because of this concern for converting a single arrest into the solution for many crimes, whenever a suspect sought by another station is arrested, the number of separate offenses with which he may be charged has an effect upon the decision to transfer him to another station. For example, in one case, the detective said, "Check it out; if there are separate offenses, we will say we're sorry, but we'll keep him at this station. If he doesn't say anything, we will send him to that station [that had put out a request for the suspect]."

Besides the effort to improve clearance rates, there is an awareness that in dealing with the prosecutor's office, a detention filing and the indictment are easier to obtain if there are separate offenses. For example, regarding detention in Case 11, a theft crime detective said, "As to why we didn't request a warrant based on the other [earlier] offense, the reason was that we want to be able to get detention." In relation to indictment, also in Case 11, it was stated that "indictment will be on the 12th. The supporting facts will of course be those of the main case, but in fact on the main case alone we are weak [because the suspect had returned the stolen money]. We have two separate offenses stitched up besides, and we will support it with those." Therefore, even when investigation of separate offenses is not treated as the sole purpose of investigation, it figures prominently as a means to obtain detention and indictment.

In many cases, the pursuit of separate offenses produces expected results. The detectives told me, for example, "Today he admitted another offense. That brings it to eight so far," and that "he talks a lot more freely about separate offenses."

This attitude and conduct in relation to separate offenses, which is connected with their attitude and conduct previously seen in relation to detention, also is tied closely to at least two other patterns. One of these is that the method of investigation inclines toward pursuit of confessions. Since pursuit of confessions is essential to uncover separate offenses, there is a need to seek detention and its extension at the police station detention cell.

A second pattern is that when the detectives make an arrest they often expect to discover a totally different, more serious type of separate crime, rather than merely to find separate cases of the same type. This practice is considered more questionable because the arrest is used to create an opportunity to investigate a crime not indicated in the arrest warrant application.

Skolnick (1966: 177) has described a case in the United States in which suspects "were arrested on minor charges in order to give the police an opportunity to interrogate them [for more serious charges]." McBarnet (1981: 41) has reported a similar practice in Great Britain, "using one charge to take a person into custody then interrogating him in the isolation of the police station on another offense." On similar practices in Japan, I quote from a conversation that took place one night in the duty room:

- Detective Abe: (working on papers for a child molestation case) By itself, this is a dull little case, but we get an arrest warrant for this, and I expect a big one [as a separate offense].

- Detective Baba: You mean an arrest to investigate a *bekken*, don't you?

This conversation also mirrors a finding reported by Ericson about Canada (Ericson, 1981: 72): "Minor occurrences were seen in terms of their potential for generating information about possible major occurrences."

The detectives have a very strict idea of the level of proof required for investigation. It is for this reason that in Case 17 they bought a plastic bag identical to that with which the fire was allegedly started and experimented with starting a fire using the same tools and equipment. In reality, however, they often have to compromise. In the same case, confronting differences between the statements of the witnesses and the confession of the suspect concerning the site of the crime, a detective complained, "We should expect one or two minor errors, otherwise we cannot get anywhere."

There is also recognition of the need to prove motive. As a theft crime detective said, "Courts feel that way now, and so proof of motive is extremely important."

Like the supervisors, detectives believe that prosecutors expect strict proof. For example, a detective observed, "If all we had to do was prove the facts of the criminal act, there's nothing to it. And the prosecutors, for all their claims that they will indict if the facts are clear, will still say, 'Let's tighten up the motive on this.'" Proving the subjective element of intent means reliance upon confession.

Among the detectives, there is an attitude that procuring confessions is primary in investigations and that other investigative activities must follow from this. For example, a theft crime detective said that generally, "The best method is to get the confession, and then cross-check it." As another said, "Confession is king. You really get to the truth." Like supervisors, they doubt they can prove guilt without confessions. "If they don't say anything, there's nothing you can do," a detective said in Case 17, "They don't leave stuff behind at the scene when they leave, there is no proof."

The statement by an organized crime detective that "courts and prosecutors require confessions even if there is evidence" demonstrates a belief that a confession is necessary for indictment and conviction. When a prosecutor refused to indict in one case, an organized crime detective remarked, "I wonder if the real reason wasn't because there was no confession. No matter how solid your proof is, I guess without a confession they won't indict for you."

Of course, the confession must be corroborated. This is manifest in the statement in Case 17: "We will see whether the room [the scene of the crime] fits the description in the confession, and whether anyone had seen these papers in the drawer or not." However, evidence is occasionally made to fit the confession. For example, in a theft investigation, a detective said that they "make up a damage report [of the victim] following the confession."

The need for post-confession collection of important evidence is reflected in their notion of a good confession. Like the supervisors, detectives believe that the good confession is made up of "facts which only the criminal could know." Detectives firmly believe that only such confessions prove guilt. An organized crime detective stated, "What is absolutely necessary is the confession to facts which only the criminal would know, and their confirmation." In Case 17, the arrested suspect stated to detectives that he "went in from the back door of the noodle shop, rolled up a white coat that was hanging on the wall, and set fire to it." A detective pointed out, "Even the detectives don't know this, and there has been no report of a white uniform lost. If this is in fact true, it will be something that 'only the criminal knows.'"

This implies that detectives often spend much time in interrogation before they seriously search and examine physical evidence. Detectives as a policy do not collect too much evidence before the confession. In Case 17, we find the statement, "If we run a complete investigation at the scene, there will be a question of whether we have gotten a statement that conforms to our own preconceived ideas." Detectives thus believe that in order to make a confession credible and voluntary, it should be obtained through long confinement, and that thereafter materials should be collected on the basis of the confession.

What interrogation methods should be used to obtain a confession?

The most interesting point on this subject is that there is no detective who repeated the supervisors' preferred method: allowing the subject to speak freely and then following up on contradictions. A large number of detectives described that confessions generally are taken after establishing a "human relationship" with the suspect. "Exchanging talk about parents and family, discussing human nature, you loosen up their feelings and coax out a confession," and, "If you can't develop a human relationship with the suspect, he won't talk for you. Then you take care of his needs, but be strict in interrogation." In one case, a detective said that "he has softened up quite a bit, but we're not there yet.... We can't make him angry when he denies the offense. We have to build a good human relationship."

It is thought that the "human relationship" is something which builds "naturally." One organized crime detective stated, "We have interrogations like this every day, so we can build up a human relationship naturally. In any case, we go into everything from the family situation to finances."

This relationship, however, is not one between equal partners. In the "human relationship," the suspect is both physically and emotionally dependent upon the detectives and usually cannot but respond to their expectations. Whether or not the detectives subjectively see things in this way, where they have the power to control the situation of the suspect entirely, this result is the only one we should expect. Indeed, when a detective, after investigating a wrong suspect, says, "I just start over, looking for a new customer," it appears that the suspect is taken as a resource to be used in boosting the clearance rate. In Case 11, a detective said, "If she [the suspect] were a little smarter woman, we could do nothing, but this one has no brains, you can fool her easily." Here, the suspect is seen as an object to be manipulated. The treatment of a sick suspect from Case 11 ties this attitude with the pursuit of separate offenses and the desire for enhanced clearance rates. The detective said first, "We will transfer Yamada [the suspect to the outside detention center]. When we had her examined by a physician, he found she had an adhesion where her appendix had been operated on." Afterwards, however, interrogation was continued, and the detective proudly reported, "She just admitted another offense."

Bayley (1976: 145, 150) has described the relationship that exists between Japanese detectives and suspects. According to Bayley, "The Japanese policeman can devote so much more time to considering appropriate treatment" because a Japanese confronting the police is more submissive than an American. "A Japanese accepts the accusation and tries to kindle benevolence. In response,...the Japanese policeman is sympathetic and succoring." My observation indicates, however, that Japanese police detectives are far more manipulative than Bayley indicates and do not hestitate to take advantage of the suspect's submissiveness to obtain as many confessions as possible.

Even if this "human relationship" develops as "naturally" as the detectives claim, their efforts do not stop at that point. For example, sometimes a lighter sentence is held out as an instrument of persuasion. In an embezzlement case, the detective describes how he persuaded the suspect. He urged, "Why don't you admit it, and later ask for leniency? Isn't that better? What do you think?" Skolnick (1966: 176) has argued that in the United States "criminality becomes a commodity for exchange." At least the possibility of such an exchange is one of the instruments Japanese detectives use in dealing with suspects.

Ericson (1981: 159-61) has described the methods of interrogation he observed in Canada:

- Detectives did not use physical force. They proceeded by way of the carrot rather than the stick, although threats with coercive consequences were prevalent.

- Detectives employed a variety of tricks and threats to obtain information from suspects. The tricks all involved playing upon the suspect's lack of knowledge about some aspect of the case and/or about procedures.

The situation seems similar in Japan. Violence is rarely observed, but tricks and threats are employed. Particularly when the suspect stubbornly denies the charge against him, detectives react forcefully. The following statement is illustrative: "You take care of his [the suspect's] needs, but be strict in interrogation." In Case 17, I witnessed a detective swear, "We will make you talk." In another case, I heard the voice of a forcible crime detective through the door of the interrogation room: "Yamada! (striking the desk and shouting) Let's have some talk. Sit down! 'I'm sorry' won't cut it. Get it out and get it over with!" From these situations, it is clear that forceful language is not out of bounds. I also heard a detective's voice booming from the interrogation room in still another case, "If you are lining up your stories, you should do a better job of it!... That woman asked for 10,000 yen [approximately $33 U.S.] in front of you. Didn't she!" Regarding this exchange, the detective explained, "You don't get anywhere with this kind of gangster, unless you start with an all-out argument. After that you begin to *understand* one another." While we were riding out together, a theft crime detective told me, "There aren't any confessions that are really voluntary. They're told that if they don't talk, they won't eat, won't smoke, won't meet with their families."

If confessions are so critical, it follows that it is difficult to honor a suspect's request to exercise the right to remain silent. In Case 17, a detective admitted, "We say first, 'You don't have to tell us anything,' and then say, 'Now talk.' It's not like they're going to talk for you." This reveals the ambivalent feeling of the detectives.

Further, Cases 11 and 17 show that interrogation, regarding separate offenses at least, sometimes continues beyond indictment.

Despite such aggressiveness, however, some detectives have doubts about the chance of arriving at the truth through confession. In Case 17, a detective mused, "He [the suspect] doesn't remember very well. The guy made his statement saying, 'Now that you mention it, maybe that's the way it was.'" These could not be facts known only to the criminal.

Detectives are of course aware of the voluntariness problem. A forcible crime detective stressed the need for voluntariness, saying, "At public trial, if we have voluntary confession and corroboration we will get a conviction." In Case 17, a supervisor told me, "Yesterday, we didn't interrogate him [the suspect]. If the content of the confession wanders too much, its voluntariness comes under suspicion."

But these comments do not demonstrate obedience to law. What they show is detectives' practical concern for losing the case due to doubts about the voluntariness of the confession. In other words, efforts to corroborate confessions are not motivated by a firm conviction for procedural propriety. If a confession is unlikely to be questioned, detectives may be easily tempted to take legally questionable actions.

The survey responses below conform to the observational material.

Table 10.1 deals first with perception of the actual state of separate crime investigation (items 1 and 2). Here, a majority of detectives not only acknowledge that upon entry into the detention phase, the focus of investigation is upon separate offenses, but also that there are cases in which, despite the relative unimportance of detention in the main case, a detention filing should be requested for the sake of the investigation of separate offenses.

Table 10.1   Attitudes about Separate Offense Investigation

SITUATION REGARDING SEPARATE OFFENSE INVESTIGATION

1. Do you believe that there are many cases in which the greatest part of the detention period is devoted to the investigation of separate offenses?

Yes	Undecided	No	Total Respondents
53.5	32.6	14.0	(43)

2. Do you believe that there are also a large number of cases in which the main case has been pretty well put in order, but detention is obtained because there is a need to investigate separate offenses?

Yes	Undecided	No	Total Respondents
53.5	25.6	20.9	(43)

EXERCISE OF THE RIGHT TO REMAIN SILENT

3. Do you believe that many suspects know of the right to remain silent from the outset?

Yes	Undecided	No	Total Respondents
51.2	34.9	14.0	(43)

4. Do you believe that such cases are increasing in number?

Yes	Undecided	No	Total Respondents
58.1	30.2	11.6	(43)

Table 10.1 *(Continued)*

EFFECT OF THE RIGHT TO REMAIN SILENT

---

5. Do you believe that the existence of the right to remain silent interferes with procuring confessions?

Yes	Undecided	No	Total Respondents
58.1	18.6	23.3	(43)

CONNECTION BETWEEN SILENCE AND SUSPICION

---

6. Do you believe that silence is proof that the suspect had something to do with the crime?

Yes	Undecided	No	Total Respondents
60.5	27.9	11.6	(43)

THE EXPECTED METHOD OF PURSUING CONFESSION

---

7. Of the following types of statements, A and B, which do you believe is the more desirable?

Note: The answer "A" signifies either "A" or "Of these two, A," while the answer "B" signifies either "B" or "Of these two, B."

A: "First I let the suspect speak freely; I listen to what he says, and I pursue any contradictions."

B: "I question the suspect in an effort to determine whether what has been learned through investigation is true."

A	Undecided	B	Total Respondents
79.1	14.0	7.0	(43)

OFFICIAL POLICY ABOUT METHODS OF PURSUING CONFESSION

Note: Regarding the meaning of the answers "A" and "B," please see item 7.

8. Which do you believe to be in accordance with the official policy within the Hokkaido police Department?

A	Undecided	B	Total Respondents
67.4	32.6	0.0	(43)

9. Which do you believe to be in accordance with the thoughts of the supervisors of the police station to which you are attached?

A	Undecided	B	Total Respondents
67.4	32.6	0.0	(43)

Table 10.1   *(Continued)*

NEED FOR AUTHORITY FOR POLICE DECISIONS

---

10. Don't you think that larger authority should be given to the police? For instance, how do you feel about the decision about whether a confession is voluntary?

Yes	Undecided	No	Total Respondents
60.5	18.6	20.9	(43)

The pursuit of separate offenses also is singled out as one of the actions that must be taken as part of investigation. In items 332 and 333 of Appendix A, most detectives not only acknowledge the general importance of the pursuit of separate offenses, but also indicate a belief that even after the conclusion of the main case, the remaining detention time should be devoted to the pursuit of separate offenses.

The importance of separate offenses noted in field observation is supported by the survey data.

In items 3 and 4, I inquired about the suspects' knowledge of the right to remain silent and the detectives' attitude towards it. Most detectives believe that many suspects know about their right. They believe that the number who remain silent is large and increasing. In item 5, we find that a majority of detectives believe that the right to remain silent interferes with their ability to obtain confessions.

Do such attitudes affect the way the right to remain silent is advised by the detectives to the suspect? According to Appendix A, item 310, a majority of detectives deny that the need for efficient investigation affects the method of informing suspects of the right. Even so, the interrogation of a suspect who remains silent is harsher than that of one who cooperates. Item 6 reveals that a suspect's silence deepens most detectives' conviction that he is guilty.

What sort of investigative methods are considered appropriate? Let us look first at item 7.

Most detectives believe that the better method is to allow the suspect to speak and to follow up on any contradictions. This is the point that is stressed by the supervisors. Pursuit of contradictions evidently is as important as developing a "human relationship" with the suspect. From items 8 and 9, we learn that most detectives know that this approach is expected by the supervisors and it is the official internal policy of the police force.

It is important then to examine what detectives believe to be the expectations of others in order to gain a full understanding of their attitudes and conduct. The next part of this book takes up this issue.

In Appendix A, items 368 through 380 indicated that the attitude of detectives regarding concrete methods of pursuing confessions are quite conservative, perhaps because they judge the queried methods to be clearly illegal. However, one must look carefully at item 368. Although most detectives indicate restraint when concrete questions are posed, they also believe strongly that confessions must be extracted. Obviously this conviction can lead to problematic actions which reach the level of illegality. In fact, field observation indicated that detectives made promises of lighter sentencing, promises to look after the suspect, interrogation late into the evening, and the like.

The attitude that confessions *must* be extracted is related to the previously noted attitude that the detective must succeed in attaining the goal of his investigation and absolutely must not fail.

Finally, item 10 of Table 10.1 indicates that a majority of detectives believe that larger authority should be given to the police in determining whether a confession is voluntary. This again demonstrates the detectives' concern over confessions.

4. Legal Implications of the Interrogation Practice

In the eyes of the detectives, interrogation and particularly the pursuit of confessions are necessary to prove motive, to establish factual details, and to collect evidence. They attempt to extract a statement containing facts which "only the criminal would know." The method promoted by supervisors is to allow the suspect to speak freely and then pursue any contradictions in his account. However, the detective's duty to secure confessions is all-important and serves to justify other methods.

If necessary to solve a case, detectives will take actions that are in some way questionable. At times they use some of the methods of which they themselves disapprove. Of course, they do so because they believe that without such action, the aim could not be achieved.

How would the detectives' practices have been judged by the law at the time of my research?

On the issue of continuing interrogation beyond the indictment, the Supreme Court has held that "it is a thing to be avoided if possible, but we cannot say that such interrogation is necessarily illegal, or that the evidentiary force of a confession obtained by such interrogation is lost" (November 21, 1961, *Keishu* 15, 1764). However, in 1974, a statement made by the defendant six days after the indictment was refused evidentiary force by a lower court, which cited the fact that counsel had not been selected for the defendant (Osaka High Court, July 18, 1974, *Hanji* 755, 118). In another case, a confession resulting from interrogation four and a half months after indictment on other charges was ruled illegal by a lower court. The court held that "the use made of detention here put the cart before the horse, so to speak, and detention was used almost entirely for confining the suspect for interrogation." Therefore the interrogation violated the constitutional warrant requirement and was illegal (Hiroshima High Court, December 14, 1972, *Kokeishu* 25, 993). I cannot say that any of the cases I observed were as questionable as this last-cited case. Neither can I say, however, that they showed no hints of the questionability of the same nature.

Regarding interrogation methods, a lower court decision denied the voluntariness of a confession obtained after an interrogating officer promised to release the suspect once he admitted guilt (Osaka District Court, April 2, 1970, *Hanji* 606, 104). In a decision in another case, a lower court struck down a confession obtained by an officer's suggestion that the suspect would be let off with a fine (Osaka District Court, September 27, 1974, *Keisaigeppo* 6, 1002). The voluntariness of yet another confession was denied "because the questions were arranged so logically [for detail, and consistency in answers] that they were difficult to answer, and because of the psychological distress produced thereby...." Therefore, "the statement, not necessarily true, was made without deep thought, and as an attempt to ingratiate oneself with the detective; these considerations argue against the voluntariness of the statement" (Tokyo District Court, July 6, 1971, *Keisaigeppo* 3, 991). Another case involves interrogation by the prosecutor. In that instance, a number of suspects each were interrogated from one to ten times after 10:00 p.m., over a detention period of forty-seven days. This was interpreted as "persistent logical interrogation [which sought minute details and consistency]" by the court which denied the voluntariness of the confessions thus obtained (Utsunomiya District Court, November 11, 1970, *Keisaigeppo* 2, 1175). I observed no practices in my field research as clearly problematic as the ones in these cases, but was witness to problematic instances of a similar character.

* * * * *

The attitudes and behavior of the supervisors and detectives at each stage of criminal investigation now have been reviewed. The basic pattern that occurs commonly at every stage is a mixture of aggressiveness and reserve in the attitudes and conduct of the supervisors, and a more general inclination toward aggressiveness in the detectives. Even the very enabling legal framework of criminal investigation does not always satisfy the police, particularly the detectives.

This aggressiveness is not always something that clearly can be termed illegal. Nonetheless, the conduct is problematic under such standards as the judicial precedent, the guiding policy within the police force, or the thoughts expressed in some situations by the detectives themselves.

My next objective is to seek the causes for the ordinarily conservative supervisors' orders of aggressive investigations at times and the causes for the inclination toward aggressiveness in the detectives. We must look for the cause in the strong drive to solve cases. In this regard, I direct attention to the attitude manifested repeatedly in this analysis that the detective must succeed, that failure is not permissible. This motivation must be something that grips detectives with great force.

I should reiterate that problematic actions are taken even when the supervisors and detectives themselves are aware of their nature. This indicates their perception that controls and demands exist capable of displacing even their own evaluations. I examine this matter in part 3.

Part III

Explanation of Investigative Activity:
Why Do They Think and Behave as They Do?

11

The Forms of Detectives' Involvement in Investigative Actions

In part 2 I indicated that the very enabling legal environment does not always satisfy detectives and their field supervisors. Because of the accommodating nature of the legal environment which allows prolonged interrogation of the suspect in custody without meaningful intervention of the defense counsel, detectives rarely apply physical force or engage in overtly illegal actions. I did not observe any physical abuse of the suspect during my field research. It is clear, however, that detectives nevertheless engage in questionable actions. It is not uncommon for them to use investigative measures for purposes other than those recognized by the law, to hide their real purposes when they apply for a warrant or request detention, to use coercive words in interrogation, or to otherwise manipulate the suspect. Even at the Eastern Police Station which is known for its procedural restraint, the supervisors and the detectives tried to expand their already great advantage over the suspects in their efforts to build a case. The purpose of part 3 of this book is to explore explanations for this aggressiveness.

First, there is a significant difference in aggressiveness between the supervisors and the detectives. The supervisors generally express more reserved policies. Their behavior demonstrates an ambivalent mixture of aggressiveness and reserve. Compared to the supervisors, the detectives manifest a more general inclination to be aggressive in their action. I need to attempt to explain this difference.

Second, the supervisors and the detectives express their own doubt about the legality of some of their actions. They engage in questionable actions in spite of their own doubts, and I seek to understand why they do so.

My strategy is to explain the behavior of the supervisors and the detectives as a specific response to the controls and expectations they perceive, both internal and external. I will try to explain their behavior through understanding the meaning it has for them, that is, their own perspective about their work environment.

Amitai Etzioni (1961: 4–14, 55–65) has presented a typology of the congruent relationship between the types of power wielded by organizational elite and the types of involvement exhibited by organizational members. I use his scheme as a heuristic framework to characterize the relationship between the perceived environment and the response of the supervisors and the detectives.

Power is an actor's ability to induce or influence other actors to carry out one's directives or any other norms one supports. Etzioni classifies this power into three types, according to the means employed to make the subject comply. These are (1) *coercive power,* power arising from use of physical punishment or the threat of physical punishment; (2) *remunerative power,* arising from control over material resources and rewards; and (3) *normative power,* arising from the management and distribution of symbolic rewards and penalties.

Involvement means the actor's emotional and evaluative orientation toward the subject of action. Etzioni distinguishes three types of involvement by the degree of approval or disapproval in the actor: *moral involvement,* meaning strong approval; *alienative involvement,* meaning strong disapproval; and *calculative involvement,* meaning weak involvement, whether of approval or disapproval.

According to Etzioni's review of past research, there is an adaptive relationship between pairs of these typological classifications: coercive power with alienative involvement, remunerative power with calculative involvement, and normative power with moral involvement. The exercise of one specific form of power is most effective in mobilizing organizational members who manifest a specific form of involvement. When subordinates express only calculative involvement, elites exercise utilitarian power. When subordinates indicate moral involvement, elites apply normative power.

In my analysis of investigative activities, I eliminate the combination of coercive power and alienative involvement. In alienative involvement, the participant outwardly displays compliance in actions, but his involvement is totally negative. The police organization does not use force to keep members, and those who feel only negative orientation toward police work will sooner or later move out of the force.

If aggressive problematic actions have a character of moral involvement, we should examine what normative controls the detectives perceive. If aggressive actions are merely calculative, in the sense of that term as used by Etzioni, then we should examine to which remunerative controls the detectives respond.

Following this approach, the question of whether the involvement driving aggressive activity by detectives is characterized as moral or calculative is extremely important to the nature of our explanation.

Here, moral involvement will indicate a high degree of approval in the emotional and evaluative orientation to the subject. Therefore, even where an aggressive action is problematic, if the detective acts with confidence about the legality and legitimacy of the action and believes that the action is a natural responsibility, and if he feels satisfaction simply in carrying it out, the involvement in this case may be termed moral. In such a case, the detectives may not deny that taking such aggressive action would be appropriate as a technical means of efficiently resolving the case, but engaging in such action is based upon an evaluation that the action is right rather than upon a sense that it is technically appropriate. Thus we will not find large differences in such conduct between cases. If detectives always take aggressive actions, their working conditions will become very stressful. Therefore, the typical detective who shows moral involvement also must have a high degree of self-acceptance of the general situation surrounding work and private life.

On the other hand, calculative involvement means a weak degree of emotional and evaluative orientation, whether this be of approval or disapproval. Where an aggressive investigative action is not accompanied by much confidence in its legality or legitimacy but is made based upon a decision that the action is a technical means of efficiently resolving the case at hand, this may be termed calculative involvement. In such a case, even where an action is taken in which at first glance the detective appears to be morally involved, the detective may not report feeling satisfied with the action. Further, if he does not demonstrate strong approval for aggressive investigative action, we can hypothesize that a detective will not show acceptance of such action as a natural part of his job because the work condition deteriorates his personal situation.

These are two typical complexes in the perceptions of the detectives derived from application of Etzioni's typology of involvement to problematic aggressive actions by detectives. The description in part 2 indicates that calculative involvement is more common than moral involvement among the detectives I observed.

Regarding the means of control through the exercise of power, normative control by means of normative power is that which operates through the management and distribution of symbolic rewards and penalties which have normative meaning to the person who is the object of control (Etzioni, 1968: 397). To the detectives, this may refer to control through management of a commendation, the reputation and status as a master detective, a career as an investigative specialist, and the position of an actual leader in the investigative processes.

On the other hand, utilitarian control over the exercise of remunerative power means control over material resources and rewards (Etzioni, 1968: 397). Needless to say, to detectives working within a salary structure which corresponds to rank and seniority, there is no utilitarian control through management of financial rewards. Therefore, in the context of my research, any reward that is of more than symbolic significance may be considered a utilitarian reward. A higher rank or assignment to the city or station of one's choice may be considered a utilitarian reward. Assignment to a large city such as Sapporo is particularly valued by detectives where they can then build a private house and provide their children with a better education. Since they are relocated from one station to another every few years, and transfer to a remote place disrupts established family life, relocation is their critical concern. Of course, it is not only the prospect of reward, but also the prospect that such reward may be delayed or withheld that serves as an effective means of utilitarian control. When an officer is presently assigned to a station or city that fulfills his expectations, it is the prospect of losing this "reward" that serves as a means of utilitarian control. Given our understanding of the aggressive actions shown in part 2, the form and level of utilitarian control perceived by the detectives should be a special object of our attention.

We should also be aware of an apparently paradoxical but not unexpected situation. It is not necessary for the elite to exercise controls in order to maintain aggressive investigations by detectives who already have reached the level of moral involvement. Constant engagement in aggressive investigations already is internalized, and a supervisor will accomplish his objective without further action.

The position of a supervisor confronted with detectives who exhibit merely calculative involvement is more difficult. These detectives are not convinced of the legality and legitimacy of aggressive investigations, nor do they take pleasure in the process of investigation. Thus, the supervisor who requests aggressive investigations must exercise some utilitarian control. Of course, because of the very nature of these rewards, opportunities for field supervisors to manipulate the utilitarian rewards specified above are not common; thus, they generally will use negative rather than positive controls. They may exercise these by stressing that as supervisor they are in a position to have an effect upon the distribution of utilitarian rewards, particularly through their recommendations for promotion and relocation if their expectations are not met. Because negative controls are less effective than positive controls, we may hypothesize that the tone of the expressions of supervisors with only negative controls at their disposal tends to be extremely strong.

I have characterized the dominant form of detectives' involvement in aggressive investigative actions as calculative, on the basis of their lack of confidence in the legitimacy of their own behavior. Before proceeding to the main body of this part, in this chapter I check the validity of this characterization through analysis of detectives' attitudes to other aspects of their work. I do not mean, of course, that no detectives showed moral involvement. I certainly encountered such detectives and will describe them in the first section. Nevertheless, I believe that most detectives manifested calculative involvement. I will present evidence for this conclusion in the subsequent sections.

1. Moral Involvement in Aggressive Investigations

a. Desire for Unrestrained Aggressive Behavior

Moral involvement of the detectives exists when they wait expectantly for a case to break. For morally involved detectives, a busier day is a better day. An interesting finding in this regard is a perception at the police academy that some people "attract" cases. A student in the assistant inspector class said, "Some officers really attract cases.... It is true that you get a feeling that maybe something will break tonight." Another student said, in his evaluation of an instructor, "He is an instructor blessed with cases."

I find this idea of a case as a blessing even with officers assigned to duty at a police box. For example, in Case 3, a squad leader was enthused when he made an arrest, "Professor, you brought a case with you.... Today is our day, eh?" When his deputy squad leader said, "Sweating away writing up papers for someone else's case, I don't know what to say," he was complaining that as a patrol officer, he rarely has a chance to make an arrest and is required to hand over the case to detectives.

After transfer to this station and assignment to patrol duty, another complained about how boring patrol duty was, indicating the individual's desire to have direct contact with cases.

Detectives want to be "blessed with cases." A detective who does not "attract" cases is made to feel inferior. For example, in one case a theft crime detective confided, "Without a case I hated coming in to work, to tell the truth."

Therefore, when the opportunity arrives, detectives feel that they must "make something out of it." Those who are first associated with an investigation hope to continue with it to the end. In Case 9, when a supervisor suggested letting the sections decide between themselves which one would handle the case, a detective responded, "Let's assign it to the section on duty watch. Otherwise their morale will suffer."

Detectives remember well the cases in which they have been involved. In one instance a detective said, "I just remembered; Yamamoto, isn't he the guy that stole a camera from a construction site?... I remember because I did the interrogation in that case."

Naturally, detectives who "attract" cases have many suspects in custody. The more one has in custody, the higher morale becomes. In the words of one theft crime detective, "With someone in custody, your head clears, and you have spirit. No one in custody, and you feel low."

The result of this desire for cases is to foster competition among detectives. Ericson (1981: 60–63) has reported that in Canada "general investigation detectives did not compete for cases in an effort to obtain individual credit" and "the general rule of cooperation" prevails "within the general investigation units." Japanese police detectives appear to be more competitive. At the police academy, an assistant inspector student said, "When you recognize the M.O. of a guy with a record, you act as if you don't know it in front of other detectives." If another detective arrests a person you suspected, "you feel like he 'got your thief,' because you feel you are in competition." In fact, an instructor of a patrolmen's class had to warn, "Officers must not conceal information out of competition for accomplishments."

Detectives themselves acknowledge the existence of this sort of competition. A theft crime detective said, "There is a circle, an information network of each detective, made up particularly of young patrol officers picked by him. You don't give any news out about yourself; you might get clobbered for it." This practice has been described by Ames (1981: 131) as "cultivating the field." Ames reports that the field of a detective "consists of various types of collaborators or tipsters," including ex-convicts, just as "former suspects being kept 'on the line'" are reported by Ericson (1981: 120) in Canada. My data indicate that a detective's tipsters also include young patrol officers working for him on a personal basis.

This competition is visible between the sections as well. At the Eastern Police Station, it was explained, "There is competition between the First and Second Sections [of theft crimes] in a positive sense." In Case 9, the detectives of one section complained to another, "Because you put two into custody last night, we may take this case over if it's alright. Looks like you're getting someone in every other night, so *your* record is the only one that gets polished!" In an investigation report I saw in Case 10, although another unit's detective was connected with the case from the outset, the report listed a detective from the report-writer's own unit.

It also appears that there is competition between police stations. For example in Case 10, a detective explained, "The Northern Station and the Eastern Station are fighting over him [a single suspect]."

Detectives are irritated when another station outstrips their investigation. For example, in Case 9, in response to the request to prepare papers about a suspect arrested by the headquarter Mobile Investigation Squad, a detective at the Eastern Station responded, "It was the Mobile Squad that caught him, and the suspect in custody and the witnesses have all been taken over there, so the Mobile Squad should take statements."

The Mobile Squad far exceeds the investigative strength of detectives at police stations. An executive at the Hokkaido Police Headquarters proudly told me, "How can their record be that good? They're first in Hokkaido and in the nation as well." However, the attitude of the field detectives toward the Mobile Squad is replete with animosity. When one detective was transferred to the squad, another exclaimed, "Star Squad! Number One in arrests!" The jealousy was clear when a detective moaned, "Damn, the squad's done it to us again," after it had arrested a thief his section had flushed out.

Detectives who engage in such competition crave praise. "Detectives are lovable and foolish," a theft crime detective said. "Flatter them and they feel like working their tails off for the boss." The boss who makes a detective feel like "working one's tail off" is one who typically approves of the aggressive style of investigation by detectives. Supervisors who urge procedural restraint, paperwork without error, and organization-wide cooperative investigations are not at all popular among this type of detective. "If in the end the Detective Department chief does not approve of me, I plan to turn on him," a detective proudly told me. "I work with the idea that it is not the policemen's police, but the citizens' police." The "policemen's police" refers to an investigative officer who acts with procedural restraint out of fear that the reputation of the police will be damaged. The "citizen's police" refers to an investigative officer who plunges forward with bold investigations in response to citizens who demand the arrest of criminals and the reparation of injuries. Other detectives most respected by this type of detective are those who work around the restrictive directions of the supervisors, utilize methods they feel to be the most effective, and single-handedly promote aggressive investigations.

This type of detective takes pride in hard work and commitment. "In all of the government agencies, I guess it must be the detectives who are the hardest working," they say.

In a sergeants' class at the police academy, an instructor said, "What motivates the citizen to make a loss report? It is [merely]...the restoration of the goods.... But the sense of justice of the police officer is not satisfied simply by restoration of the goods."

These attitudes comprise the "guts" (*konjo* in Japanese) of detectives. As a student in a class of assistant inspectors said:

> Pride leads the way. This lacking, guts are lacking. You're off the mark if you just putter along satisfied with reaching your own objectives. The test of whether you have "guts" hangs on whether it digs at you when another station carries off what you did not. If they pursue

their case well, and the arrestee is taken from you, it pisses you off. This is not because your case clearance rate does not rise, but because your pride is hurt. I want guys with "guts" as detectives.

A theft crime detective explained, "Guts is number one." Older, retired detectives often complain, "The young officers today do not have 'guts.'"

The detectives with "guts" take satisfaction in the act of investigation. Their attitude demands that they arrest the suspect with their own hands, extract confessions, resolve multiple separate offenses, and secure a strict penalty. This is not due to an expectation of economic rewards, nor is it a reflexive effort to raise arrest rates, nor is it necessary that actions be considered appropriate by citizens. This type of detective has in his personality a strong sense of aggressive investigative action as expressive behavior. It is only natural that supervisors who do not regulate detectives' actions in detail are the most popular among them. If one wants aggressive investigative actions, it is sufficient to provide normative encouragement.

The survey makes it clear that most detectives find satisfaction in being detectives. In Table 11.1, they indicated they are satisfied with the department to which they are currently assigned (item 1). Items 2 and 3 show that most detectives are proud of getting at the truth of the cases in which they are involved and of knowing the reality of crimes and criminals.

Table 11.1   Attitudes about Their Work

LEVEL OF SATISFACTION IN DEPARTMENT ASSIGNMENT

1. Are you satisfied with the department to which you are currently assigned?

Yes	Undecided	No	Total Respondents
65.9	12.2	22.0	(41)

PRIDE IN UNDERSTANDING THE ACTUAL STATE OF CRIMES, CRIMINAL ACTIVITY, AND CRIMINALS

2. Do you feel that detectives, more than judges, prosecutors, and attorneys who handle these matters, understand the concrete truth about the cases they handle?

Yes	Undecided	No	Total Respondents
66.7	26.2	7.1	(42)

3. Do you feel that such detectives understand the actual circumstances of crime and criminals best?

Yes	Undecided	No	Total Respondents
66.7	19.0	14.3	(42)

Table 11.1 *Continued*

THE MEANING OF INTERROGATION AND INTERROGATION SKILLS TO DETECTIVES THEMSELVES

4. Do you believe that the life of the police officer is in interrogation skills?

Yes	Undecided	No	Total Respondents
54.8	28.6	16.7	(42)

Item 4 demonstrates that a majority do believe that interrogation skills are the soul of the detective.

In summary, many detectives feel that they are evaluated in terms of the excellence of their skills—perceiving themselves, so to speak, as craftsmen—and find satisfaction in the realization of the craftsman's skill. We may infer from this that they have great confidence in the image of people and society that they have acquired through their work.

b. Harsh Working Conditions

Evidence of detectives' moral involvement in investigations becomes stronger when we examine their working conditions.

A morally involved detective's sense of duty is not commanded by the supervisors, but arises spontaneously. As one supervisor stated, "It isn't something ordered from above, but independent duty that is precious." Without orders, detectives will remain at the station for after-hours interrogations and head out for voluntary accompaniments and arrests. One day, despite the fact that they were not on duty, five theft crime detectives remained and carried on with document preparation and similar jobs. The supervisor asked, "Going to eat?" and the others declined, answering, "No thank you—we can't eat [because we are too busy]."

A full accounting of the duty record would call for quite a substantial overtime bonus, but in reality there is a "cut-off payment" in the budget system. For example, a supervisor announced that for a certain month for detectives "the total of overtime pay will be 2,000,000 yen [approximately $6,670 U.S.] for this month—about two thirds of the amount in months past. It will be paid next month. You are notified that it will be less than in months past."

Under these circumstances, it is not surprising that the actual record of overtime shows less time than was actually spent on duty. For example, I overheard the following exchange:

- Detective: But even if I turn it in, it won't all be paid, will it?
- Supervisor: I do turn in all of it.
- Detective: But if I have ten hours of overtime, only about half of it...
- Supervisor: You couldn't have ten hours of overtime.
- Detective: Just supposing.
- Supervisor: Stop talking to me about what-ifs.

Under these circumstances, detectives do not even attempt to maintain a record of overtime hours put in. The work planned each day for individual detectives is set out in the "Investigators' Scheduling Ledger" by the supervisors. The detective writes in a description of the operation and of its results in response to the supervisor's instruction. However, there are those who will not enter the time if it is beyond duty hours. A detective explained, "In the end, the Detective Department head looks it over and puts in the numbers." An elder detective said, "I have plenty of salary, so I don't file any requests."

Overtime is usually a continuation of regular duty, but detectives are also sometimes called in after returning home. A supervisor told me that "aside from sickness, school time [training at the police academy], and private trips...you must be prepared to respond to an emergency call to the station." Therefore, there was an admonition, on the occasion of a going-away party for a transferee, that "we will be stuck if there is a late call, so please avoid a party afterward." The station must always be notified of one's location. When a call is put out, the officers respond promptly.

Once every six days, detectives are assigned to overnight duty. They sometimes continue to work after the overnight assignment. Around noon one hears, "I was assigned to it yesterday, so I'm a bit sleepy," or "I got back from the scene at five o'clock this morning, so I am too sleepy." In addition, continuing investigations are sometimes ordered on days off.

A detective generally cannot get a day off with pay. "Last summer, I couldn't take a day off," a police academy student noted. "Even if I can't take time off myself, I see that my subordinates get vacation time. No one takes time off for themselves." Among the detectives as well:

Vacations! You can't get time off. Even just one day off, you'll be told it's impossible. The station chief talks like we should take days off, but it gets tied up and dies somewhere in the administration.

The working conditions of the detectives may be described as almost cruelly strict. Ericson (1981: 44) has reported for Canada that "detectives were able to use 'credits' they had obtained in working overtime in order to take time off from their regular shift schedule." There can be no such arrangement in Japan. However, the detectives continue in their work whether or not the supervisors clearly demand them to do so. In appearance at least, this is a spontaneous response to duty. From these circumstances, it can be inferred that detectives derive satisfaction from conducting aggressive investigations.

2. Dissatisfaction and Criticism about Working Conditions

The previous evidence may give the impression that moral commitment by the detectives to aggressive investigations is the dominant form of work involvement. However, examination of other data makes it clear that this cannot be so.

First, there are complaints regarding working conditions. Ames (1981: 201) has reported the resentment of lower-ranking police officers about unpaid overtime:

> There are irritations within the police organization that work against police solidarity.... One of these is overtime pay, which is not based strictly on hours worked, but is apportioned to police stations and divided among police officers according to a set pattern. Young officers...are particularly bothered by the amount of overtime demanded in police work.

I found similar attitudes at the Eastern Police Station. A theft crime detective bitterly complained:

> I will submit this as overtime, but that doesn't mean I'll be paid for it. In any case, the money is limited. If you charged correctly for it all, I think it would come to a large sum of money.... It really should be paid out, but in the end it doesn't come around. That's strange, isn't it? We just keep on quietly slaving away.

There are signs of dissatisfaction with orders for in-station on-call time, as well. For example, in the case of a strike by a public employee's union, the detectives were mobilized and an order was given that they were to stay on station alert. After 9:30 p.m. when the station alert was extended, a low murmur of discontent could be heard among the remaining detectives.

There is also discontent in regard to emergency calls. For example, "We are called on every occasion. They could exclude those of us who have just returned from an overnight shift."

The same is true of continuing investigations. In one case a detective complained about an order for continuing tails and stakeouts in shifts, stating, "It's tight. On outside duty or in the headquarters there are vacations, which would be fine. But this [detective work] is tight."

Nor do detectives like continued duty after night watch. "I would really like to go home, but...," a detective admitted. He continued:

> If I were a Detective Department head it would be different. But [merely] as an assistant inspector, I want to go home. If I were a Detective Department head, I would say, "I'll stay, so you guys go home." At night, your efficiency isn't going to improve. Even if you stay, you don't get much work done.

Detectives complain about the impossibility of getting paid vacation days. A detective who was retiring told me, "Write all you want about the vacation situation. There is no order 'Don't take time off,' but you can't get time off, and nobody takes time off." The atmosphere is not conducive to filing for vacation days, and although there is no order against taking a vacation, the detectives feel a policy exists against applying for vacations.

On the other hand, detectives sometimes are forced to take paid vacation days irrespective of their own plan:

> They tell us they will give us a vacation, but they are just giving us our regular paid vacation days. It's strange. "Take a vacation" means "Use your paid vacation days when I order." And I guess the guy at the top figures he has given you a vacation that way.

Of course, what this detective wants is to take a real vacation, at a time when he really needs or wants it.

True, there are those detectives who say, "Even if there are vacation days, I don't know what to do with them." But, there are others who admit, "I concealed my real feelings about my job, with so much overtime and without any vacation, because of what they call the guts, or the pride, of the detective."

This evidence, thus, indicates that there are detectives with many complaints about the system who do not accept it as a matter of course. If detectives put up with the system despite their criticisms and dissatisfactions, there must be very effective control imposed upon them.

Dissatisfaction and criticism are leveled at the basic structure of the police organization, in one area in particular: the rule stating that all decisions are made according to rank within the organization. Detectives often refer to their organization as a "police society." They mean a society in which decision-making depends entirely upon rank. "When policemen talk, what really counts is rank," a police academy instructor stated. A crime lab officer complained, "In the police, the lab officer is pathetic, because what matters is rank." A detective acknowledged, "It probably looks feudal from the outside. Obedient to the end."

There are supervisors who speak about this proudly. A supervisor told me, "To the end, rank cuts sharply. We carry it to the full extreme. If I gave just one word, it would be a piece of cake to cover up the truth from you." He then assured me that such an order would never be given.

But it is with this "sharp cut" of rank that dissatisfaction particularly begins. "It's a totally hierarchical society. In the end, we have to work based on the orders supplied to us," a theft crime detective complained. Those who are dissatisfied with this arrangement probably experience moments in which they would like to quit. A detective noted, "When I said, 'Maybe I'll quit,' my wife told me to quit in an instant. Even my wife knows how it feels to live in a police society." Another responded, "This should be a place that is easy to work in even without a union [as it is right now]. This year there will be a lot of people quitting out of dissatisfaction with personnel changes."

Bayley (1976: 81) has described how Japanese police officers are discouraged from criticizing the organization:

> In small ways too [*sic*] criticism of the organization is discouraged among policemen. For instance, there are no formal grievance procedures.... Several times, however, junior officers have confessed that they found the organization's view of itself intimidating. Having been told almost daily that an individual with "police spirit" does not count his days of holidays or pay much attention to the precise amount of his pay check, policemen are reluctant to express dissatisfaction about these matters to superiors.

Likewise detectives at the Eastern Station fear criticizing their "police society." A good example is the response of detectives to the announcement by the National Police Agency about a new system in which the department compensates officers who are at home on alert. This proposal was very unpopular among the detectives. A detective started to criticize it, saying, "Even if they're talking about home alert payments...," but he immediately stopped. "Nope [I can't talk]!" he said. "If I speak out, it will just take more time. And then, too, you will write it down." Another detective told me, "Look, if I say too much...it's police society," and cut himself off.

There is dissatisfaction and criticism in regard to personnel matters as well. Ames (1981: 192) has reported the following particularly about transfers in Japan:

Transfers are a subject of keen interest and rumors within the police because of the uprooting and isolating effect they have on the lives of police officers and their families. Transfers occur en masse in the spring and tension mounts as the time approaches. Police officers speculate whether they will be transferred and try to read meaning into new assignments.

Officers I met in Sapporo complained about other things as well. At the police academy, for instance, one instructor said:

> I want you to write down that personnel matters are decided in absolute secrecy. You are not assured of the course you have set your hopes on. You can't say we have the right man for the right job. Even in the academy, there are some who are terribly disappointed.

At the Eastern Police Station, upon seeing a list of personnel to be transferred there, a supervisor complained, "Ah, this is trouble. Nobody to do lab work is there. What a mess." A detective explained the problem to me, "A young man from Tokyo University moves in as superintendent of police and makes personnel decisions without understanding the feelings of the common cop on the beat."

Reassignments at unexpected times or to unexpected locations are bitterly resented. I observed one officer who without warning received a transfer to a remote location. He was unable to conceal his shock and talked with his colleagues, trying to understand the reason for the transfer. In the end, he went dejectedly to his new assignment, without taking his family with him.

For some detectives transfer is a kind of surprise attack, and if one asks about departments or places to which they would like to transfer, they are wary in their response. After the announcement of transfers one day, it arose as a subject of conversation during watch. But at that point someone warned, "When somebody says, 'If I were transferred...,' they figure, 'Well, let's transfer him!' and he's off to some godforsaken place or other." The officers quietly changed the subject.

Naturally, everyone can't be transferred to the location of his own choosing. One reason is that the greater number of officers aspire to a transfer to the large cities. In Hokkaido, the chief of the Eastern Station said:

> Hopes concentrate on Sapporo. For example, within the jurisdiction of the Asahikawa Regional Headquarters [in northern Hokkaido], eighty percent of the officers hope for Sapporo. Here the greatest number want Sapporo. But the five stations making up the Sapporo force are fixed at 1,300 men. We can't satisfy everyone.

He continued:

> You move from Sapporo to Kushiro [in eastern Hokkaido] and there is
> a jinx that keeps you from forgetting Sapporo for a good ten years. At
> the Nakatonbetsu Station [in the Kushiro region], with only thirty six
> officers on the staff, there is nothing but a night time high school, so
> the officers send their kids to Asahikawa and Sapporo.

On the other hand, an officer sometimes desires a transfer. "When you
are being transferred for a promotion, there is a strong chance that you will
get to go where you want," one detective explained. One supervisor ordered
to transfer said with satisfaction at his going-away party, "Yes, the people
upstairs think carefully about transfers. They match us carefully."

Sometimes a person who is dissatisfied by personnel decisions while
on first-line duty will change mind when he is later assigned to the personnel
department. An assistant inspector at the Hokkaido Police Headquarters said:

> When I was with the first-line, and saw personnel from the outside, I
> figured that the personnel department was an irresponsible place, just
> matching up the number of bodies needed. But no, it really is a big job.
> It isn't completely successful, but they try to assign people who are
> generally compatible with one another. And now there is a strictly
> unofficial prior consultation, and they inquire into the circumstances of
> the person himself.

Nevertheless, the detectives' dissatisfaction with personnel, particularly with
transfers, is quite strong.

Survey data support these observational materials. Table 11.2 deals
with working conditions.

Table 11.2   Attitudes about Working Conditions

1. Do you believe that the time spent in overtime duty is accurately submitted?

Yes	Undecided	No	Total Respondents
30.2	16.3	53.5	(43)

2. Do you believe that pay for overtime accurately matches the time submitted?

Yes	Undecided	No	Total Respondents
9.3	20.9	69.8	(43)

3. Do you believe that, even if there is pay for overtime, the amount of overtime duty ordered should be reduced?

Yes	Undecided	No	Total Respondents
27.9	18.6	53.5	(43)

Table 11.2   *Continued*

4. Do you agree with the statement, "We should have a fixed work schedule in order to know in advance when will we be able to take a vacation?"

Yes	Undecided	No	Total Respondents
65.1	18.6	16.3	(43)

5. Do you believe that police officers should be able to exercise the right to paid vacation like other people?

Yes	Undecided	No	Total Respondents
95.2	4.8	0.0	(42)

6. Do you believe that currently there is an atmosphere that makes one hesitate to file for paid vacation?

Yes	Undecided	No	Total Respondents
67.4	11.6	20.9	(43)

7. Do you believe that even when one finally gets a vacation or a day off, it is often interrupted by a call to duty?

Yes	Undecided	No	Total Respondents
60.5	9.3	30.2	(43)

8. Do you believe that in making calls to duty, the ordinary working conditions should be maintained, and duty calls should be used minimally, only when necessary?

Yes	Undecided	No	Total Respondents
58.1	20.9	20.9	(43)

9. Do you believe that, if there is compensation for home alert, it would not bother you if you were assigned to it often?

Yes	Undecided	No	Total Respondents
16.3	9.3	74.4	(43)

10. Do you believe that even if there is compensation for home alert, the ordinary working conditions should be maintained as much as possible?

Yes	Undecided	No	Total Respondents
57.1	23.8	19.0	(42)

11. Do you believe that frequent overtime is correct for the policeman, to be accepted as a matter of course? Or do you believe that while it is not correct, there is no choice, viewed from the perspective of police strength?

Correct	No Choice	Neither	Total Respondents
2.4	92.9	4.8	(42)

Regarding the overtime situation, most detectives do not believe that all overtime hours are submitted by supervisors to the overtime register, nor that overtime pay is issued commensurate with hours turned in. Nevertheless, they accept it as a necessary condition for the resolution of crimes. Nothing can be done about it, they feel.

Aside from overtime, many detectives oppose other aspects of present working conditions. In regard to vacations, most detectives resent that they hesitate to file for vacation time. They believe there should be a scheduled duty system to indicate when they will have vacation. Ninety percent feel that they should have a right to use vacation time at their own discretion.

Regarding calls to duty, most detectives complain that they often are called to duty even on vacation days and a majority feel that calls to duty should be minimized.

Most detectives deny that the home alert problem is solved by compensation, and a majority feel that even if there is compensation, ordinary working conditions should be maintained. The program of payments for home alert is not welcomed by most detectives.

In sum, although many detectives feel that nothing can be done about the need to continue duty beyond normal hours, they do not wish to be on call when they are supposed to be on vacation, or when they are supposed to be off duty.

Table 11.3 inquires about perceptions of and desire for opportunities for more free expression by detectives within the "police society." I divided the subjects of expression into the three categories of "general affairs within the station," "means of proceeding in cases," and "treatment," but the pattern of responses is common to all three. Many detectives say that there are insufficient opportunities for expression and wish for more such opportunities.

Table 11.3   Attitudes about Opportunities for Expression

1. Do you believe that in regard to general affairs within the station, there is sufficient opportunity for patrolmen and sergeants to express themselves and offer suggestions?

Yes	Undecided	No	Total Respondents
27.9	20.9	51.2	(43)

2. Do you believe that, generally speaking, opportunity of this kind should be made available?

Yes	Undecided	No	Total Respondents
66.7	26.2	7.1	(42)

3. Do you believe that in regard to the means of proceeding in actual cases, there is sufficient opportunity for patrolmen and sergeants to express themselves and offer suggestions?

Yes	Undecided	No	Total Respondents
27.9	20.9	51.2	(43)

Table 11.3   *Continued*

4. Do you believe that, generally speaking, opportunity of this kind should be made available?

Yes	Undecided	No	Total Respondents
76.7	18.6	4.7	(43)

5. Do you believe that in regard to treatment within the Hokkaido police force, there is sufficient opportunity for patrolmen and sergeants to express themselves?

Yes	Undecided	No	Total Respondents
14.0	27.9	58.1	(43)

6. Do you believe that opportunity of this kind should be made available?

Yes	Undecided	No	Total Respondents
83.3	11.9	4.8	(42)

Table 11.4 inquires about promotion. Most detectives indicate that striving for promotion is important, although they do not feel that the promotion examination reflects true ability. They also believe that working in some departments is more beneficial as preparation for the examination than working in others, with the General Affairs Department most frequently indicated as the most advantageous place. Most detectives wish that promotion on the basis of seniority and clearance record be expanded. In view of such criticism of the examination and promotion, it is inaccurate to characterize detectives as feeling satisfaction.

Table 11.4   Attitudes about Personnel Matters

1. Do you believe that promotion by examination reflects one's true ability?

Yes	Undecided	No	Total Respondents
18.6	14.0	67.4	(43)

2. Do you believe that preparation for the promotion examination is easier for those in certain departments?

Yes	Undecided	No	Total Respondents
65.1	18.6	16.3	(43)

3. Which of the following is best in this regard?

General Affairs	Security Police	Others	Total
59.3	33.3	7.4	(27)

Note: Respondents to this item are those who answered "yes" to the preceding question.

Table 11.4 *Continued*

4. Do you believe that the road to promotion by seniority should be broadened?

Yes	Undecided	No	Total Respondents
72.1	20.9	7.0	(43)

5. Do you believe that the road to promotion upon one's clearance record should be broadened?

Yes	Undecided	No	Total Respondents
69.8	23.3	7.0	(43)

6. Do you believe that it is extremely important, as police officers, to strive for promotion?

Yes	Undecided	No	Total Respondents
65.1	30.2	4.7	(43)

7. Do you believe that in assigning staff to the various departments of patrol duty, detectives, etc., careful thought is given to the nature of the individual officer?

Yes	Undecided	No	Total Respondents
51.2	27.9	20.9	(43)

8. Do you believe that in assigning officers to the various departments of patrol duty, detectives, etc., more attention should be paid to the desires of the individual officer?

Yes	Undecided	No	Total Respondents
88.4	11.6	0.0	(43)

9. Do you believe that in regard to transfers, careful thought is given to the circumstances of the individual officer?

Yes	Undecided	No	Total Respondents
7.0	30.2	62.8	(43)

10. Do you believe that in regard to transfers, more attention should be paid to the desires of the individual officer?

Yes	Undecided	No	Total Respondents
76.7	18.6	4.7	(43)

11. Do you believe that university graduates are treated too well?

Yes	Undecided	No	Total Respondents
11.6	30.2	58.1	(43)

The same basic pattern exists with regard to transfers. Most detectives believe that little thought is given to individual circumstances at the time of transfer and wish that attention be paid to individual desires in assigning and transferring personnel to different departments.

If police detectives value and take pleasure in conducting aggressive investigations, then we might expect that they would overlook dissatisfaction with working conditions, treatment, opportunities for expression, and promotion. They also would believe it unprofessional to engage in criticisms and demands of this kind. Such a morally involved detective would rather hold a positive view about harsh working conditions because they signify the higher status of one's job among various police functions. Table 11.5, however, indicates that few detectives take that posture.

Table 11.5   Attitudes about Expression of Demands, Dissatisfactions, and Criticisms

1. Do you believe that to complain about orders given by one's superior disqualifies one as a police officer?

Yes	Undecided	No	Total Respondents
16.3	32.6	51.2	(43)

2. Do you believe that stating that one wants opportunity for expression and offering suggestions disqualifies one as a police officer?

Yes	Undecided	No	Total Respondents
2.3	30.2	67.4	(43)

3. Do you believe that stating that one wants full payment of allowances disqualifies one as a police officer?

Yes	Undecided	No	Total Respondents
2.4	19.0	78.6	(42)

4. Do you believe that stating that one wants freedom of action outside of duty time disqualifies one as a police officer?

Yes	Undecided	No	Total Respondents
9.3	25.6	65.1	(43)

5. Do you believe that stating that one wants to exercise one's paid vacation days disqualifies one as a police officer?

Yes	Undecided	No	Total Respondents
7.0	16.3	76.7	(43)

6. Do you believe that complaining about the pay disqualifies one as a police officer?

Yes	Undecided	No	Total Respondents
4.7	23.3	72.1	(43)

7. Do you believe that stating that one wants to fully experience the life of an individual citizen disqualifies one as a police officer?

Yes	Undecided	No	Total Respondents
11.6	14.0	74.4	(43)

Table 11.5   *(Continued)*

8. Do you believe that thinking of matters beyond one's assigned duties disqualifies one as a police officer?

Yes	Undecided	No	Total Respondents
11.6	18.6	69.8	(43)

It is clear that detectives are dissatisfied and complain about many issues. Although observational data on some subjects conflict with results of the survey, there is a fundamental consistency between the two. Such dissatisfaction among detectives is a fact, and we should conclude that their investigations are accompanied by these dissatisfactions. Despite these feelings, many detectives appear to conduct aggressive investigations with great zeal. Their dissatisfaction indicates that normative controls are insufficient to explain this conduct.

Although one may say that there is great satisfaction in being a detective compared to other roles in the police organization, answers to one question in the survey indicate that satisfaction in being a police officer is not so great that detectives want their own children to become police officers. When asked, "If you have a boy, or a boy is born to you, would you recommend that he become a police officer who works his way up from patrolman?", 65 percent said no, with only 25 percent saying yes. A similar result also was reported by Bayley (1976: 43) for the Japanese police as a whole. He has said that "few of them want their children to follow in their footsteps." This result makes it hard to believe that moral involvement is dominant even among detectives.

Overall, detectives often expressed despair about their jobs. "Even if I can be called a 'veteran,' all I have done is to suppress my own thoughts, sacrificing my time, charging ahead recklessly.... It is really tough," one told me. "I would have my doubts about the character of anybody who said how happy he was that he became a police officer."

3. Doubts Regarding the Legality of Aggressive Investigations

Not only are many detectives dissatisfied with important aspects of their working conditions, they have doubts about the aggressive mode of investigation that they pursue.

Detectives doubt the propriety of using a search warrant issued for a specific past crime in order to create an opportunity for a warrantless arrest of a new, unknown crime. For example, in bookmaking cases, detectives regularly get search warrants based upon past facts. Then they make a warrantless arrest for a new crime in the location of the search, by picking up the phone and intercepting phone calls from customers. A supervisor worries, "There is a problem with that.... This breaches a confidential communication...for the officer to take incoming calls and use that to prove an offense is not really correct. But if you don't do it that way, you can't catch criminals." Similar tactics are used in investigations of illegal stimulant cases. A search warrant is secured on the basis of past selling, possession, or use. The police use it to enter the residence of the suspect and search for evidence of a new crime. When they find stimulants and related materials, they make a warrantless arrest.

Requiring a urine sample to determine the presence of stimulants is considered questionable. A supervisor stated, "Although in form it is offered voluntarily, that is doubtful. There was a case in the Crime Prevention Department where they said, 'Hey, out with it,' and locked the suspect in the men's room for forty minutes. I would have liked to get a warrant for physical examinations and expert opinions."

It is common for investigations to be particularly aggressive when the suspect is a member of an organized crime syndicate, but doubts are stated in this regard as well. One supervisor said to me:

> Isn't there some problem with the special handling of organized crime cases?... Because the syndicates are professionals at crime, we, for our part, have special techniques that we use. Is there not a problem with saying that because a syndicate is suspected, these methods will be excused...?

Detectives express further doubts about other police activities. They voice concerns about how to define what is a "crime syndicate." "'Crime syndicate,' that's a label tagged on by the police," one detective admitted. "I once was called to the court as a witness. I was asked: 'Crime syndicate' [*boryokudan* in Japanese] and 'racketeer' [*tekiya* in Japanese], how is there any difference? And there really isn't any distinction."

Detectives express doubts regarding arrest. For example, in Case 11, a detective commented, "Is it really necessary to arrest a woman like this? If I were a judge, even if I issued a warrant, I wouldn't grant detention in this case." In Case 3, police doubted the propriety of an emergency arrest of the man with the suspicious truck and steel bars. "It happened between five and nine o'clock, the report came in at ten, and he was spotted at eleven, which means that it's too spread out both in time and in distance." The officer who effected the arrest made this comment on his action. Despite the doubts of the persons directly involved, the courts approved detention in the former case and issued an arrest warrant in the latter.

Doubts also have been expressed regarding the circumstances under which confessions are pursued. A detective admitted:

> You are not going to get a confession out of someone voluntarily. You fool them into it. Plainly put, it is coercion. You won't smoke any cigarettes, you won't eat, we'll stretch out your detention, we'll appeal and you'll be stuck here for two months. Anyway, you don't think anyone is going to step forward and say, "Yes, I stole it," do you?

One detective approached me, saying, "You must be surprised at the difference between law and actual practice, Professor."

Even where detectives appear to practice aggressive investigative methods with enthusiasm, many seem to have an uneasy feeling about them. An organized crime detective said, "Ah, I told you something I shouldn't have. You'll probably write about how we do such and such at the Eastern Police Station." According to their responses to my survey question, "Do you agree with the statement that, 'If one is faithful to the procedural rules, even if efficiency were reduced somewhat by this, this must be accepted'?," 56 percent of detectives said yes, while only 21 percent said no. A majority appear to give priority to procedural propriety over investigative efficiency. Yet it is clear that, in fact, detectives do not always observe the procedures.

Some cause must motivate detectives to conduct the investigations as they do. When a supervisor states, "If you don't do that, you can't catch him," it suggests that there is a control or expectation which places high clearance rates ahead of anything else.

12

Policy and Action of Supervisors

1. Dominant Policy Stance of Supervisors

More than anyone else, supervisors at police stations are in a position to directly influence the detectives with their expectations and controls. Therefore, their attitudes are extremely important factors for explaining the conduct of detectives during investigations. However, the supervisors also are affected by factors within and outside the organization in which they serve.

Because supervisors must request warrants of all kinds from a judge, and because they must transfer a case or ask for detention from a prosecutor, they have direct contact with legal decisions made outside the police organization. In this sense, they must be more concerned with judicial judgments and procedural restraint than the detectives.

In theory, one would expect them to possess the highest respect for investigative procedures required by law. But the reality suggest otherwise.

The general policy of the supervisors is that of restraint. In one interview, a supervisor of many years experience criticized laxity in procedures. "The fuss over the false conviction cases [like those summarized in chapter 1 of this book] is overdue, since the current Code of Procedure has been in force for twenty years," he said. "There are more than a few cases [of abuses] at police stations that never surface. If that is the case, we should be more strict as a general principle." He also cautioned against old habits. "Investigations which are fashioned on experience and out of force of habit are dangerous. No case can be the same as another." "If you do it from experience and cause an irreparable violation of human rights, what are you going to do?

This is what I fear the most." Therefore, supervisors make severe demands upon the section chiefs who have direct contact with detectives. For example, at a meeting of assembled section chiefs, one supervisor cautioned:

> If you don't tell your subordinates about each mistake, they will never learn their jobs. Even if they have experience, if they develop [bad] habits, we are in trouble.

The same supervisor harshly criticized the detectives. "Detectives...there is really nothing you can do with them..." he said. He continued:

> Inside, outside, everyone kisses up to the detective; that's no good. "Work is busy, my time schedule is uncertain, I have to go out nights as well, so I can't study." They say things like that. It isn't so. Because we are professionals, to live like the beat cop at the police box doesn't cut it. I made it to where I am that way [through study]. Then they say that X [his own nickname] is special. But that isn't so. It's written there in the book, and you're okay if you do things that way.

He also criticized the training methods for detectives. For example, he stated, "You don't get anywhere just acquiring things from your superior." In any case, "There is no such thing as being unable to study because you are too busy." One must study "not for the sake of a test, but for the job."

An ideal detective not only must master regulations, one supervisor says, but he also must be conservative and precise with respect to procedures. Supervisors of course demand one ability that is critical for a detective, namely, the skill of arresting criminals. However, that skill does not necessarily mean aggressive pursuit of confessions. A supervisor commented:

> It varies from detective to detective. A guy that uses his head is best at it.... A man that uses his head can make the arrest even if he is put to other things.... They patrol the areas where prowlers are most frequent, do duty questioning and bring them in, too. A detective with ability will make his own materials, do his own research.

Conservatism also is manifested in the duties which he feels supervisors should fulfill. In his view, the duty of the supervisor is:

> Direction of investigations, conducting inquiries for filing warrants, to be at the center of compulsory investigations as judicial police officer. We operate investigations as an organization, so an officer cannot run an investigation on his separate initiative. The supervisor checks on him.

He contemplates, "In the post-war Code of Criminal Procedure, only designated police inspectors can file for arrest warrants. We have to consider why the system was set up this way." According to him, important decisions should not be left to the "impossible" detectives, but should rather be made by supervisors.

There is evidence indicating that such attitudes are common in the organization. For example, one supervisor praised the practice of another supervisor who is trying to use voluntary investigative methods even when one holds an arrest warrant for the suspect:

> This runs counter to the position of recognizing a "command" [from the judge to arrest the suspect] in the arrest warrant; and this reflects Abe's individual nature [in encouraging conservative arrests]. As an organization, we move according to a system of orders, and so the thinking of the supervisors spreads [to other members of the organization].

In Case 17, he commented, "It is our policy not to use the different crime arrest [arrest on the basis of a minor charge with the real intention to investigate another crime]." Another supervisor, in support of this, said, "In an arson case, there was a separate theft offense. But at Abe's direction, we stuck with arson to the end." In regard to the suspect's meeting with the attorney after arrest, another supervisor said, "Abe says to let them meet freely if refusal might cause trouble later on."

Of course, we cannot say that this restraint is entirely the result of commitment to legality. For example, the word "if it might cause trouble later on" indicates a concern not to compromise the case rather than to protect the suspect's rights. Nonetheless, some supervisors demonstrate real commitment. "It's not bad to have at least one investigations supervisor like myself around, is it?" a conservative supervisor boasted. Another supervisor explained his colleague's concern, "His reserve on procedures comes from the fact that he is taking the methods of intellectual crime investigation [about which he knows most] and applying them to forcible crimes as well."

The young supervisor who made this comment also generally emphasizes restraint in investigations. In Case 17, he said, "Police investigations are not, as is commonly thought, a simple sprint to the finish." He criticized one instructor at the police academy as follows:

> The thinking of Instructor X is not common in theory or practice among detectives. He hasn't studied [recent developments]. Please do not take his thinking as the common view. Among detectives, theory and practice like his is not prevalent. It is not so much that he is old fashioned, but because he doesn't study recent developments that he causes problems.

Of course, there are supervisors who do not agree with the policies advocated by these two. In one case, a supervisor said, "If it were me,... I would cart him away. But [other supervisors] would tell me not to rush things; it's depressing. Maybe I'm getting old-fashioned." A theft crime detective cast light on this point, saying, "Our ways are very different from the old way of doing things. In the old days, it was like, 'Hey you, do this!'"

Despite this, a stance of restraint is the dominant policy among supervisors at the Eastern Police Station.

This fact leads to a question: Why are aggressive investigations sometimes ordered by the supervisors who generally expressed a desire for procedural restraint? From the findings presented above, the demands of the supervisors for aggressive investigations do not appear to arise from moral involvement, but exhibit strong characteristics of calculative involvement.

Detectives are supposed to follow supervisors' orders. "Do not fail to perform the orders and directives which are our life. Do not manage things on your own initiative. Take your orders from us," one supervisor instructed at morning orders. From the perspective of the supervisors, detectives are to be admonished against excessively aggressive actions, which may be declared illegal.

In the investigative process, the supervisors will offer comments and at a certain point decide upon the course to pursue. This process can be seen in Case 17. There the supervisor summarized the results of the investigation and evaluated the pattern that had developed, and at the same time lectured on the proper methods of interrogation and the contents of the best form of confession. After this, he pointed out the kind of information that should be turned up later in the investigation.

The supervisors also make the most important decisions at each stage of the investigative process. The most obvious of these is filing for warrants, which cannot take place without the intercession of a supervisor. This decision remains his even if he has already gone home for the day. For example, after 11:10 on the night I was accompanying the outside duty watch, there was a report of an infanticide. Within fifteen minutes, a supervisor arrived at the station. His special responsibility brought him dashing in. A theft crime detective explained, "Only he can file for a warrant." Detectives also will call the supervisors at home to ask for orders. For example, in Case 10, the detective called the supervisor at home at about 7:35 p.m. to ask permission to make an emergency arrest.

Supervisors sometimes make decisions about warrants that run counter to the opinions of the detectives. For example, in one case a theft crime detective complained:

> There is a witness by the name of Honda. But the fingerprints don't match. There is circumstantial evidence, but we can't get an arrest warrant with just that. The supervisor won't get it for me.

The decision whether to proceed from a voluntary to a compulsory investigation is always made by a supervisor. In fact, there is cross-checking of this decision among the supervisors. For example, in Case 10, a Detective Department head asked for the approval by the assistant station chief of his decision to confine a suspect.

Such checking also takes place at the stage of voluntary investigations. For example, in one case a supervisor informed a theft crime detective that "Abe [the superior to the speaker] has given his O.K. to a voluntary appearance."

Interrogation also takes place under the guidance of the supervisors. For example, nearly all of the detectives were assembled and assigned to the investigation of an illegal strike by a public employee's union. The primary duty of the detectives was to question the members of the union based upon their voluntary appearance. The detectives went to work more lightheartedly than in ordinary cases, saying such things as, "Hey, it's out [a statement is obtained], it's out, this one talks too!" "And talk and talk." To ascertain that there were no errors, their report was reviewed by the section heads, the Detective Department chiefs, and the assistant station chief.

Supervisors seldom conduct interrogations themselves, although they readily can learn about the situation within the interrogation room. At the Eastern Police Station, detectives work in a large open space, and the interrogation rooms face one side of it. The Detective Department chief sits in the center of the detectives' office, so he can see all entries to and exits from the interrogation room. If voices are raised a little, what is said will easily reach his ears. Moreover, whatever the method of interrogation, it will be reported to him in detail.

Supervisors also must question judgments of the detectives. For example, when a detective attempted to apply the law against carrying swords to a suspect carrying a jackknife, a supervisor gently reproved him.

The supervisors also often visit the scene of a crime, especially in cases of forcible crimes and those involving fire. Even with a simple fire, arson is always a possibility, and I most frequently met supervisors at fire scenes.

At times, a supervisor's control extends beyond the field of investigative activity. When several detectives are reassigned and moved out or in, for example, half the detectives are assigned to assist them in moving, and the remaining half are assigned to rearranging the offices of the Detective Departments. In this case, one supervisor directed not only the detectives to assist with unpacking, but their wives as well.

However, as noted earlier, the supervisors who order strict restraint in investigations were relatively new in their positions at the time of the research. They may be termed a new breed. Although they form a dominant group at the Eastern Police Station, they may not make up a majority of field supervisors in Hokkaido or in the whole country. One special characteristic of this type of supervisor is that he studies a great deal. One supervisor asked me, "Is this book good?" and asked for my comments on the two volumes of a festschrift for a leading criminal law professor and on a volume about the criminogenic environment in a series on city planning. According to him, "Since I reached my current rank, a few years have passed, and soon I will take the examination [for the next rank], but I won't [be able to] read the books all at once, so I want to learn a little at a time as I go along." He added, "What we read mostly is books written by detectives, so our perspective gets narrow."

The supervisors strive to regulate the actions of the detectives both in general and in detail; however, it is impossible to give direct instructions to all detectives on the staff. Ordinarily, then, the supervisors give their orders to the section heads, and only where necessary directly to the lower-echelon detectives.

Orders to the section chiefs by the supervisors are very strict. Even casual request for a search warrant will be criticized. One supervisor related:

> I stopped...a request for a warrant...in a case where there was no cause for arrest. It was a theft of just 10,000 yen [approximately $33 U.S.]. There is a provision in the Code of Criminal Procedure which imposes special arrest requirements for so trivial an offense. He just called the family on the telephone once [and found that they wouldn't cooperate in a voluntary appearance]. Can you call that a cause for arrest? If the section chief is involved [in such a wrong judgment], there will be problems. If the subordinates ask for an arrest, and if the section chief does not act in a restrained manner, there will be problems.

Commonly, there is a demand that procedures be appropriate and conform to law. One supervisor said:

> Pay attention and take care that investigative procedures do not lose their appropriateness. "First get the proof, then get the man," be constantly attentive to this. Even things which are not illegal may cause trouble if they are inappropriate. You must act rationally, legally, appropriately. I want you to pay constant attention to these points.

There is also criticism regarding delayed or incomplete preparation of paperwork. One supervisor said:

> Sometimes investigation reports come in later than they ought to. I have received a report from a March case on my desk in July. And that

was an [easy] case of theft within the family, where detectives have received documents from the suspect's bank, and it still hasn't been cleared up.

Demanding prompt preparation of investigation papers, he said:

> Incomplete investigation papers catch the eye. They come up even from the section chiefs—what the hell is this? What are you, blind? Checking things carefully is supposed to be your, section chief's job! If you mess up people's names, next they'll be saying, "Ah, that's the sort of work they do at the Eastern Station"! The [headquarters] Detective Bureau chief meets with the prosecutor four times each month. And if papers are prepared carelessly for the prosecutor, he's going to tell the chief that the Eastern Station is hopeless.

Thus, the first demand made of the section chiefs is proper procedure. On this they are to make no compromise with the detectives and insist on procedural restraint.

The supervisors ask that the section chiefs stand in for them. According to one supervisor:

> In giving orders to the detectives on duty in a case requiring representation of the Detective Department chief or the assistant station chief, the section chief will always proceed and represent them; then the section chief will contact both the Detective Department chief and the assistant station chief. If the section chief doesn't go out, they can't give orders.

They also are required to convert the general orders they receive into concrete directives for the detectives. One supervisor said, "We don't have any use for a section chief who just parrots what was said to him. We would skip over the section chief and give the order [ourselves]."

Section chiefs are required to be tough with those below them. For example:

> Even when a subordinate comes in and asks for an arrest, the section chief has to be calm.... The job of the sergeant is to guide the patrolmen while he works with them. If you leave things to them, we have trouble.... The section chief has to be a bastard. If you don't berate your subordinates for every mistake, they will never learn their jobs. Even if they have experience, we are in trouble if they develop [bad] habits.

Supervisors strive to keep the actions of detectives under their control. Underlying their demand upon the section chiefs for strict procedural restraint of the detectives there is somewhat of a feeling of distrust. "Detectives, there is really nothing you can do with them," one supervisor told me. One detective had written down a wrong provision of the Criminal Code in an arrest record. "And the section chief's seal was on that; he sealed it with his eyes closed." "Adachi [this section chief] was a renowned sergeant at the Western Station, but when he made section chief, he became quiet," a supervisor complained. "It's not good to badger your subordinates, but...it is all right to be strict."

Even if supervisors consistently maintained procedural restraint, and even if the section chiefs did their jobs well, it would be impossible to oversee all of the actions of lower-echelon detectives. Unavoidably, one must rely upon their spontaneous obedience. In Case 17, a supervisor told a detective, "I explained it to the prosecutor just as you say. There is nothing I can do about it but just trust you." "Still seems like you don't trust me," the detective responded.

However, even if complete control is impossible, supervisors strive mightily to maintain correct procedures. Sanders (1977: 45) describes the situation in the United States: "[T]he manner in which a routine investigation was conducted did not depend on anything these officers [lieutenants and captains] did." Ericson (1981: 11, 56) has reported that in Canada "detective work can be conducted away from the watchful eye of police superordinates" and emphasized "difficulties in supervision of line member activity." The situation in Japan seems to be different.

Bayley (1976: 62–63) has described the close supervision of Japanese patrol officers by their supervisors, saying that "[f]or all but the most routine events, a sergeant or senior patrolman will come to the scene minutes after initial response. The chief of a station's patrol section monitors radio communications...." My data indicates that contrary to the practice in North America, Japanese detectives are even more closely supervised than Bayley suggests for patrol officers. In forcible crime, for example, at least the Detective Department chief at the rank of inspector usually rushes to the scene with detectives. Even when detectives have an arrest warrant to proceed, they call into the station and ask for permission of a supervisor. Ames (1981: 188) has reported that "[w]henever there is an incident or a crime of any consequence [in Japan]..., the commanding officer—police chief, section chief, or corps commander—is always notified, even in the middle of the night, and he assumes control of the situation and makes all the necessary decisions." My data fits this description.

Most supervisors I observed were very conscientious in maintaining close supervision. And because of this, it is instructive to examine some cases in which they fail to maintain procedural restraint.

2. Reactions of Section Chiefs

When supervisors stress restraint, the extent which they succeed in securing it from detectives depends largely upon the section chiefs. As we have seen, the supervisors place heavy demands upon the section chiefs. In truth, conferences between the supervisors and the section chiefs are a prime example of "emperor's wish, underling's action." In advance of a conference, one supervisor said of the section chiefs attending, "They're lax; we're thinking of kicking them out." After the conference, another supervisor told me, "We are strict. It's because we get paid for this."

In the following exchange between supervisors and a section chief, whose errors in a statistical table were criticized, we can see the pressure he is placed under to relay harsh instructions and yet maintain the morale of his direct subordinates.

- Section Chief Akino: I looked at the data prepared by the sergeant, but was there something wrong with it? I, at least, thought it was all right.

- Supervisor Abe: It's fine if you just look at that table, but if you set it against the others, they don't conform. It shows he tried to cover up by combining figures that don't match.

- Section Chief Akino: The sergeant seems to have confidence in what he was doing, so I will try to broach it to him in a way that won't damage his pride.

- Supervisor Abe: Learn to be a bastard.

- Section Chief Akino: The best thing would be for me to just do it myself.

- Supervisor Baba: That is not a section chief's responsibility. If you do everything yourself, efficiency will suffer.

Even if the orders of these supervisors require strict observation of procedures, there is a danger that burden of some controls will arouse the opposition of the section chiefs and may frustrate the supervisors' policy, not because they disagree with it, but because they resent having to enforce it.

The section chiefs have no power to file for a warrant. When they feel a compulsory investigation is necessary, they must make a request to the supervisors for a warrant filing. Therefore, in Case 11, "We had planned to request a warrant based on the other offense, but it was held up from above. The lost article in that case was cash, so it probably can't be found. In that case, there won't be direct proof of the charge." As this indicates, there are cases in which the supervisors do not allow the request.

The central authority of the section chiefs is to define the applicable legal provisions. For example, in a case in which a man stole a television set from his employer's dormitory and had his friend take it to a pawn shop, the investigating detective said, "I am sure of it. There was a conspiracy. Both of them can be called theft offenders [rather than offender and accomplice]." But his section chief directed, "With regard to the original criminal, there is nothing criminal after the original act, and [as to] the guy who pawned the goods, you might get 'receiving stolen goods' against him, but accessory to theft, that's out."

The detectives also report to the section chiefs on even the smallest details of the investigative process and often seek their direction. When news was received that a man resembling the suspect was seen working at a certain place, the detective called the section chief at home and asked for directions about going out and secretly confirming the identity. Also in Case 11, although they were already in receipt of an arrest warrant, the detectives called the section chief for instructions upon arriving at the residence of the suspect.

However, the type of detective who is inclined to develop aggressive investigative action often feels that the orders of section chiefs are troublesome. In one case, upon calling in for orders from the section chief and being told to "act with restraint," the detectives had the following conversation:

- Detective Akita: I mean, we act in response to circumstances at the scene.

- Detective Bando: If the section chief came along, the operation would fail, with him meddling on the sidelines.

- Detective Akita: It's all right for the section chief to work as correspondent and arrange the paperwork. If he comes along, we can't run things our way, like in the old days.

- Detective Bando: I'm one to run things my way.

The section chiefs are aware of this. One supervisor said, "The section chiefs sometimes go along themselves, but while they are reviewing papers and preparing materials, everyone seems to disappear. From the detective's perspective, they feel that if the section chief is along, they can't do as they want." The section chief also finds it impossible to take care of all of his business and also to directly supervise numerous subordinates outside the station.

Aggressive detectives will oppose directives from the section chiefs. In one case, in regard to a plan to take a witness along to confirm the identity of a suspect, the section chief said, "It is not proper investigation to use an ordinary citizen." In response, the detective argued, "The witness is looking forward to it. He says, 'Unless I see the man, I won't know for sure.'" Cutting short the section chief's objections, he called the witness' home.

An organized crime detective recalled how he opposed a section chief, stating, "I have argued with a section chief. A guy in a hospital was buying stimulants. After he was released, we tried to get a search warrant for him, but the section chief said, 'It's unbelievable that any of the drugs that he got there would be left,' and he wouldn't go for it." Detective Department chiefs and section chiefs are separated by only one rank, but the former have considerably more authority over patrolmen and sergeants.

However, since the section chiefs are closer in rank to the detectives than the supervisors, they share with them a similar sense of the harshness of the duty structure imposed upon them. They also react to the severe demands of supervisors in a similar way. As a result, they cannot usually maintain a tough demeanor before the detectives. "Even though I can be called a 'veteran,' all I have done is to suppress my own thoughts, sacrifice my time, and charge ahead recklessly," a section chief explained. "That's how the hardship of the detective has sunk into me. I know the facts of it, so I can't talk harshly to my subordinates." Another section chief stated, "There are detectives who are called 'guests [who don't work],' but the guys themselves know it. Because even though the others are making progress all around him, he can't get anything done. You can't rub that in."

Even though the orders of the supervisors consistently demand procedural restraint, section chiefs would be unable to enforce such strict orders, and even if they try, there will be areas in which detectives elude their direct control. Morally involved detectives may feel free to carry out investigative activities as they wish, and as a result, questionable actions may occur.

3. Reactions of Aggressive Detectives

The detectives are well aware that supervisors stress a fundamental procedural restraint. A theft crime detective said, "Our supervisors are the most insistent on restraint...of those whom I have served." A crime lab officer said, "They believe that even if ten escape, it is best to have one about which there is no mistake."

When we look to the detectives who exhibit moral involvement in aggressive investigative action—who are satisfied by that in itself and are the chief subject of this strict supervision—it is not unnatural that they would regard their supervisors as "lukewarm [to criminals]."

Such detectives hope that the supervisors will approve aggressive investigative actions more widely. For example, "We have trouble if we can't get wider approval of search warrants. The brass is strict in thefts.

Ways have changed here. Didn't used to be this way," a theft crime detective complained. "My former supervisor would get a warrant for the suspect's nickname. Abe [a supervisor], now, he makes us get it under the suspect's actual name." Organized crime detectives are especially pleased when they discover that a strict supervisor's replacement favors aggressive investigative action. "Looks like it will be easy to work with Supervisor Yashiro," they say. A veteran enthused when an aggressive supervisor took over:

> Since Yashiro arrived, the atmosphere in the Organized Crime Section is different, isn't it? Probably seems brighter, eh? He has always done things his way, so he knows how to manage his staff. Under Abe, it was like death around here. There's just one thin wall between them [the Organized Crime Section] and the Forcible Crime Section, but I'll bet the impression is totally different.

Opposition to lenient supervisors affects the evaluation of section chiefs also. A theft crime detective said:

> In the old days, they would just call out, "Oh!" and you would go out. It wasn't the section chief's job to tell you where the staff were, or where they had gone. Detectives had to know what to do on the order "Oh!" We had grit, guts. Now, going out and coming in, both, we do reports.

Supervisors demand that section chiefs strictly supervise detectives. But the section chiefs often must rely upon detectives' reports secondhand, and aggressive detectives take this as proof of incompetence. Thus, the section chiefs are likely to be belittled by those very same detectives who call for the strongest supervision. One hears such comments as, "I think there are a lot of mistakes in the orders from my superiors.... They only give orders, without listening to the subordinates. They push forward their way. They pull rank, and push their point on you."

In truth, supervisors do take such opinions into account, because in the end crimes must be solved. So even supervisors will not deliberately injure the morale of this type of detective. In Case 10, a supervisor said, "The station chief would not allow it [arrest]," and rejected the request of detectives for an emergency arrest of a teenager. Finally, however, they compromised, deciding that if he had no fixed address, no vocation, was not in the custody of parents, and had an arrest record, the detectives should proceed with the arrest. If detectives can obtain such compromises from supervisors, it is also likely that they can negotiate similar compromises with section chiefs.

13

Perceptions of Internal Demands
for Improved Records

1. Demands for Improved Organizational Records

We have discovered that while the supervisors essentially demand restraint, at times they expect aggressive action from the detectives. In this chapter, I explore the reasons why supervisors demand such action in violation of their own general policy.

It is extremely important to understand the causes of supervisors' demands, as they can precipitate aggressive action even by those detectives who dissent or who harbor doubts. We focus on the demands on supervisors to improve the overall records of their stations.

At the police academy, attendees hear a demand for "resolution of all cases [*zenken kaiketsu* in Japanese]." There is generally no explicit declaration from the instructors, but, for example, one instructor said, "Internally, there is a demand for resolution of all cases.... Even in traffic matters, we have an 'All Case Resolution' policy."

As an unofficial policy, then, there is an implicit goal of all-case resolution. The problem we deal with below is whether or not the organization and the individuals within it are evaluated upon the basis of case resolution, and whether any sanctions are associated with this issue.

Among the supervisors, there are those who maintain that further improvement of crime resolution records is impossible. For example, one said:

> At the Eastern Station, the per-officer crime rate is number one or number two in Hokkaido. Since we can't catch any more than we do

now, an increase in crime rates will only result in a worsening of our average. That would be mainly because we cannot subject all suspects to investigation.

Despite this, record improvement is demanded. One supervisor complained, "Higher-ups [at the headquarters] tell us that they transfer superior detectives to the cities; so we are told that clearance rates should improve [at the Eastern Police Station]." Supervisors who feel detectives cannot accomplish any more with current methods may come to expect detectives to undertake aggressive actions of a more problematic nature.

There are also supervisors who believe that improvements in clearance rates are possible. One supervisor said, "It is true that they transfer superior detectives to the cities. For example, the Detective Department chiefs don't include anyone newly promoted; all of them have experience at other stations. And many of the detectives are young men. That's why we should be able to catch more here."

There is no doubt that the latter type of more optimistic supervisors believe that this is possible to achieve. Therefore, such supervisors have higher expectations of detectives. Where detectives have more pessimistic attitudes about improvement of their record, we should expect a greater risk of their engaging in questionable activity.

The detectives also are aware of the demands that the clearance record of the organization be improved. For example, in a case of bribery in violation of election law in which goods were disguised as midyear gifts [*ochugen* in Japanese], two detectives had the following conversation:

* Detective Ando: On the midyear gift case, if we had waited a couple more days, we could have arrested forty people at once.
* Detective Bando: Isn't it good for a police officer to prevent it, before the event, by early intervention?
* Detective Ando: No, there's a big difference between filing on one person in a single case, and filing on forty. You want to become the one with the best record in Hokkaido. If you think about the budget, you will understand.

Whether or not there is a connection between arrest records and budget and staff allocations is unclear. However, there is no doubt that the detectives themselves believe that they must devise the means to improve the record of their station.

Some detectives act accordingly. For example, one detective urged, "If we solve a case that arose at another police station, the Eastern Station's rate of case resolution will increase."

There are also those who do not hide their opposition to supervisors who impose harsh demands to improve the clearance rate. Upon hearing that a certain supervisor believed it possible to improve the record of the Eastern Station, one theft crime detective groused, "I don't know what he said, but maybe we could do that if we all worked without sleep. That old-fashioned spirit isn't around much in today's world. I feel gloomy about that whole thing."

Detectives' statements indicated that the orders they receive from the supervisors may lead them into questionable, aggressive investigative actions. "There was a section chief someplace that hanged himself, and I think I understand that feeling," one detective said. "From the gang with the higher ranks you get this pressure to work and work; you have to go beyond what is possible."

In fact, the supervisors are also aware of the danger of "going beyond what is possible." In Table 13.1, we see that most detectives acknowledge the official policy of "all crimes resolution," and most feel this is the standard for evaluating individual police stations. Also, half of the detectives feel that even if no amount of effort could improve a station's record, this would count as a negative in evaluating the station.

Table 13.1   Evaluation of Police Stations

"ALL CASE RESOLUTION" AS A STANDARD OF EVALUATION

---

1. One sometimes hears that there is a 'goal of resolving all cases'; do you believe that this slogan is actually an official policy?

Yes	Undecided	No	Total Respondents
73.8	19.0	7.1	(42)

2. Do you believe that such a slogan is a standard against which the record of the police station is measured?

Yes	Undecided	No	Total Respondents
75.8	15.2	9.1	(33)

Note: Respondents include only those who answered "Yes" to the previous item.

EVALUATION OF CLEARANCE RATES

---

3. Do you believe, in a case where, even after mobilizing all available staff to the greatest possible degree, and managing the greatest amount of overtime duty physically possible, the clearance rate of the station does not improve, that this would count as a negative in evaluating the record of that station?

Yes	Undecided	No	Total Respondents
53.5	18.6	27.9	(43)

It is clear that many detectives believe there is a demand within the organization that clearance rates be improved, and that this is why supervisors place severe demands upon them. One can further infer that their response will be aggressive investigative actions.

In the next section, I examine those expectations and controls which operate upon detectives to make them generally willing to engage in aggressive investigative action.

2. Demands for Improved Individual Records

This section examines the nature of demands upon individual detectives. Part 2 revealed that the supervisors sometimes insist upon more aggressive investigative actions, contrary to their generally conservative stance, and that the detectives are more responsive to directives demanding aggressive action than those seeking procedural restraint. This chapter also explores why aggressive directives play a larger role than do directives that are aligned with the policy of procedural compliance.

As was discussed earlier, I believe that a majority of detectives at the Eastern Police Station do not have a moral involvement in aggressive investigative action. Therefore, I explore the incentives and sanctions of a utilitarian nature. Below I examine the perceptions of detectives regarding internal control measures and their relationship with clearance effectiveness of individual detectives.

a. Police Academy

It is very clearly acknowledged at the police academy that there are demands upon individual detectives for improvements in their performance. One teacher described the ill effects of such demands, saying, "Below the level of sergeant, they feel the pressure from the section chiefs, and so they tend to violate the law."

Students believe that the goal presented by superiors becomes the standard for evaluating their work. An assistant inspector student explained, "[They say that] the goal [they set] is not the norm [to evaluate us].... In reality, that is the standard against which you are evaluated, and it is even considered in [promotion] examinations." "In rating conduct, there is a demerit system. You start with one hundred points and go down from there," added another assistant inspector.

Students believe that such demands inhibit cooperation among detectives. In explaining the reason why detectives keep the identities of their informants a secret from their mates, a sergeant student told me, "It is because [if they lose informants to other detectives and clearance rates go down] their individual performance will end up being criticized. Though organizational investigation is the policy, what really counts is the individual record." Another student also criticized the system stating, "Management by target [employed in the organization] requires us to clear a certain number of cases. [But, because that inhibits cooperation among detectives] we may fail to resolve cases which we might have resolved if we cooperated."

b. Supervisors

It is supervisors who are in a position to directly demand improvements of individual performance and evaluate individual detectives. Therefore, we need to scrutinize supervisors' actual behavior. On one occasion, I witnessed a detective supervisor criticizing the evaluation system of another department. The detectives explained to me, however, that supervisors in Detective Departments also were involved in this system:

- Detective Ando: Evaluation of the Patrol Department works on a demerit system.

- Detective Bando: For duty questioning, if you turn in thirty [duty questioning cards a month], there are no demerits. That comes out to three cards per watch.

- Supervisor Abe: That's a little strange, isn't it? I don't think that the station chief knows about that. He's against that sort of thing.

- Detective Bando: Maybe it's the Patrol Department chief's idea.... When duty questioning cards come in, they are stamped for approval by a Detective Department chief and the Forcible Crime Section chief.

- Detective Ando: When an officer figures that he is short, he starts automobile questioning from around midnight. Although that's not exactly the way to fall within the requirements for duty questioning under the Police Duties Execution Act.

- Supervisor Abe: (visibly irritated) I don't think that automobile questioning is based on the law.

- Detective Bando: The blanket questioning of autos in emergency alert is under the Act, no?

- Supervisor Abe: That is [legal] duty questioning, [not automobile questioning Bando mentioned].

- Detective Ando: Some of them run away, but there's nothing you can do. They turn off their lights and run, so you can't get a license number, either.

- Supervisor Abe: It's no good to take an average and use that for the standard [to evaluate individual officers].

- Detective Ando: When we don't have enough duty questions, we try at other things. If you do that, you can get the points, see.[1]

In comments such as these, the supervisor is not seen as evaluating the performance of the individual detectives. But in fact he does.

The most important data on this point is on one meeting I observed between the supervisors and the section chiefs. There, confronting the declining record in thefts, they discussed the subsequent policy to be followed. There was almost no talk from the section chiefs; it was the supervisors who declared the policy.

First, the evaluation of individual detectives was announced. Setting down burglary cases as an important area, a supervisor announced, "During this period, there will be no points for theft crime detectives outside of burglary work." Publication of points also was announced, "We will set up a public chart of those whose points are worse than they should be."

The supervisors then stressed the connection between points and personnel management. One supervisor warned:

I am going to be transferred myself in April of next year. At that time, I'm throwing out the garbage. I cannot leave trouble for the successor. This year there have been two transfers to get rid of the trash, and talent has come in its place. The [remaining] trash will get too much attention.

Unfortunately, I was unable to continue my observations to confirm the publication of points and to witness the transfer of personnel. However, I

---

1. This system of evaluating individual performance of patrol officers by the number of duty questionings and other objective measures was revised in 1989 (Murayama, 1990: 206–9, 441–43). This system had been criticized as one that makes police box officers seem less interested in crime prevention and community service functions than in criminal investigation, contrary to an accepted view about patrol officers in Japan (Bayley, 1976). The new system emphasizes house visits (*junkai renraku* in Japanese) and other indices that are ostensibly more closely related to crime prevention and community services. However, Ames (1981: 37–40) has already reported that the primary use of information about individual households collected through house visits is also for criminal investigation.

did find some evidence of the supervisors' influence over personnel matters in the way they handled affairs within the station.

When one supervisor learned of the assignment of transferees to the station, he called their present superiors on the phone and asked about their age, experience, and for an evaluation of their performance. Then he worked to prevent a fifty-five-year-old sergeant and another sergeant (who allegedly took twice the normal time to prepare reports) from being assigned to his two Detective Departments. When there were too few transferees with the necessary skills and ability, he lamented, "Ah, we are in trouble. There is no one to deal with intellectual crimes. What a mess." Blame is placed upon the Hokkaido Police Headquarters. "At the meeting of Department chiefs, I will try to skim off the cream," he boasted.

c. Detectives

Observational data clearly indicates that the detectives believe that they are evaluated solely in terms of investigative efficiency, and that procedural compliance does not count at all.

A theft crime detective said, "A detective is just like a salesman. He is evaluated by his performance." Another detective elaborated on the theft crime sections: "Report and clearance records, those are the individual diary of the theft crime detective. The theft sections are very strict." Still another detective explained the system at the Mobile Investigation Squad of the headquarters in a cynical tone: "At Mobile, they are spurred to get custody in eight cases in one day; that's good." These statements show their exhaustion and imply a criticism of the demands placed upon them.

Many detectives expressed the hope that the difficulty of combining investigative efficiency and respect for procedures be taken into account in evaluating their performance. When I asked in my survey, "Do you believe that close respect for rules of procedure in investigation is highly touted in evaluations of performance?", 53.5 percent said yes.

However, I never observed individual detectives who were publicly praised for procedural compliance in the police station. Even though I witnessed morning orders many times, never once was a concern raised about procedure or information disseminated about legal regulations. On one occasion, three awards from the Hokkaido police chief were given to the members of the First Detective Department, all for clearance of a string of connected thefts. Fifteen awards were given by the station chief to the Traffic Department: one award for controlling double parking, one award for collecting information about the same, two awards for hit-and-run and drunken driving, two awards for driving without a license and drunken driving, five awards for drunken speeding without a license, and four awards for regulating minor traffic offenses.

On another day, detectives received awards for an exhibitionist case and two cases of crime lab work that resulted in the arrest of a nationally wanted criminal. Officers of the Crime Prevention Department received five awards for handling more than five hundred missing persons, for dealing with more than six hundred cases of business regulations, and for taking care of more than two hundred and fifty cases of crimes against children.

All of these were based upon clearance record, not respect for procedures.

One detective described his dilemma, "When they tell us to stick to procedure, and to increase the clearance rates, we are caught between a rock and a hard place." What the detective actually perceives as the tangible expectation is efficient investigation, and thus solves his role conflicts by pursuing efficiency. The presence or absence of clear policy and even the physical presence or absence of supervisors in the station can cause a dramatic change in the actions of most detectives.

One day, before the supervisors had introduced the evaluation policy based on individual performance and when these same supervisors were attending a meeting at the Hokkaido Police Headquarters, a detective jubilantly shouted, "At least when the brass isn't around, let's take it easy." Detectives joked among themselves; some called friends at other stations; and some smoked cigarettes idly. The station took on a quite relaxed atmosphere.

Three days later, after the conference of the supervisors and the section chiefs in which the supervisors had stated what they wanted, I was told, "The station detention cells are full. There's been a push, you see." Twenty-two persons had been confined; the station detention area had no more free space.

We should reemphasize here how detectives fear removal from the detective department and reassignment to patrol. Ames (1981: 191) has reported on a survey on the preferences for assignments among Japanese police officers. While more than 80 percent of officers in criminal investigation (i.e., investigation of adult crimes), crime prevention (i.e., investigation of juvenile offenses), and security (i.e., investigation of politically motivated crimes) did not want to change their department, nearly 60 percent of officers assigned to patrol activities at police boxes wanted to alter theirs. Even though patrol activities at police boxes have been praised as the uniquely effective aspect of the Japanese police (Bayley, 1976), many Japanese officers despise them. As Ames (1981: 192) has reported, "Work that emphasizes investigation and the catching of criminals is usually thought of as 'real police work' in Japan as in the United States and is considered very desirable duty." Ames has noted the following episode:

An old sergeant...who was switched from criminal investigation to patrol work a couple years before retirement, was certain it was a punishment for some mistake, but was perplexed as to what he did wrong.

My data indicates that supervisors effectively use the possibility of transfer to patrol as a means of mobilizing aggressive investigative actions on the part of lower-ranking detectives.

3. Meaning of Statistics

Bayley (1976: 8) has written that "[t]here have been no revelations or even accusations of this kind [falsification of official statistics] in Japan." In 1982, however, just such a case occured in the Chiba Prefecture near Tokyo. Nearly all the police stations there underreported the number of reported crimes in order to improve the clearance rate. This practice was so widespread there that it seems unlikely the technique is not used in some other areas of the country. My data indicate that "stats" (Sanders, 1977: 82) are important to the police officers at the station level.

Bayley (1976: 8–9) has written, "Senior police officers serve short tours of duty in any jurisdiction, so...[i]t is not especially in their interest to make a particular locality look good with respect to crime." This may be true with regard to executives sent from the National Police Agency. They do not directly affect police work at the station level, including the preparation of statistics. Field supervisors at the station do have such an effect, however. They are very much concerned with the statistical local performance and they direct lower-ranking detectives with this in mind.

The findings here indicate that Japanese police detectives are somewhat different from those described earlier by Ericson (1981) and Sanders (1977). Ericson (1981: 53, 55, 63) has reported that in Canada "there was no apparent pressure on detectives to produce a specifiable monthly volume of arrests, charges and other clearances," so that "emphasis was upon collective cooperation among detectives rather than on individual productivities." Only those on a probationary status in the detective department were "production conscious," and "many of the detective practices related to 'easing' the pace of their work." Sanders (1977: 82–83) has presented a slightly different picture of his American detectives because "the rates were one indicator of how well the department was doing." He has argued, however, that "the focus in any single case was not on 'stats' so much as it was on identifying a 'real criminal' or a 'real crime.'"

It is true that when supervisors are absent, Japanese detectives tend to "ease" the pace of their work. It is also true that detectives are especially satisfied when they are able to resolve more serious crimes. Still they know that statistics are a factor in deciding their assignments. This was most apparent when supervisors enunciated their policy of individual evaluation. It also was discernible from the casual conversations and behavior of detectives.

Among American researchers studying detective work, Skolnick (1966: 110, 167, 168, 231) has been the one who most emphasized the pressure for productivity and a higher clearance rate and its impact on police behavior. He has argued that "[f]or detectives, the most important measure of accomplishment has come to be the 'clearance rate,'" and "the demand for police 'efficiency' creates a type of 'professional' police practice in which the concern for legality is minimal." Skolnick studied special duty detectives, while I, in contrast, did research on general work detectives. Still, they are same in their perception of the significance of investigative productivity to a successful career.

Skolnick (1966: 239) has argued that "[i]f the police are ever to develop a conception of *legal* as opposed to *managerial* professionalism, they will do so only if the surrounding community demands compliance with the rule of law by rewarding police for such compliance." This argument applies very well to the reward system inside the Japanese police organization. My data indicate that rewards are all directed to higher productivity through aggressive investigations. In spite of official policies of the police organization as a whole, and of supervisors at the Eastern Police Station in particular, procedural compliance was not rewarded. When caught between the two conflicting expectations of aggressiveness and compliance, the detective would solve this dilemma in favor of the former.

14

Perceptions of External Controls and Expectations

This chapter examines the effect of controls and expectations that arise outside the police organization. I will examine supervisors as well as detectives because supervisors' perceptions and actions influence those of detectives.

While there is an almost infinite variety of individuals and groups outside the police organization whose expectations and controls exert an influence on the organization, some interact almost constantly with police and belong to the "organization set" (Evan, 1966) around police. I focus my discussion on such individuals and groups.

I examine police perceptions about the expectations and controls of four types of members of the organization set around police: prosecutors (and the prosecutor's office); judges (and the courts); attorneys (and the bar associations); and the public or, more realistically, the mass media. The main point of the analysis is that expectations and controls from these sources work mainly to demand, excuse, or ignore aggressive investigative action.

There is no effective incentive in the police organization to support procedural restraints. Whether normative or renumerative, all rewards are designed to promote aggressive investigation. Still, most of the time the detectives' aggressive behavior is not clearly illegal. There must be some factors outside the police organization that set what might be called the upper limit of aggressiveness.

In determining the degree of external controls, I evaluate the nature of dependency between outside individuals and organizations and the police organization. To the degree that one organization depends on the other, expectations and controls of the other organization will exert a larger effect (Aiken and Hage, 1968; Benson, 1975; Pfeffer and Salancik, 1978).

An important question in determining the degree of dependence is to what extent the one organization supplies resources necessary to the operation of the other. For example, we may suppose that the relationship between the courts and the police is one-sided. The police need a warrant and detention from the judge to continue with an investigation, and at the end of an investigation the police hope for a guilty verdict and a heavy sentence. On the other hand, the judge does not need the officer's cooperation and, in fact, if the officer's investigation is incomplete or found to be inappropriate, judgment may go against the officer. We may expect that while the court has a large impact on the police, the police do not exert much influence on the court.

The relationship between the police and the prosecutor may be more mutually dependent. The police request that the prosecutor file for detention and hope for an indictment by the prosecutor. The prosecutor, in turn, must have the aid of the police to collect evidence and dispose of cases. The full extent of such a relationship is of course an empirical question, but I approach the influence of judges, prosecutors, defense attorneys, and the mass media through this analytical framework.

1. Defense Attorneys

Theoretically, the person who stands in the position of greatest opposition to aggressive investigative action by the detectives is the suspect's attorney. The attorney can advise the suspect to exercise his constitutional rights and resist interrogations; he can rob the detectives of opportunities to get a confession. The frequent meetings between the suspect and the attorney can interrupt the investigative process. After indictment, the attorney may challenge the actions of the detectives, challenge the merit of evidence, present mitigating evidence to secure a lighter sentence, and even secure an acquittal or overturn a guilty verdict. The attorneys, thus, are in a position to hamper the supply of various resources to detectives.

However, as I have explained in chapter 2, a state-appointed attorney is not available until indictment, many suspects do not have the resources to hire an attorney, and the Japanese courts have interpreted the attorney's right of intervention very narrowly. Ericson (1981: 144) has reported that in Canada, "In maintaining control over suspects, detectives also strategically regulated the suspect's access to a third party." Police in Japan literally have a *right* to do this. Even on a rare occasion when an attorney was retained by the suspect before indictment, the prosecutor could direct the police to limit or deny meetings in order not to impede the convenience of investigation. As I have explained in chapter 2, meetings were permitted only after the suspect admitted his guilt. Police perceptions about the impact of defense attorneys reflect this situation.

One supervisor told me, "Sometimes attorneys attach at the suspect stage. Abe [another supervisor] says that if refusal will cause trouble later on, we should let meetings occur freely. I can't say that evidence is never concealed because an attorney attached, but an attorney at least does improve the suspect's spirits." This "trouble later on" refers of course to actions by the attorney at the trial. However, letting it occur "freely" indeed may reflect the perception of the supervisors that an attorney only results in a rise in "spirits," without much tangible threat to their goals.

There is also a perception that even this rise in "spirits" happens rarely. One supervisor said, "Attorneys attach at the suspect stage mainly in intellectual crime cases and public security cases; maybe one case in thirty overall." In fact, I did not see any case in which an attorney was privately retained before indictment.

Retained attorneys do not present much threat either. Detectives even criticize attorneys because most of them fail to use opportunities to challenge them on behalf of clients. A theft crime detective told me:

> Attorneys, they are slick. I know that after I've been in the station detention cell with them. I don't go to interviews, of course, but I can overhear them talking. All they say is, "How much will you pay me to get bail?" Domon is especially forward. He specializes in the defense of people in organized crime. He is ripping off the mob. When they are selected for state-appointed defense work, a lot of these guys don't show up for the interview with the client, and beg off when we call them on the phone. We aren't supposed to mediate on the phone like that, but once you get familiar with them, you can't refuse it. "I won't go to any meetings with you. I'll be there at trial," they tell the client. And at trial, it's "Will you admit the facts of the offense as stated by the prosecution?" that they are asked. And they answer, "Yes, I will." There should be a weakness they could find somewhere in any case. The serious ones are the young attorneys. They're green, but they are at least for real.

In Case 17, a forcible crime detective commented, "If the case is run by a state-appointed defender, there won't be much of a problem."

Attorneys are not taken very seriously by supervisors and detectives alike, in ordinary cases. Attorneys do not have a great impact upon the operation of criminal investigation.

2. Prosecutors

Prosecutors have an ambivalent relationship with the detectives similar to that of supervisors. While excessively aggressive investigative actions must be prevented to save the case at trial, if investigative actions are not satisfactorily aggressive, they usually cannot indict the suspect, get a conviction, and secure a heavy sentence. While it may be the policy of the prosecutor's office to "educate" policemen, it is also true that "[s]ince the district attorney depends largely upon the policeman for evidence, the policeman has a good deal of influence over the district attorney's excercise of discretionary authority" (Skolnick, 1966: 179, 201). Furthermore, prosecutors are in a more difficult position than supervisors in that they cannot directly observe and direct detectives.

Under these circumstances, the prosecutors have two primary ways of encouraging the detectives to exercise restraint. One is not to file for the detention which is necessary for the detectives to engage in efficient interrogation and investigation. The other is to refrain from indictment or refuse the acceptance of cases that exhibit procedural irregularities. (I presented one such case in chapter 4.) Through such methods, the prosecutor presumably can exercise his control over resources necessary to the police.

On the other hand, where the prosecutor needs aggressive investigative action by the police, police supply a needed resource and take more of a dominant role in the relationship. In ordinary cases, the prosecutor has no chance to investigate and interrogate. Although the prosecutor may conduct supplemental inquiries, he lacks the staff and facilities for more extentive work and must rely upon evidence collected by the police. Moreover, when the prosecutor does conduct a supplementary investigation, his power is limited to giving general directives to the police. The prosecutor usually allows the police to pursue aggressive investigations freely, without requesting specific evidence or confessions.

Prosecutors also are under pressure for efficient case disposition. If this demand is strong, prosecutors are unable to insist on restraint from detectives, although the exact nature of the interrelationship and its consequences remains to be explored with empirical data.

How do the police officers actually define their relationship with the prosecutor? When the supervisors at the Eastern Police Station discuss it, they stress the independence of the police and express displeasure at direction received from prosecutors. In Case 17, one supervisor proudly explained, "The police are not an auxiliary unit of the prosecutors as they were under the old Code of Criminal Procedure. Prosecutors [now] do not have concrete, distinct power to command [police officers in individual cases]." Another supervisor elaborated:

> In the police, authoritative interpretations of law based upon Supreme Court precedents come down from the Detective Planning Section of Headquarters. These sometimes differ from interpretations offered by the prosecutor's office.

He stressed independence in legal interpretation as well as in decision-making.

Despite this, prosecutors think they have a monopoly on decisions that have an importance to the police. This belief is especially strong regarding decisions about indictment, which irritates the police. In Case 17, the supervisors complained, "As police, it is damaging to our pride to have a case dismissed for 'lack of proof,'" and, "We don't like to see judgments that there is 'insufficient proof' for a finding of guilt."

The supervisors essentially have confidence in their investigations and do not hide their mistrust and dissatisfaction when there is a decision not to indict. Again in Case 17, a supervisor commented, "Prosecutors, especially in intellectual crime cases, reason politically," and expressed their frustration: "[When they tell us the evidence is insufficient] We ask them, 'Send us the document of the decision of the prosecutor's office,' but they don't get around to sending it. Eventually the concerned prosecutor is transferred, and it gets lost in the shuffle."

Despite their complaints, there is no question that the police must abide by the prosecutor's decision. When the prosecutor offers strong guidance, such as a demand for restraint, we may predict that the supervisors will accordingly demand for restraint from the detectives.

However, supervisors perceive that the demands from prosecutors are ambiguous. On the one hand, a supervisor told the section chiefs, "The headquarters' Detective Bureau chief meets with the prosecutor four times each month. And if papers are prepared carelessly for prosecutor, he's going to tell the chief that the Eastern Station is hopeless." On the other hand, as in Case 17, a supervisor complained, "The prosecutor says, 'Hurry up and interrogate Wakamatsu [for a different offense],' but as a policeman, I want to proceed after firming up my primary investigation." Pressed sometimes toward restraint and other times toward aggressiveness, the supervisors must improve their clearance records, and typically they will find it easier to comply with a request for aggressive investigation.

The detectives know that in ordinary cases prosecutors almost never engage in investigation themselves. A forcible crime detective told me:

> It is true that on-site evidence gathering for the prosecution is directed by the prosecutor, but we do most of it all by ourselves. Even if a prosecutor comes, all he does is watch. So since the prosecutors don't come to the scene, we have no choice but to do it ourselves, and sometimes a prosecutor will ask who directed us. We have fights with the prosecutors all the time, but they are understaffed over there.

The detectives understandably believe that they have more experience and superior skills in investigation than do prosecutors. A detective told me,

"It only happens in about one case in ten that someone tumbles [confesses] to the prosecutor when he doesn't talk to the police." Detectives clearly resist receiving directions from prosecutors.

A forcible crime detective explained the supervisors' decision about one case (Case 17), stating, "I think the first case [separate offense] will go across [to the prosecutor] today.... Supervisor Bando says to send it across today, so we are working on it.... Supervisor Bando says, 'Send it across anyway, and transfer any stuff that we get afterward.'" Under these circumstances, detectives feel that a demand for continued investigation and interrogation from prosecutors is a hardship. In Case 17 again, a detective complained, "The prosecutor keeps picking at this and that aspect," and "He can't rest easily until he nails Yamamoto [a man indicated by the arrested suspect as also involved in the case]." A supervisor responded, "The prosecutor is trying to slow down with obstructive requests." Another detective added, "There was a call from the prosecutor. He said, 'If you plan to send the first arson case across, let me know first.' Seems he does not want the case sent to him in the current form of investigation. Sounds like we have to get Yamamoto to save the case."

Such demands arouse the opposition of detectives, and they tend to label the prosecutor as a coward. In this same case, the detectives exchanged their views, stating, "The prosecutor is complaining. Says that white coat was not in the right place and stuff." "That prosecutor is always making noise about something." "Probably he has no confidence in himself."

Nevertheless, detectives cannot totally ignore demands from the prosecutor. In Case 17, one detective stated, "The prosecutor has asked for the clothing worn at the time of the crime. I sent the socks; I'll send the shirt next. I guess the kerosene [which was allegedly used to set fire] won't be found, will it?" The detectives perceive that prosecutors basically are concerned with a necessity for more evidence. In this case, a detective told me, "The prosecutor's reputation is on the line if he loses, so he is asking us to do an experiment under the same conditions," and they tried a makeshift experiment.

To the detectives, a requirement of more evidence means longer detention of the suspect and tougher interrogation. Thus, from the initial understanding that full investigations are demanded of them, they also conclude that longer and more aggressive investigations are expected. One forcible crime detective said:

> The prosecutor is afraid to carry a case that results in an acquittal, so he wants especially strong investigations. When his feelings crystalize against indictment, even if you send him papers sufficient for a guilty verdict, he will not use it in the prosecutor's report, but throw it away.

We should note that the detective does not perceive that the case might be lost because of illegal conduct, but only because investigations were not aggressive enough to produce an adequate confession and adequate physical evidence.

Beyond preventing clearly illegal actions which might easily be detected, the expectations and controls of the prosecutors do not appear to demand restraint. Ericson (1981: 16, 211) has reported about Canada that "[d]etectives are able to produce accounts which give [an] appearance of conformity to the rules because...Crown attorneys...rarely have the inclination or the capability to undertake an independent investigation," and "Crown attorneys were rarely consulted in the initial laying of charges." In Japan, the lengthy detention period provides the prosecutor with a means for independent investigation simply because he has more time than a Canadian prosecutor to evaluate the police work and reach his own decision. The ironic result is that the police perceive prosecutorial interventions and resistance as a demand for more aggressive investigation.

3. Judges

As I have already discussed, the police appear to depend on the court for essential resources. In spite of the potential impact judges have, however, there are limitations in their ability to restrain illegal police actions. One difficulty is that their control is even more indirect than prosecutors'. Not only is it exercised after the fact, but even in the post hoc examination at trial, they rely upon the efforts of defense attorneys, whose limited effectiveness we already have examined. Judges cannot proactively control the detectives.

Bayley (1976: 5) has reported that:

> Japanese detectives...are more outspoken about their own shortcomings than those of others. Getting them to evaluate the effect of judicial decisions on police performance or criminality is like pulling teeth. They seem to have given the matter very little thought.

My observations indicate, however, that Japanese detectives are strongly concerned with the judicial behavior, especially in a case on which they are personally working. Skolnick (1966: 175) wrote that "the severity of the sentence is the most important consideration to all of the active participants in the system...[including] the police." My data indicate that Japanese detectives are no different from their American counterparts.

Observations at the police academy indicate a strong concern with the outcome of trial. An instructor told me that they "take an interest in the judge's decision in the cases we are working on."

Criticism of the judiciary focuses almost exclusively upon its opposition to aggressive investigations. The following are examples of detectives' opinions:

- Young judges know nothing of the detective's real life. That's why they deny warrants and refuse detention.

- Judges turn down the requests of the police because they know nothing about investigations. If they themselves were victimized by the thieves and others, they might understand better.

- The assistant judge who denies a warrant may be sticking to the law, but that's because he knows nothing about the real world.

Controls exercised by judges are of keen interest to the police. But do judicial actions affect their actions, and if so, how?

Perceptions of the supervisors at the Eastern Station differed depending on their basic orientations.

Those supervisors who manifested a policy of restraint were also most acutely conscious of the possibility of criticism at trial. In Case 17, a supervisor worried:

> Wakamatsu [a person indicated by the arrested suspect as the principal criminal of the case] owes money for mahjong gambling, so there is at least a possible motive. But without Yamamoto [a man indicated by the arrested suspect as also involved in the case] in the case, there is a risk that Matsuda [the arrested suspect] will recant the confession even if we could get one. If an attorney gets mixed up in the case, recantation would be certain.

Another supervisor commented on this fellow supervisor:

> Ando says that if refusal [of the meeting between the suspect and his counsel] will cause problems later, we should let the suspect and the counsel have meetings freely when they wish.

On the other hand, other supervisors who generally stressed aggressive actions strongly criticized the court. One such supervisor said:

> Professor, you will go out to see the Susukino area [a downtown drinking area], won't you? If you don't go there, you won't know the real

circumstances, what sorts of things organized crime syndicates do in their business. These young judges fresh from the bar exam, they don't understand that. The ones who understand are the older judges in the summary courts.

Such supervisors are less concerned about the possibility of judicial control. A supervisor commented on the questionable procedure of taking urine from a suspect, stating, "You can be blamed for falling short in your search for evidence [if you do not take urine], so there is merit in it [to take risk]."

The perceptions concerning the judiciary held by the second group of supervisors (those more aggressively inclined) appear to be closer to reality. As we have seen in part 2, in none of the cases I observed did the court turn down applications for warrants and detention. This suggests that either the judges did not know the actual circumstances, or if they did know, they consciously accepted them and proceeded to decision without examining the problematic elements of police actions.

Like generally aggressive supervisors, detectives see no significant threat in judicial control. This is particularly so regarding warrants. One theft crime detective said:

> I go to pick up the warrants myself in the cases I am working on. That is because, if someone else goes, and there is some question posed by the judge, they can't answer. Even so, there are questions in only about one case in ten. If your evidence and case history is all in order, there is never a call for further explanation, because they just tick off the points in a quick reading.

The detectives believe that it is easy to satisfy the requirements for a warrant and that the inquiry itself is a simple matter.

The detectives express more concern over trial. They often said, "Whatever you do, try to support your case at trial with your investigations." When they lack confidence, as in Case 17, they hope the trial will end smoothly and say things such as, "Looks like the prosecutor will recommend sentencing only after one hearing. I heard that the state-appointed defender consented to [the introduction of] the record of the suspect's statement [as evidence]. The decision will probably be handed down at the second hearing."

However, such sensitivity to judicial scrutiny does not produce restraint on the part of the detectives. They worry that confessions may be undermined and holes found in prepared evidence. Therefore, judicial scrutiny serves to promote longer, more aggressive investigations and interrogations.

Even if the legality of an investigation is challenged at the trial, and detectives themselves are called to trial as witnesses, they never alter their position. This is because there are no direct witnesses of procedural illegalities except the suspect and themselves in most cases. They perceive that the chances of evidence being excluded, or of a verdict being overturned are very low. A forcible crime detective told me about his experience:

> I look at a trial like a sporting event, see, so I try to keep a good stance with what I say, so as not to be caught off balance. What I hate the most is a question asking me to describe the course of the investigation from the beginning. While you're talking, you can let something that sounds bad slip. Once I was asked whether I had eliminated all other suspects, and I answered that no others were under suspicion. The prosecutor had a report on his desk that showed otherwise, and he scolded me badly for that afterwards.

Other detectives added:

- I look at trials as a sport, so when an attorney tells me, "Mind you, you are a witness here," I say, "I am only going to tell you the truth." Sometimes the circumstances are bad, you know. At trial, if I am asked, "You squared your story with the prosecutor, didn't you?" I answer, "What's wrong with that?"

- Once they tried to make out a voluntary appearance as an act of arrest. In fact, when the suspect started to run away, I had called out, "Catch him!" and that is an act of arrest. So I answered that I had said, "Wait!" instead.

Thus, unfavorable judicial decisions are considered to be rare. The principal concern of the police regarding the court is to carry aggressive investigative action forward as far as necessary to gain a conviction and a heavy sentence.

Ericson (1981: 180) has written that in Canada there is a "general requirement of bringing a suspect before a Justice without reasonable delay and within a maximum of 24 hours." This is more stringent than in the Japanese system. Yet, Ericson (1981: viii, 16, 153) has argued that "Justices routinely grant warrants, releases, and bail conditions in accordance with detective requests," and "Justices of the Peace could do little else in any case because they had no means of validating the information presented to them by detectives." These restraints on the judicial control of investigative actions apply to Japan, too. Moreover, the dominant perspective in the Japanese judiciary discourages active use of any leverage judges possess.

4. The Public and the Mass Media

The preceding three sections examined the effect of the controls and expectations from those directly participating in the legal processes regarding detectives behavior. This section looks at the effect of the expectations and controls from the public and the mass media.

At the police academy, I observed great sensitivity to public reactions to the police, particularly as represented in the mass media. One assistant inspector student told me, "We are conscious, foremost, of criticism in the media. Generating explanations [for them] takes a great deal of work." Does this sensitivity lead to procedural restraint or increased aggressiveness?

An assistant inspector student argued in a class discussion, "We are easily criticized by the public. We should do our best to find a judicial precedent to follow." This was in response to a particular question: During pursuit, when a suspect flees into a governmental office and the officers lose sight of him, should a representative of the office being searched be present during the search? The answer reveals that although in fact this student wants to avoid anyone else's presence, he thinks it safer to take the conservative course when the risk of criticism is considered. To this extent, concern about public criticism appears to mitigate aggressive investigative actions.

However, police officers firmly believe that the public expects them to carry out aggressive investigative actions. For example, in a sergeants' class, a teacher boasted:

> Let us be aware of the Hokkaido Police chief's instructions when he took his post: "Truth, strength, benevolence." The Japanese love "truth, strength, and benevolence." Let us look at the detective programs on television. The "License to Be Cold-Hearted" [a T.V. drama] does not conform to reality. They engage in illegal investigations as a matter of course. Nonetheless they are accepted by the public. This is because the police have "truth, strength and benevolence."

In another class, the instructor told the students, "The police are an investment, a savings account for the people. They want their interest on that account. They demand service and the protection of their safety from the police."

The officers also believed that the public wants the full resolution of all cases. One instructor said, "Resolution of all cases is demanded within the organization. The world at large demands it as well."

Thus, officers at the police academy believe that the central expectation of the general public is for aggressive investigations and that the police must continually prove their record on that point. This is also the basic perception of detectives at the Eastern Police Station. They think that the general public will criticize excessive or illegal actions, but procedural compliance, in and of itself, is not expected.

For detectives who exhibit moral involvement in aggressive investigative actions, the perceived demands from the general public for such investigations strengthens their sense of the legitimacy of their actions. For example, one theft crime detective said, "I think of myself not as a policemen's policeman [who is worried about internal regulations], but as a citizens' policeman [who responds to the public expectations]." For these detectives, supervisors who do not allow them to freely engage in aggressive actions are not ultimately satisfying public expectations.

The supervisors at the Eastern Station were more sensitive to these conflicting components in the public's expectations.

On the one hand, they expressed concern over public criticism of excessive aggressiveness. In regard to Case 17, a supervisor told me, "Use of the arrest for different crimes [to create a chance to investigate the crime they really want] may be within the law, but the practice is criticized by the public as irrational and inappropriate." In a case where it was decided not to arrest a woman thief, a supervisor explained, "From the amount of money involved, we should arrest in this case. Why didn't we use compulsory measures [such as arrest]? The reason is concern over our image before the public—the negative reaction that says, 'Why do you have to arrest her?'—you know." Thus, even if a certain method is possible under law, it may not be used for fear of public criticism.

On the other hand, the supervisors were keenly aware of the public demand for aggressiveness. Also in regard to Case 17, a supervisor told me, "The [newspaper's] report that the suspect has been 'transferred to the prosecutor' was not correct, but we had to make the announcement to ease the minds of the people in the neighborhood; and I suppose that it's all right to add some name value [exaggeration] in order to do so." Another supervisor said in regard to the handling of a complaint, "When we cannot prove the alleged criminal facts, we try to persuade the complainant to withdraw. But then we can be criticized for failing to cooperate with the public."

The irony is that, in spite of this two-sided perception of the supervisors, public expectations, particularly those of the mass media, clearly favor aggressive investigative actions. Crime articles published in the newspaper of widest circulation in Hokkaido during my research provide good examples of this.

A sample of headlines:

- Man runs and hides; Cafeteria operator arrested; Pretends ignorance at interrogation.

- Criminal remains absolutely silent; Shiraoi town mayor stabbing death; Background investigation continues.

- Appearance of great calm; Explanation in a gesture; Inspection made of the scene by Haruyama, the enemy of the woman.

- Saito is calm; Faces of his family color suddenly.

It appears that the expressions "calm" and the like are not based upon direct observations by the reporter. In the last article, "In contrast to the shock of the family, *it is said that* Saito has gotten out of bed to drink water, and sat calmly smoking cigarettes" (emphasis supplied).

Even when a news story reports an investigation that contains questionable elements, the story begins and ends with simple description. For example:

- Wife-beater arrested; Connection sought with murder.

- Confession to murder of police officer; Re-arrest of Harada for murder, formerly arrested for assault.

- Drivers from Shiraoi; Young team of two [murder suspects] surface; Arrest on warrant for different offense [theft].

These cases involved arrest on charges other than the offense the police actually wanted to investigate. The articles give the impression that such pretext arrests for different offenses are not questionable.

On the other hand, when a difficult crime was solved, the news report was enthusiastic. For example, one item stated, "The heavens do not forgive; Crime solved after two years," and "Violent attack by Hyde, Haruyama, after offer of ride." Moreover, the newspaper did not hesitate to criticize the clearance record even when it praised the police. For instance, reports such as "Hokkaido Police carries many unresolved cases," were combined with "A big hit, which has been long overdue by Hokkaido Police with its mass of unsolved cases; Investigation personnel rejoice." These reports were peppered with reports of a public demand, such as "Local people...angry voices heard."

One should note here the difference between crime news and court reports. The summaries of police crimes and other illegalities in chapter 1 are based on newspaper articles. Those articles clearly criticized police practices. However, one should note that most of them were based on court decisions. Otherwise, they were the result of aggressive media campaigns by defense attorneys. The mass media rarely investigates and criticizes ongoing criminal investigations in regard to procedural issues.

Defining the relationship between the media and the police in Japan, Bayley (1976: 68–69) counts it as one of the outside sources which elicit the highest degree of discipline from the Japanese police. The same is true of the Human Rights Bureaus of the Justice Ministry, the prefectural legislatures, and the Public Safety Commissions at the national and prefectural levels. Bayley argues that "the media in Japan is a very important though diffuse mechanism of accountability. It is free and vigorous and not reluctant to publicize police misdeeds." A different view is presented by Ames (1981: chapter 10), who casts serious doubt on the effectiveness of outside controls by Public Safety Commissions and the prefectural government. He argues, however, that "[t]he most effective check on police impropriety in Japan is thus an unfettered and aggressive press. The police establishment has the potential of great power and abuse, but it is sensitive to public desires and criticisms as articulated in the media."

It is true that the Japanese media strongly criticizes the police when it reports cases like those presented in chapter 1. But publicizing illegality of police actions in these well-known cases is not the most important role of the media. The real problem is the daily coverage of routine cases. Ames (1981: 72–73), in emphasizing the value of the media as an instrument of police control, argues that:

> The police make effective use of the media both in improving their image and in eliciting cooperation from the community. The media, in general, are supportive of the police, especially in the regional press.... The media cover police-related matters and incidents by way of writers' clubs located in the prefectural police headquarters and in the city offices.... The media can be a particularly powerful tool in the hands of the police because one of the strongest factors in social control in Japan is the fear that if one is arrested one's name will appear in the newspaper.

This picture is close to the reality of the media-police relationship in everyday situations in Japan. The media rarely conducts its own investigation and routinely relies on information provided by the police. Therefore, when serious cases such as those presented in chapter 1 occur, the media also has been criticized by victims of the police misbehavior. Particularly in false accusation cases, the media had stigmatized the victim as a "criminal" from the beginning of the investigation and that stigma hindered the victim's effort to exonerate himself. Indeed, this problem is called "the crime of crime-reporting" in Japan, and various groups have been formed by activist lawyers, victims of police-media cooperation, and concerned journalists to improve the situation.

In any event, given the role of the mass media, supervisors at the Eastern Police Station seemed overly sensitive to possible public criticism of extreme aggressiveness.

The detectives were more realistic. The survey data indicates that they believe that what matters most to the public is efficiency of criminal investigations. If performance records do not improve even when the duty structure is stretched to its limits, most detectives feel that the public or mass media will criticize them (Table 14.1, items 1 and 2). They also believe that even if it is caused by procedural restraint, a drop in performance records will also not escape criticism from the public (Table 14.1, item 3).

Table 14.1   Attitudes about Public Criticism

1. Do you believe that even despite such efforts, the general citizenry of Hokkaido would be critical? (see note)

Yes	Undecided	No	Total Respondents
69.8	20.9	9.3	(43)

2. Do you believe that the mass media would be critical as well?

Yes	Undecided	No	Total Respondents
74.4	18.6	7.0	(43)

Note: Items 1 and 2 are based upon the following question: "Do you believe, in a case where, even after mobilizing all available staff to the greatest possible degree, and managing the greatest amount of overtime duty physically possible, the clearance rate of the station does not improve, that this would count as a negative in evaluating the record of that station?"

3. Do you believe that even if one remains within the rules of investigations, and because of that the rate at which cases are solved drops, there will be criticism from most of the members of the general public?

Yes	Undecided	No	Total Respondents
53.5	16.3	30.2	(43)

Note the implication of these perceptions for supervisors and detectives who are engaging in questionable investigative actions. Such perceptions neutralize their own doubts and make it easier for them to engage in such actions. The effect on detectives is to strengthen their sense of legitimacy.

15

Conclusions: Irony of Effective Supervision and an *Enabling* Legal Environment

Most detective supervisors at the Eastern Police Station generally maintained remarkable procedural restraint in spite of their very heavy work loads. Police executives at the Hokkaido Police Headquarters made a shrewd decision when they chose the Eastern Police Station as my research site. Supervisors at the Eastern try hard to keep their control over every major action of police detectives even when detectives are away from the station. For instance, detectives are required to telephone the station to get approval for arrest even when they have a warrant in hand. In cases of violent crime, supervisors immediately rush to the scene and take command of the investigation. Moreover, at least two supervisors are usually involved in a single case. It is typical for the assistant station chief in charge of criminal investigation and head of one of the two Detective Departments to work together to direct an investigation.

This system of tight control makes the job of section heads a particularly difficult one. Section heads do not have independent authority as police supervisors to apply for warrants to the court and see themselves as lower-ranking detectives. They feel more in sympathy with detectives than with supervisors, yet they must direct their co-workers according to the demands of supervisors.

Previous studies of Japanese police suggest that this situation is more or less true of all police stations in Japan. We may conclude therefore that internal control of police detectives in Japan is more effective than is reported for police in the United States, Canada, and the United Kingdom. The visibility of detectives' actions to field supervisors is higher in Japan, and it is

233

difficult to imagine that clearly illegal actions would go unrecognized by supervisors.

However, this effective internal control is double-edged. Supervisors can push detectives in either direction of procedural restraint or of aggressive investigation. Moreover, the internal reward system makes one edge sharper than the other. Aggressive detectives with higher productivity in the solution of crime are rewarded either morally or with tangible benefits, while there is no significant reward for procedural restraint.

It is also apparent in this research that detectives are not necessarily morally committed to aggressive criminal investigation. In chapter 11 I presented strong evidence that a substantial number of detectives question the legality and legitimacy of their own behavior and complain about many aspects of their working conditions. Even these detectives, however, do not hesitate to take questionable actions when they perceive strong internal pressure for higher productivity.

We have seen in chapter 13 how this combination of effective internal control and rewards for aggressive behavior works. Criticized by the Hokkaido Police Headquarters for poor performance in theft crime investigation, supervisors at the Eastern Police Station announced that they would rigorously evaluate individual performance of theft crime detectives and tie in that evaluation with personnel relocation. Detectives had an instant response to this policy. Police station detention cells immediately filled up. That can quite adequately explain their apparent devotion to hard work by the institutional arrangement of rewards and controls.

Case studies in chapter 4 and descriptions of investigative tactics in part 2 have clearly indicated that Japanese police detectives can be quite cynical in their relationships with suspects and will manipulate a detained suspect to their advantage. In this sense, detective work in Japan is fundamentally the same as that reported in other countries. The former image of a Japanese police detective as a benevolent caretaker of the suspect and his family is not accurate.

I should note, of course, that even the most aggressive and questionable forms of investigative behavior at the Eastern Police Station look benign compared to the situation often reported for North American police forces. For instance, I did not observe any physical abuse of a suspect, much less a shooting, not an uncommon event in the United States.

That is so because Japanese police officers need not behave as aggressively as their North American colleagues. As I have argued in chapter 2, police work loads are generally lighter, serious crimes are more rare, firearms are prohibited, and, most importantly, the legal environment is more enabling in Japan. Japanese detectives rarely need to apply physical force to a suspect because the legal system of criminal investigation is designed and implemented to give the detained suspect sufficiently strong psychological pressure to admit guilt.

In routine cases, the police do not need to worry about judicial scrutiny of their tactics. The court, when requested, routinely issues warrants and routinely approves detention at a police station detention cell. There is no need for the police to hurry an investigation. Detention is often lengthy enough to allow them to investigate separate offenses as well. Moreover, most suspects confess to a crime even without detention; they know what will happen if they refuse. Coupled with these very enabling legal resources, relatively benign tactics still can have a significant impact on a suspect.

Ease of getting a confession has long been the most important foundation of criminal investigation in Japan. Japanese detectives work on the assumption that the suspect will confess and that this confession will match the physical evidence. Therefore, they do little other than interrogate the suspect. Their enabling legal environment has precluded the development of other investigative skills. Indeed, the detectives' single-minded pursuit of the constantly changing confessions in Case 17, for instance, can be frustrating and puzzling to the uninitiated observer.

Japanese police detectives panic when they discover that a confession does not match the physical evidence. A clear example is Case 17. Detectives were caught in a vicious cycle of coercive interrogations and false confessions. When one confession did not fit the physical evidence, the detectives simply pressed the suspect to make another confession, which again failed to match physical evidence. It did not occur to the detectives that their original hypothesis was incorrect.

Fortunately, there was another crime for which to indict and detain the same suspect, so the detectives earned additional time to continue the investigation. Otherwise, they might have been tempted to use more coercive and manipulative tactics in interrogation in order to *make crime* which fits their hypothesis within the approved time limit.

Herein lies the seed of more serious cases of coerced false confessions and other procedural illegalities such as those capsulized in chapter 1. Serious cases are not qualitatively different from more routine ones. They simply magnify the problems inherent in criminal investigation in Japan.

Here we can see an essential irony of the enabling legal environment and effective internal control.

While the legal system allows detectives to spend more time in investigating each case, the internal control system allows supervisors to closely manage subordinates. Ericson (1981: 210) concluded in his study that both the structure of formal legal rules and the condition of low visibility sets the organizational framework for detective work in Canada, which allows the police to dominate the interactive process of *making crime*. The organizational framework of Japanese police detectives shares only one of these two elements, and one might expect that the higher visibility with tighter control more effectively restrains detectives.

However, the reality is that this organizational framework in Japan does not necessarily result in a higher degree of civility and restraint on the part of investigators. The legal system has caused detectives to rely heavily on interrogation of the suspect and the internal control system is administered in such a way as to demand higher productivity. If detectives fail to get an expected confession at an early stage of investigation in an important case, they are tempted to take more abusive or manipulative actions.

From a detective's perspective, emphasis on proving motivation at a trial is also a major reason for a preoccupation with confessions. In 1987, trial courts in Japan passed judgment on 76,483 defendants (Saiko Saibansho, 1988: 157). Among them, 69,851 completely admitted their guilt. Therefore in most cases, the real issue becomes sentencing, and mitigating and aggravating circumstances are central concerns for the court and, thus, also for the prosecution and defense. Motivation naturally plays a leading role in sentencing, and confession of the defendant becomes indispensable as evidence.

Reform proposals in Japan focus on the enabling legal environment, with the basic idea to make it less enabling by increasing direct intervention by the defense counsel during investigation, particularly in regard to questioning of the suspect in police custody. For instance, in chapter 1 I referred to a survey of falsely accused people which was administered by the three bar associations in Tokyo in order to find support for their proposal to abolish or limit the use of police station detention cells as substitute detention centers (Tokyo San Bengoshikai, 1984). It is no surprise that prosecutors oppose any such proposals.

A more serious problem is that influential judges are also against many of reform proposals, or at least reluctant to support them. A recent publication in which well-known judges, prosecutors, and attorneys wrote on the same subjects from different perspectives (Mitsui et al., 1988) provides some ideal material to see this pattern.

Attorney Kumamoto (1988) proposes, for instance, the following measures for crimes punishable by a prison term of three years or longer:

(1) Require the judge to provide the suspect with a state-appointed attorney when he authorizes the suspect's detention.

(2) Establish a clear rule which specifies minimum requirements on frequencies and length of meetings with the attorney during detention.

(3) Require the prosecutor to provide the defense attorney with a record of interrogations upon indictment.

(4) Give the defense attorney a right to read and xerox all the statements taken from the suspect upon indictment.

It is apparent that the Miranda decision in the United States in 1966 has influenced Kumamoto's proposals. However, Judge Sato (1988) compares Kumamoto's paper with another by a prosecutor (Harada, 1988) on the same subject and comments:

> In light of my practical experience of more than twenty years, I do not believe that the present system requires a radical reform, except some needs for improvement in its implementation. Of course, as Prosecutor Harada admits, secret interrogation always contain the danger of coercion, and the interrogator should always keep it in mind that he should not go beyond the limits allowed by the law. From this perspective, too, the proper attitude of mind [*kokorogamae* in Japanese] proposed by Prosecutor Harada for interrogators is truly important.

What Sato means by "the proper attitude of mind" is the following: an effort to understand the suspect's perspective; the patience to listen to the suspect and prudence to see the truth; and an understanding about the inevitable limits of human perception and memory (Harada, 1988: 184). No one would deny the wisdom of these recommendations. However, this influential judge still denies the need for reform of the system itself.

Akiyama (1988), another attorney, makes proposals similar to these of Kumamoto and offers additional recommendation. First, he wants to provide a state-appointed attorney for every arrested suspect. In 1985, excluding traffic offenses, there were 124,000 arrested suspects, about ten suspects per each attorney. He argues that this is not an impossible figure and that the bar has to make such a system possible. Second, he proposes the establishment of minimum standards for meetings of suspects with an attorney. Third, he argues that Article 34 of the Constitution, which says that "[n]o person shall be arrested or detained...without the immediate privilege of counsel," guarantees a right to effective defense, so that the suspect should be able to secure the presence and advice of an attorney during interrogation. Fourth, he proposes to introduce various measures to make the suspect's right to remain silent more meaningful. He advocates, for instance, the suspect's right to refuse interrogation even after arrest or detention, and also recommends the tape-recording of interrogations. Fifth, he proposes to reduce the time allowed between arrest and the detention application from forty eight hours to twenty four hours, as well as to introduce bail before indictment. Finally, he argues for the need for exclusionary rules in regard to illegally obtained evidence.

Judge Horigome (1988) comments on Akiyama's paper, and is sympathetic to some of the proposals. He says that "[i]t seems worthwhile to explore the feasibility of state-appointed attorneys and bail before indictment." Horigome argues, however, that "while interrogation of the suspect should be a voluntary measure,...it is not true that voluntary investigation is permitted only when the suspect consents," and that "within the limits deemed reasonable under concrete circumstances, some investigations can be permitted as lawful voluntary investigations even when the suspect does not consent." He argues that investigators may continue to persuade the suspect to confess even after a refusal to be investigated, otherwise, large-scale cases of bribery or election law violation would never be indicted. He also points to the difficulty of investigating briberies and election law violations in order to justify his opposition to other proposals by Akiyama. Since these represent only a small portion of crimes in Japan, we can question the general validity of Horigome's argument. However, he strongly believes that confessions are indispensable in criminal justice as well as in criminal investigation. Judge Horigome says, therefore, that "we should also pay attention to the recent tendency in the United States to limit applicability of the Miranda rule and exclusionary rules," implying that the Japanese judiciary has stayed on the right track from the beginning in its rejection of such rules.

Similar patterns appear in other exchanges between defense attorneys and judges. For instance, Attorney Ishii (1988) argues that detention at a police station detention cell should be the exception, but Judge Nakayama (1988) counters that, in spite of the language of the Code of Prisons, "in practice, there is no relationship of principle and exception between detention centers and police station detention cells, and the judge uses his discretion and considers all the factors of each case." Attorney Muraoka (1988) argues that the suspect's right to retain counsel as provided in Article 34 of the Constitution implies the counsel's right of meeting and communicating with the client, and this right should enjoy priority over the right of investigation. Judge Nakayama (1988) argues, however, that while that right of counsel is recognized by the Code of Criminal Procedure on the basis of a principle established by the Constitution, it is not in itself a constitutional right, and thus does not have priority over the right of investigation.

Given these judicial opinions, reform proposals of these nature are not likely to find many supporters among judges. Some judges in the same publication went further. For instance, Judges Nitta and Yasui (1988) doubt even the necessity of a court procedure to disclose the cause of detention to the suspect.

Even if the judiciary becomes more supportive of reform proposals, legislative changes would not be made easily. Under the parliamentary cabinet system of Japan, major legislative proposals always come from relevant governmental agencies (Upham, 1987: 14). In the case of criminal procedure and policing, these would be the Justice Ministry and the National Police Agency. No one would expect the ministry and agency to propose legislations which reduce their power. Rather, the National Police Agency has made every effort to pass a bill called the Confinement Facility Act in order to legitimize confinement and detention in a police station detention cell. Prosecutors also want to increase their power. Prosecutor Masui (1988), for instance, argues that weekends, national holidays, and periods around New Year's Day should be excluded from the calculation of the detention period, even though convenience of interrogation is not recognized as a cause for detention in the Code of Criminal Procedure.

A remote possibility for change may lie in following the path toward improvement of procedural protection of the suspect introduced by the English Police and Criminal Evidence Act of 1984 (see, *The Criminal Law Review*, 1985; Dixon et al., 1990).

The Japanese bar could point to the English system of a ninety-six-hour limitation of police detention (Section 44), the availability of a duty solicitor at the police station (Section 59), and tape-recording of interrogations (Section 60) as comparative law evidence of the feasibility of some of its own proposals. However, "the thrust of the 1984 Act...has been to facilitate their [suspects] removal into police custody to a greater extent and for a longer period than previously" (Gibbons, 1985: 566). Procedural safeguards are strengthened in order to protect the suspect from the enabling apparatus which favors relatively unimpeded police work.

Likewise, the Japanese defense bar may consider legitimizing detention at a police station detention cell to a limited extent, in return for the introduction of state-appointed attorneys before indictment, counsel's prerogative to meet with the client, tape-recording of interrogations, and a shorter detention period. Judge Horigome (1988) mentions, for instance, that criminal immunity for collaborators and the use of police decoys could be alternatives to interrogation. The bar might consider such measures for white-collar crimes in return for improved procedural safeguards in other kinds of cases.

Unfortunately for reformers, however, there is no real impetus for prosecutors and the police to make such a deal with the bar. The present system is sufficiently enabling for them. Application for detention at a police station detention cell is granted routinely, and investigators can interrogate the suspect without interference of counsel for a long period of time. The prosecution and police do not have any need to make concessions to the bar.

Another possibility is a unilateral act on the part of the defense bar to establish a Japanese version of the duty solicitor scheme in England. With an annual budget of only 380 million yen in 1989 (approximately $3 million

U.S.), the Legal Aid Society in Japan is extremely small compared to the legal aid systems in other developed countries. Its official purpose is civil legal aid and the government contributed only 100 million yen limiting its use for that. With the contribution of 136 million yen, attorneys were the largest contributor, and, in fact, the activities of the prefectural offices of the Legal Aid Society are managed by officials selected from among local attorneys. In spite of this small budget, the society established in 1990 the Pretrial Criminal Defense Assistance System in six prefectures, including Tokyo and Osaka. This system provides a suspect with an attorney with a fund of up to 100 thousand yen (approximately $720 U.S.) on a loan basis. The number of the beneficiaries will be small, but this is nonetheless a good start.

However, not every attorney is willing to take a state-appointed case, even under the present system. According to a national survey of attorneys in 1980 (Nihon Bengoshi Rengokai, 1988: 102), 57 percent of the respondents were willing to take state-appointed cases. The major deterrent is the small compensation for such work. The overwhelming majority of such attorneys receive only 50 thousand yen or so (approximately $360 U.S.) per case. Then the question becomes, how many attorneys are willing to volunteer their time for pre-indictment suspects without meaningful compensation? If only one quarter of the attorneys are willing to participate in a Japanese version of duty solicitor scheme, each attorney will have to take four times the estimate by Akiyama, namely, forty cases a year. We cannot be too optimistic about the feasibility of such a blueprint.

There are no criminal defense specialists in Japan, much less organized specialists such as public defenders or legal aid attorneys in the United States. Celebrated cases such as those summarized in chapter 1 are often handled by activist lawyers with a strong commitment to civil rights. However, even these lawyers spend most of their time on civil cases. Most criminal work is carried out by an individual attorney who work on the case in his spare time. Most likely the attorney lacks expertise in criminal defense and cannot effectively challenge the police and the prosection. Therefore, the Japanese Federation of Bar Associations recently decided to establish so-called Criminal Defense Centers in major cities as depositories of information about successful defense actions, so that less experienced attorneys might learn from them. This is another good beginning; however, it is still very far from an organized defense bar with full-time specialist attorneys.

Finally, the public will very likely be opposed to any significant steps to make the legal environment for the police less enabling as the preceding section of this chapter demonstrated.

In 1977, researchers at Kyoto University asked a national sample of adults in Japan to name both a "violator" and a "protector" of "individual liberty and rights" (Kyoto Daigaku Hogakubu, 1978: Question 8). The largest category of responses to both questions was "none" (45.7 percent about "violator" and 29.6 percent about "protector"). A very interesting pattern appeared for other response categories. Mass media was the most frequently named "violator" (25.5 percent), followed by big business (21.9 percent) and then the government (9.3 percent). The police were named as a "violator" only by 2.8 percent of the respondents and were the most frequently named "protector" of individual liberty and rights (31.9 percent), followed by the family (30.4 percent) and the court (25.5 percent). Only 3 percent of the respondents regarded the mass media as a "protector." This finding tells us that most people in Japan do not view the police as part of the government, nor do they define liberty and rights as requiring protection from the governmental infringement. They rather think of more immediate interests such as safety of property, person, and privacy as examples of liberty and rights. Thus, other than the most intimate protectors (family members) of their interests, the police and court who apprehend and punish criminals are seen as the particularly important protectors of their liberty and rights.

The Japanese also do not perceive themselves as potential targets of police activity. This attitude appears in public opinion regarding *junkai renraku* or house visits by patrol officers. The official justification of house visits is the need for detailed information regarding each household for public service purposes, particularly for helping a visitor locate an address. Ames (1981: 39) has reported, however, that the real purposes of collecting such information include the potential use in criminal investigation and the surveillance of gangsters, ex-convicts, and leftist organizations. This has been understood for many years by police observers in Japan. Nevertheless, the Japanese public generally welcome house visits. For instance, in 1984, the Office of Prime Minister asked a national sample of adults about their impressions of contacts with police officers (Naikaku Sori Daijin Kanbo, 1985: survey number 8). Fifty-one percent of the respondents said they had no contact with the police in the preceding year; the most frequent contacts were house visits (21.1 percent). Fifty-five percent of the visited respondents reported a good impression, while only 0.2 percent said they harbored a bad impression. Similar opinions were found in a survey conducted by the National Research Institute of Police Science (Nishimura and Suzuki, 1986). In 1984, a sample of residents of seventeen urban police jurisdictions were asked about house visits. Sixty-four percent answered that "they understood well the purposes of house visits," compared to only 1.4 percent who said that they did not. Thirty-seven percent answered that "the officer was kind and courteous," while only 1.6 percent said that "the officer asked too much about details." Thirty-two percent wanted "more visits," compared to only 0.9 percent who denied the necessity of house visits. Only a small minority in Japan view house visits as an invasion of their privacy or appreciate the possibility that information collected during house visits might be used against them.

Of course, these surveys by governmental agencies were conducted to support the government's position that present police practices were acceptable to the public. It is also very likely that most people did not know the real purposes of house visits. Given the attitudes found by the Kyoto University survey, however, I doubt if people would criticize house visits even when they were told the real reasons. Since police are the most important public protectors of their private interests, the surveys suggest that they support more effective use of information about undesirable neighbors for more aggressive crime control.

Thus, I have to reach a somewhat pessimistic conclusion. It seems unlikely that effective measures will be introduced very soon to mitigate this combination of strong internal control over police detectives and the very enabling legal environment. The prevailing attitudes of the judiciary, the structure of the legislative process, the present situation of the bar, and dominant public opinion all contribute to maintain the present environment of criminal investigation in Japan.

In spite of some of their own doubts about the legitimacy of aspects of police practices and related working conditions, many detectives may continue to be forced to manipulate the suspect and to otherwise engage in questionable actions. If this hypothesis is correct, then for as long as this situation continues, morally involved detectives will appear in the ranks of the detectives exhibiting primarily calculative involvement.

Police behavior illustrates the principle of cognitive dissonance (Festinger, 1957). If the action cannot be avoided even where it is against the person's original will, cognitive dissonance may be reduced by placing a positive value on the behavior. If a reward is associated with the behavior, then to the extent that this reward is provided, the behavior will tend to become more pronounced.

In the Hokkaido police internal magazine, *Hokkai-keiyu* (Police Friends of Hokkaido), it is possible to locate some information suggestive of this process.

Initially, we find these statements by young officers:

- I am making the efforts I should to conform to the police organization.

- Because I entered this society as a police officer, and because in police society, those who persist in their own way will likely be banished from the organization, that is what I must do.

- It is a great thing to live with pride in one's work. We are drawn to such a man.

- For a man whose thoughts are on his paycheck, every day exhausts his body and his spirit, but for the man with passion and fight, rigor and stress awaken his enthusiasm, and become the vitality of the next day.

From such statements, it seems that there are many individuals who are making positive efforts to conform. However, there are others:

I took the exam [to join the force] in an offhand way, and after I had joined up, I felt resistant. However, with the passage of time, in the course of my transformation as a member of the force, this resistance gradually began to fade.

Also, a junior member of the riot squad mustering out for guard duty against a demonstration wrote:

When asked "Are you a human?" [by a demonstrator], I became agitated. But thinking, "I grow agitated because I have no confidence," I read the notes of a member headed for service in the Asamasanso case [in which a squad leader was shot to death by extreme leftists], seeking confidence and pride in myself. Now I carry my chest out further than anyone, and can declare in a full voice, "Yes! Send me, sir!" (on the Asamasanso case, see Bayley, 1976: 160-62).

And from another:

I was distressed to be caught between youth and duty, but as I listened to the mustering-out song, "To make this world a flower" while setting out, I came to think, "What is the matter with you?" There is work to do to foster a peaceful society. What's with this stupid whining?

Of course, these statements were written and published with the full anticipation that supervisors and family members would read them. However, they still suggest that the perception of many recruits, who are initially plagued by resistance and doubt, is transformed gradually toward a feeling of satisfaction in the performance of their duty. If a similar process of cognitive modification were to exist in a detective department, the involvement of detectives in aggressive investigations may more readily change from calculative involvement to moral involvement. Geertz (1973: 126–27) argues that culture is a device through which people accept reality as morally right and cognitively natural. My data indicate that many police officers in Japan perceive aggressive actions and stressful work conditions in this light.

As recent experiments of police effectiveness in the United States have proven, styles and levels of police activities often are not causal factors in determining crime levels (for a summary of these studies, see Skolnick and Bayley, 1986: 1-6). Still "the police have been assigned, and have taken on, an impossible responsibility for controlling crimes as the key indicator of their success at reproducing order" (Ericson, 1982: 4). Only when the public ceases to demand the impossible of the police will there be any hope for a corresponding change in the direction of internal controls, and in the attitudes and behavior of lower-ranking police officers. With general public support of the status quo, increasing "professionalism" now means an emphasis on increased efficiency, rather than a deeper concern over legality (Skolnick, 1966: 238).

Recently, there has been a growing number of articles by police executives boasting of the competence of the Japanese police, often citing the great regard for the Japanese police system overseas. Indeed it is safe to say that in relative terms, the international standing of the Japanese police is very high. This does not deny, however, that they have their own problems. Given the lively international interest in Japanese police today, this book offers important new data on the day-to-day functioning of police departments, in order to present a more realistic picture of everyday criminal investigation and a deeper understanding of the perspective of lower-ranking police detectives.

Appendix A

Survey on Duties of Officers in Criminal Investigation

This is the response distribution for the forty-one questions that deal with the kinds of actions that should be taken at each stage of investigation.

Item numbers given come from the second half of Part 2 of the survey. For all questions except the personality tests, see the appendix to the Japanese edition of this book (Miyazawa, 1985).

In the answers, "1" indicates "I believe so" as well as "If called upon to choose, I believe so"; "2" indicates, "I can't decide"; and "3" indicates "I do not believe so" as well as "If called upon to choose, I do not believe so."

Figures are given for the entire sample of 199 and separately for the forty-four detectives. The total number of respondents is given in parentheses; these figures were used to calculate percentages. Because of rounding, some sets will not total to 100%.

ITEM	CONTENT	RESPONSE	OVERALL	DETECTIVES
62	In duty questioning, one must	1	56.3	55.8
	always accomplish one's	2	30.5	16.3
	objective.	3	13.2	27.9
			(197)	(43)
63	In duty questioning, always	1	29.4	34.9
	pat down the surface of the	2	39.1	23.3
	clothing.	3	31.5	41.9
			(197)	(43)
64	In duty questioning, always	1	31.5	37.2
	pat down the surface of anything	2	38.1	30.2
	that is carried.	3	30.5	32.6
			(197)	(43)

ITEM	CONTENT	RESPONSE	OVERALL	DETECTIVES
65	In duty questioning, always open anything that is carried.	1 2 3	26.5 40.3 33.2 (196)	31.0 33.3 35.7 (42)
66	In duty questioning, in the event that the subject runs away, always give chase, catch, and restrain the subject.	1 2 3	61.1 29.3 9.6 (198)	76.7 14.0 9.3 (43)
67	In voluntary accompaniment, when the subject refuses, take his arm and have him accompany you.	1 2 3	14.6 39.9 45.5 (198)	9.3 30.2 60.5 (43)
84	Once going out into the field for the purpose of securing voluntary appearance, definitely accomplish the purpose of the excursion.	1 2 3	39.9 40.4 19.7 (198)	51.2 27.9 20.9 (43)
85	In voluntary appearance, in the event that the subject runs away, always give chase, catch, and restrain the subject.	1 2 3	43.3 36.1 20.6 (194)	55.0 22.5 22.5 (40)
86	In voluntary appearance, when the subject vacillates, take his arm and have him accompany you.	1 2 3	12.2 39.6 48.2 (197)	4.7 25.6 69.8 (43)
101	After gaining assent to a voluntary accompaniment or voluntary appearance, ask the necessary questions without fail.	1 2 3	55.8 34.5 9.6 (197)	76.8 16.3 7.0 (43)
102	After gaining assent to a voluntary accompaniment or voluntary appearance, if the subject rises to leave in the middle of questioning, take his arm and restrain him.	1 2 3	18.7 43.4 37.9 (198)	9.3 23.3 67.4 (43)

ITEM	CONTENT	RESPONSE	OVERALL	DETECTIVES
103	After gaining assent to a voluntary accompaniment or voluntary appearance, box the subject in so that he cannot run away on the way to the destination.	1 2 3	11.1 40.9 48.0 (198)	7.0 16.3 76.7 (43)
104	After gaining assent to a voluntary accompaniment or voluntary appearance, continue the questioning until all necessary matters have been covered, even if questioning continues into the middle of the night.	1 2 3	8.7 41.0 50.3 (195)	4.7 20.9 74.4 (43)
105	After gaining assent to a voluntary accompaniment or voluntary appearance, stick with the subject when he eats, satisfies his bodily functions, and during rest periods.	1 2 3	13.2 45.2 41.6 (197)	9.5 28.6 61.9 (42)
106	After gaining assent to a voluntary accompaniment or voluntary appearance, do not let the suspect eat, satisfy his bodily functions, or rest until a certain amount of the necessary matters have been covered.	1 2 3	5.6 35.4 59.1 (198)	0.0 11.6 88.4 (43)
107	After gaining assent to a voluntary accompaniment or voluntary appearance, in the event that the subject runs away, always give chase, catch, and restrain the subject.	1 2 3	20.2 41.4 38.4 (198)	20.9 25.6 53.5 (43)
120	When requesting voluntary appearance, extract a confession and carry out an emergency arrest.	1 2 3	24.2 49.0 26.8 (198)	18.6 39.5 41.9 (43)
197	When carrying out a search, be certain to find the object of the search.	1 2 3	39.8 46.2 14.0 (186)	50.0 28.6 21.4 (42)

ITEM	CONTENT	RESPONSE	OVERALL	DETECTIVES
198	When carrying out a search, be certain to look for evidence of other crimes.	1 2 3	31.0 49.2 19.8 (197)	48.8 27.9 23.3 (43)
199	Even if the suspect has evaded arrest, perform any searches that could have been made without a warrant at the time of arrest.	1 2 3	30.6 46.9 22.4 (196)	37.2 25.6 37.2 (43)
200	When going to arrest a suspect, in the event that he is not there, while waiting for him perform any searches that may be performed without a warrant at the time of arrest.	1 2 3	17.9 43.9 38.3 (196)	16.3 18.9 65.0 (43)
201	When carrying out a search pursuant to a warrant, operate in such a way as to conceal the suspected crime from the suspect.	1 2 3	12.2 43.9 43.9 (196)	7.0 18.6 74.4 (43)
294	When requesting the voluntary submission of materials necessary to the investigation, be certain to accomplish the objective.	1 2 3	41.3 45.9 12.8 (196)	48.8 34.9 16.3 (43)
310	When informing the suspect of his right to remain silent, speak in such a way that the efficiency of the investigation will not be impeded.	1 2 3	17.3 50.0 32.7 (196)	14.0 27.9 58.1 (43)
311	When informing the suspect of his right to retain an attorney, speak in such a way that the efficiency of the investigation will not be impeded.	1 2 3	14.2 51.8 34.0 (197)	9.3 27.9 62.8 (43)
332	Once the investigation has begun, be absolutely thorough in checking for the existence of separate offenses.	1 2 3	44.8 42.7 12.5 (192)	65.1 25.6 9.3 (43)

333   Even if the investigation of the main
        offense is completed early, use the

ITEM	CONTENT	RESPONSE	OVERALL	DETECTIVES
	remaining time to pursue to the	1	46.9	71.4
	end investigation of any separate	2	42.3	21.4
	offenses.	3	10.7	7.1
			(196)	(42)
334	Even if the investigation of the	1	26.9	37.2
	main offense is completed early,	2	53.8	37.2
	obtain detention and pursue	3	19.3	25.6
	investigation of any separate		(197)	(43)
	offenses to the end.			
368	When performing interrogation,	1	43.4	62.8
	be certain to get a confession	2	42.9	30.2
	in the end.	3	13.8	7.0
			(196)	(43)
369	When performing interrogation,	1	12.2	4.7
	get a confession, even by promising	2	37.6	20.9
	that you will lighten up on	3	50.3	74.4
	subsequent treatment of the subject.		(197)	(43)
370	When performing interrogation,	1	10.2	7.0
	get a confession, even by promising	2	37.6	14.0
	that you "will look after the needs"	3	52.3	79.1
	of the suspect.		(197)	(43)
371	When performing interrogation, get a	1	42.6	58.1
	confession, even by questioning the	2	42.6	23.3
	logic of the suspect's statement.	3	14.7	18.6
	(Note: What I mean here is		(197)	(43)
	interrogation which seeks			
	unrealistically fine details and			
	complete consistency in the suspect's			
	statement, so that the suspect will			
	eventually abandon his effort to			
	maintain the statement and admit that			
	what the interrogator says is the truth.)			
372	When performing interrogation,	1	19.8	18.6
	get a confession, even by	2	41.1	20.9
	persuading the suspect that he	3	39.1	60.5
	"has a duty to confess."		(197)	(43)

ITEM	CONTENT	RESPONSE	OVERALL	DETECTIVES
373	When performing interrogation, get a confession, even by suggesting that "we already have proof."	1 2 3	21.6 44.3 34.0 (194)	20.9 30.2 48.8 (43)
374	When performing interrogation, get a confession, even by showing sympathy for the motives and circumstances of the suspect.	1 2 3	33.2 45.4 21.4 (196)	39.5 37.2 23.3 (43)
375	When performing interrogation, use fairly harsh language in pursuing a confession.	1 2 3	31.1 49.0 19.9 (196)	48.8 34.9 16.3 (43)
376	When performing interrogation, limit visits with outsiders until the suspect has confessed to some extent.	1 2 3	17.9 45.9 36.2 (196)	20.9 20.9 58.1 (43)
377	When performing interrogation, limit food, smoking, and rest periods until the suspect has confessed to some extent.	1 2 3	9.8 35.9 54.3 (184)	5.0 12.5 82.5 (40)
378	When performing interrogation, continue interrogation until the suspect has confessed to some extent, even if interrogation lasts into the middle of the night.	1 2 3	10.4 35.4 54.2 (192)	7.5 12.5 80.0 (40)
379	When performing interrogation, get a confession even if the right to remain silent is suspended temporarily.	1 2 3	8.7 35.2 56.1 (196)	4.7 11.6 83.7 (43)
380	When performing interrogation, get a confession, even by making maximum use of detention and extensions thereof.	1 2 3	29.1 41.8 29.1 (196)	46.5 20.9 32.6 (43)

Appendix B

List of Japanese Court Cases and Relevant Statutes

Court cases are arranged by date.

Abbreviations of the reporters:
Hanji=Hanrei Jiho (Current Court Decision Reporter)
Hanta=Hanrei Taimuzu (Court Decision Times)
Kakeishu=Kakyu Saibansho Keiji Saibanreishu (Lower Court Criminal Decision Reporter)
Keisaigeppo=Keiji Saiban Geppo (Monthly Reporter of Lower Court Criminal Decisions)
Keishu=Saiko Saibansho Keiji Hanreishu (Supreme Court Criminal Decision Reporter)
Kokeishu=Koto Saibansho Keiji Hanreishu (High Court Criminal Decision Reporter)
Minshu=Saiko Saibansho Minji Hanreishu (Supreme Court Civil Decision Reporter)
Saibanshu-kei=Saiko Saibansho Saibanshu: Keiji (Sepreme Court Decision Reporter: Criminal Cases)

	Page of
Abbreviation is followed by volume or number and page.	this book

June 30, 1948, Supreme Court, *Keishu* 2, 715. Art. 38, Constitution; Art. 319, Code of Criminal Procedure.	23
December 13, 1949, Supreme Court, *Saibanshu-kei* 15, 349. Art. 218, Code of Criminal Procedure.	23
November 25, 1952, Supreme Court, *Keishu* 6, 1245. Art. 319, Code of Criminal Procedure.	23

Bibliography

Japanese titles of journal articles and book chapters are translated, but Japanese titles of journals and books are retained for readers who might have access to them.

Aiken, Michael, and Hage, Jerald. 1968. "Organizational Interdependence and Intraorganizational Structure," *American Sociological Review* 33: 912–30.

Akiyama, Mikio. 1988. "Defense Activities of the Suspect and Counsel before Indictment" (in Japanese), in Mitsui, et al., 1988: 347–63.

Ames, Walter L. 1981. *Police and Community in Japan.* Berkeley: University of California Press.

Asahi Shinbun (*Asahi* Newspaper) (ed.). 1989. *Asahi Nenkan* (Asahi Almanac), *1989.* Tokyo: Asahi Shinbunsha.

Bayley, David H. 1976. *Forces of Order: Police Behavior in Japan and the United States.* Berkeley: University of California Press.

Benson, J. Kenneth. 1975. "The Interorganizational Network as a Political Economy," *Administrative Science Quarterly* 20: 229–49.

Cicourel, Aaron V. 1976. *The Social Organization of Juvenile Justice.* London: Heinemann.

The Criminal Law Review. 1985. September 1985, Special Issue on the Police and Criminal Evidence Act 1984.

Dando, Shigemitsu. 1965. *Japanese Criminal Procedure.* Translated by B. J. George, Jr. South Hackensack, N.J.: Fred B. Rothman.

Dixon, David, et al. 1990. "Safeguarding the Rights of Suspects in Police Custody," *Policing and Society* 1: 115–40.

Do Keisatsu Honbu (Hokkaido Police Headquarters). 1974. *Keihohan Ninchi Kenkyo no Jokyo to Nenjibetsu Suii* (Reported and Cleared Criminal Code Offenses and Yearly Changes), *1973.* Unpublished internal document.

Ericson, Richard V. 1981. *Making Crime: A Study of Detective Work*. Toronto: Butterworth.

Ericson, Richard V. 1982. *Reproducing Order: A Study of Police Patrol Work*. Toronto: University of Totonto Press.

Etzioni, Amitai. 1961. *A Comparative Analysis of Complex Organizations: On Power, Involvement, and Their Correlates*. New York: Free Press.

Etzioni, Amitai. 1968. "Social Control: Organizational Aspects," in David L. Sills (ed.), *International Encyclopedia of the Social Sciences* 14, New York: Macmillan, 396–402.

Evan, William. 1966. "The Organization Set: Toward a Theory of Interorganizational Relations," in James D. Thompson (ed.), *Approaches to Organizational Design*, Pittsburgh: University of Pittsburgh Press, 173–91.

Festinger, Leon. 1957. *A Theory of Cognitive Dissonance*. Evanston: Row, Peterson.

Geertz, Clifford. 1973. *The Interpretation of Cultures*. New York: Basic Books.

Gibbons, Thomas. 1985. "The Conditions of Detention and Questioning by the Police," *The Criminal Law Review*, 1985: 558–68.

Harada, Akio. 1988. "Interrogation of the Suspect: From the Perspective of a Prosecutor" (in Japanese), in Mitsui et al., 1988: 177–86.

Hobbs, Dick. 1988. *Doing the Business: Entrepreneurship, the Working Class, and Detectives in the East End of London*. Oxford: Clarendon Press.

Homusho (Ministry of Justice) (ed.). 1987. *Hanzai Hakusho* (White Paper on Crime), *1987*. Tokyo: Okurasho Insatsukyoku.

Homusho (Ministry of Justice) (ed.). 1988. *Hanzai Hakusho* (White Paper on Crime), *1988*. Tokyo: Okurasho Insatsukyoku.

Horigome, Yukio. 1988. "Comment [to Akiyama, 1988]" (in Japanese), in Mitsui et al., 1988: 364–67.

Igarashi, Futaba. 1984. "Forced to Confess" (in Japanese), *Sekai*, February 1984: 220–32.

Igarashi, Futaba. 1986. "Forced to Confess," translated by Gavan McCormack, in Gavan McCormack and Yoshio Sugimoto (eds.), *Democracy in Contemporary Japan*, Sydney: Hale and Iremonger, 195–214.

Igarashi, Futaba. 1989. "Abolish Substitute Prisons: Regular Detention Centers Are Not Full" (in Japanese), *Horitsu Jiho* 61–7: 103–5.

Ishii, Yoshikazu. 1988. "Place of Confinement and Detention: From the Perspective of a Defense Attorney" (in Japanese), in Mitsui et al., 1988: 281–88.

Itoh, Shigeki. 1988. *Shuso Retsujitsu* (Autumn Frost and Fiery Sun). Tokyo: Asahi Shinbunsha.

Keisatsucho (National Police Agency) (ed.). 1974. *Keisatsu Hakusho* (White Paper on Police), *1974*. Tokyo: Okurasho Insatsukyoku.

Keisatsucho (National Police Agency) (ed.). 1986. *Keisatsu Hakusho* (White Paper on Police), *1986*. Tokyo: Okurasho Insatsukyoku.

Keisatsucho (National Police Agency) (ed.). 1988. *Keisatsu Hakusho* (White Paper on Police), *1988*. Tokyo: Okurasho Insatsukyoku.

Koshi, George H. 1970. *The Japanese Legal Advisor*. Rutland, Vt.: Charles E. Tuttle.

Kumamoto, Norimichi. 1988. "Interrogation of the Suspect: From the Perspective of a Defense Attorney" (in Japanese), in Mitsui et al., 1988: 187–95.

Kyoto Daigaku Hogakubu (Kyoto University Faculty of Law) (ed.). 1978. *Ho Ishiki to Funso Shori* (Legal Consciousness and Dispute Processing). Unpublished research report.

McBarnet, Doreen J. 1979. "Arrest: The Legal Context of Policing," in Simon Holdaway (ed.), *The British Police,* London: Edward Arnold, 24–40.

McBarnet, Doreen J. 1981. *Conviction: Law, the State and the Construction of Justice*. London: Macmillan.

Manning, Peter K. 1980. *The Narc's Game: Organizational and Informational Limits on Drug Law Enforcement*. Cambridge: MIT Press.

Masui, Kiyohiko. 1988. "Comment [to Nitta and Yasui, 1988]" (in Japanese), in Mitsui et al., 1988: 266–69.

Mitsui, Makoto et al. (eds.). 1988. *Keiji Tetsuzuki* (Criminal Procedure), 1. Tokyo: Chikuma Shobo.

Miyazawa, Setsuo. 1985. *Hanzai Sosa o meguru Dai-issen Keiji no Ishiki to Kodo: Soshikinai Tosei eno Ninshiki to Hanno* (The Attitudes and Behavior Concerning Criminal Investigation of the First-Line Detectives: Perceptions and Responses Regarding Intraorganizational Controls). Tokyo: Seibundo.

Miyazawa, Setsuo. 1989. "Scandal and Hard Reform: Implications of a Wiretapping Case to the Control of Organizational Police Crimes in Japan," *Kobe University Law Review* 23: 13–27.

Muraoka, Keiichi. 1988. "Meeting and Communication of the Counsel and Client: From the Perspective of a Defense Attorney" (in Japanese), in Mitsui et al., 1988: 329–42.

Murayama, Masayuki. 1990. *Keira Keisatsu no Kenkyu* (A Study of Patrol Police). Tokyo: Seibundo.

Naikaku Sori Daijin Kanbo (Office of the Prime Minister) (ed.). 1985. *Seron Chosa Nenkan* (Almanac of Public Opinion Surveys), *1985*. Tokyo: Okurasho Insatsukyoku.

Nakayama, Yoshifusa. 1988. "Comment [to Ishii, 1988]" (in Japanese), in Mitsui, et al., 1988: 289–90.

Nihon Bengoshi Rengokai (Japanese Federation of Bar Associations) (ed.). 1988. *Nihon no Horitsu Jimusho* (Law Offices in Japan). Tokyo: Gyosei.

Nishimura, Haruo, and Suzuki, Shingo. 1986. "Citizen-Helping Role of the Police and the Attitudes of Residents in the Community (2)" (in Japanese), *Kagaku Keisatsu Kenkyujo Hokoku Bohan Shonen Hen* (Research Report of the Department of Crime Prevention and Juvenile Delinquency, the National Research Institute of Police Science) 27–1: 54–63.

Nitta, Mutsuo, and Yasui, Hisaharu. 1988. "Detention and Bail: From the Perspective of Judges" (in Japanese), in Mitsui, et al., 1988: 243–65.

Parker, L. Craig, Jr. 1984. *The Japanese Police System Today: An American Perspective*. Tokyo: Kodansha International.

Pfeffer, Jeffrey, and Salancik, Gerald R. 1978. *The External Control of Organization: A Resource Dependence Perspective*. New York: Harper and Row.

Saiko Saibansho (Supreme Court) (ed.). 1988. *Shiho Tokei Nenpo Keiji Hen* (Annals of Judicial Statistics: Criminal Cases), *1988*.

Sanders, William B. 1977. *Detective Work*. New York: Free Press.

Sato, Fumiya. 1988. "Comment [to Harada, 1988, and Kumamoto, 1988]" (in Japanese), in Mitsui et al., 1988: 196–97.

Skolnick, Jerome H. 1966. *Justice Without Trial: Law Enforcement in Democratic Society*. New York: John Wiley and Sons.

Skolnick, Jerome H., and Bayley, David H. 1986. *The New Blue Line: Police Innovation in Six American Cities*. New York: Free Press.

Tanaka, Hideo (ed.). 1976. *The Japanese Legal System*. Tokyo: Tokyo University Press.

Tokyo San Bengoshikai (Three Bar Associations of Tokyo). 1984. *Nureginu* (Falsely Charged). Tokyo: Seihosha.

Uchiyama, Ayako. 1978. "A Study on the Measurement of the Amount of Investigation per Case (2)" (in Japanese), *Kagaku Keisatsu Kenkyujo Hokoku Bohan Shonen Hen* (Research Report of the Department of Crime Prevention and Juvenile Delinquency, the National Research Institute of Police Science) 19–2: 96–105.

Upham, Frank K. 1987. *Law and Social Change in Postwar Japan*. Cambridge: Harvard University Press.

Van Maanen, John. 1978. "On Watching the Watchers," in Peter K. Manning and John Van Maanen (eds.), *Policing: A View From the Street*, Santa Monica: Goodyear, 309–49.

Wakamatsu, Yoshiya. 1987. *Sekken Kotsu no Kenkyu* (A Study on the Meeting and Communication of the Counsel and the Client in Custody). Tokyo: Nihon Hyoronsha.

Wakamatsu, Yoshiya. 1990. *Sekken Kotsu to Keiji Bengo* (Meeting and Communication of the Counsel and the Client and Criminal Defense). Tokyo: Nihon Hyoronsha.

Westney, D. Eleanor. 1987. *Imitation and Innovation: The Transfer of Western Organizational Patterns to Meiji Japan*. Cambridge: Harvard University Press.

Wilson, James Q. 1978. *Investigators: Managing FBI and Narcotics Agents*. New York: Basic Books.

Index